Imports, Exports, and Jobs
What Does Trade Mean for Employment and Job Loss?

Imports, Exports, and Jobs
What Does Trade Mean for Employment and Job Loss?

Lori G. Kletzer
University of California, Santa Cruz

2002

W.E. Upjohn Institute for Employment Research
Kalamazoo, Michigan

Library of Congress Cataloging-in-Publication Data

Kletzer, Lori G.
 Imports, exports, and jobs : what does trade mean for employment and job loss? / Lori G. Kletzer.
   p. cm.
 Includes bibliographical references and index.
 ISBN 0-88099-247-6 (pb : acid free) — ISBN 0-88099-248-4 (hc : acid free)
 1. Foreign trade and employment. 2. Labor market. 3. International trade. 4. Unemployment. I. Title.
 HD5710.7 .K5484 2002
 331.12—dc21
                                                2002013033

© 2002
W.E. Upjohn Institute for Employment Research
300 S. Westnedge Avenue
Kalamazoo, Michigan 49007-4686

The facts presented in this study and the observations and viewpoints expressed are the sole responsibility of the authors. They do not necessarily represent positions of the W.E. Upjohn Institute for Employment Research.

Cover design by J.R. Underhill.
Index prepared by Leoni Z. McVey.
Printed in the United States of America.

Contents

Acknowledgments	ix
1 Introduction	1
Outline, Objectives, and Findings	4
2 Understanding the Links between Increasing Foreign Competition and Domestic Employment and Job Loss	11
A Brief Excursion Through International Trade Theory:	
The Effects of Trade on Wages and Employment	11
Intra-Industry Trade and "New" Trade Theory	17
Measuring Industry Trade Sensitivity	21
3 Evidence from Earlier Studies	27
The Methodological Disagreement, in a Nutshell	29
Product-Price Studies	30
Factor Content of Trade (and Other Trade Flows) Studies	33
More Factor-Content Studies, Broadly Defined	38
Other Labor Demand Factors	39
What About Exports?	40
Summary	41
4 Inside Manufacturing	45
Manufacturing: Changes in Employment and Trade, in Brief	45
The State of U.S. Manufacturing, 1975–1995	47
Defining an Industry	53
Changes in Industry Employment	54
The Extent of Import Competition by Industry	56
Trends in Import Prices	60
Industry Export Activity	61
Intra-Industry Trade	65
Changes in Industry Employment: The Role of Trade and Foreign Competition	70
What About Import Prices?	75
Job Loss and Trade, 1979–1994	76
Trade and Job Loss by Industry	78
Summary	81

5 Modeling Labor Market Responses to Changes in Trade and Import Competition — 85
The Basic Empirical Framework — 86
The Basic Empirical Model, in More Detail — 95
Summary — 101

6 Measuring the Link between Changes in Industry Employment and Changes in Trade Flows — 103
Changes in Employment and Trade Flows — 103
Long-Period Changes in Industry Employment — 113
Increasing Import Competition—Measured as Changes in Import Price — 117
Assessing What the Model Says About the "Costs" of Trade for American Employment — 123
Summary — 125

7 Job Displacement and Foreign Competition — 131
Changes in the Composition of Demand and the Risk of Job Loss — 132
Summary — 141

8 Conclusions and Policy Implication — 143
Policy Implications — 145
Targeting in Enterprise Zone Jobs Credit Programs — 200
Enterprise Zones and Commuting Behavior — 204
Conclusions — 212

Appendix A — 153
Measures of Trade Volumes and Import Prices — 153
Measuring Industry Employment and Job Loss Using the CPS — 153

Appendix B — 195
Construction of Instruments — 195

References — 199

The Author — 207

Subject Index — 209

About the Institute — 221

List of Figures

4.1	Manufacturing Sector Employment and Manufacturing Employment as a Share of Total Employment, 1975–1995	47
4.2	Manufacturing as a Share of GDP, 1975–1995	48
4.3	Exports and Imports of Goods, 1975–1995	49
4.4	Exports and Imports of Goods as Percentage of GDP in the Manufacturing Sector, 1975–1995	52
4.5	Manufacturing and Total Displacement Rates, by Year (1979–1994)	77

List of Tables

4.1	U.S. International Trade in Goods and Services (Balance of Payments Basis, Billions $), 1975–1995	50
4.2	Import Shares of High-Import Industries, 1975–1994	57
4.3	Cross-Time Correlation of Industry Quartile Rankings, by Import Share	58
4.4	Export Intensities of Top Exporting Industries, 1975–1994	63
4.5	Cross-Time Correlation of Industry Quartile Rankings, by Export Intensity	64
4.6	Industry Trade Overlap, Import Share, and Export Intensity, 1994	67
4.7	Long-Period Changes in Industry Employment, Import Share, Exports, and Domestic Demand for Selected High-Import Industries	72
4.8	Top Job Loss Manufacturing Industries, Measured by Total Workers Displaced, 1979–1994	78
4.9	Industry Displacement, Import Share, and Exports	80
6.1	Changes in Industry Employment, Sales, Domestic Demand, Exports, and Imports: Within-Industry Estimates, 1979–1994	106
6.2	Changes in Industry Employment, Sales, Domestic Demand, Exports, and Imports: Within-Industry Estimates, 1979–1985 and 1985–1994	110
6.3	Changes in Industry Employment, Sales, Domestic Demand, Exports and Import Share, Cross-Section Estimates, Long-Period and Annual, 1979–1994	114
6.4	Changes in Industry Employment, Domestic Prices, and Import Prices: Within-Industry Estimates	120

6.5	Changes in Industry Employment and Relative Import Prices: Within-Industry Estimates	122
6.6	The Effect of Changes in Imports and Exports on Changes in Employment	126
7.1	Changes in Industry Employment, Sales, Domestic Demand, Exports, and Imports: Within-Industry Estimates (1979–1994)	133
7.2	Industry Displacement Rates, Changes in Sales, Domestic Demand, Exports, and Import Share, Cross-Section Estimates (1979–1994)	138
7.3	Changes in Industry Employment and Relative Import Prices: Within-Industry Estimates (1983–1992)	140
A1	Basic Trade, Output, and Employment Statistics, U.S. Manufacturing Industries, 1979–1985	156
A2	Basic Trade, Output, and Employment Statistics, U.S. Manufacturing Industries, 1985–1994	160
A3	Industry Import Shares (Imports/Imports + Domestic Supply), 1975, 1980, 1985, 1990, and 1994	164
A4	Changes in Import Prices, by Industry	168
A5	Industry Shares of Shipments and Exports, 1980, 1987, and 1994	171
A6	Industry Export Intensity (Exports/Shipments), 1975, 1980, 1985, and 1994	174
A7	Industry Import Share and Export Intensities, 1980, 1987, and 1994	178
A8	Long-Period Changes in Industry Employment, Import Share, Exports, and Domestic Demand, 1979–1985	182
A9	Long-Period Changes in Industry Employment, Import Share, Exports, and Domestic Demand, 1985–1994	186
A10	Industry Displacements, Changes in Employment, and Changes in Import Share and Exports, 1979–1994	190
B1	First-Stage Import Price Regression	197

Acknowledgments

This book has been improved by the suggestions and guidance of many colleagues. Susan Collins provided extraordinary support, advice, and encouragement. Her invitation to participate in a Brookings Institution conference in 1995 started me on a set of projects that culminate in this book. Her comments on a preliminary draft of the manuscript were invaluable. Rob Feenstra encouraged further work with his invitation to participate in a 1998 National Bureau of Economic Research conference. Susan Houseman provided helpful guidance on framing and writing the draft manuscript. Progress from draft manuscript to final version was greatly aided by the helpful comments of Ken Kletzer, Cathy Mann, Dave Richardson, and an anonymous referee. I am so grateful for Dave's support and encouragement on this book and other related projects. Randy Eberts and the research staff of the W.E. Upjohn Institute for Employment Research were gracious hosts and careful listeners when I presented preliminary results at the Institute.

Along the way, I have benefited from the helpful comments of seminar participants at the Board of Governors of the Federal Reserve System, the Center for the Study of European Integration at the University of Bonn, the University of Notre Dame, Stanford University, the University of Arizona, the University of California, Berkeley, the Danish Ministry of Business and Industry in Copenhagen, the Centre for Labor Market and Social Research, Aarhus, Denmark, and the Bureau of International Labor Affairs of the U.S. Department of Labor. Jeannine Bailliu, Ivy Kosmides, Erin Koski and Maria Unterrainer provided excellent research assistance. Finally, I gratefully acknowledge financial support from the Upjohn Institute, the U.S. Department of Labor, and the Social Sciences Division and Academic Senate Committee on Research of the University of California, Santa Cruz.

1
Introduction

The second half of the 1990s saw an extended run of strength in the U.S. economy. Both the highs and lows were notable: the government budget was in surplus, the national unemployment rate was at a historical low, the share of the population employed was high, inflation was low, and the stock market was high. These strong U.S. economic indicators stood out against more sobering statistics for virtually all U.S. trading partners. Economic downturns plagued Europe and Latin America, and financial crises rocked Asia.

In the midst of these differing states of economic health, Americans became more aware of the growing relationship between the U.S. economy and the rest of the world. It is now a familiar refrain to claim that the U.S. economy is opening up to the world. For American consumers, there are more imported goods and services to buy. Between 1965 and 1999, imports as a share of gross domestic product (GDP) rose from 5 percent to 13.1 percent. For American workers, a larger share of what is produced in U.S. factories and offices is exported now than 35 years ago. Between the mid 1960s and 1999, the share of exports in GDP rose from 5 percent to 10.3 percent. If we limit our view to merchandise trade (as we will throughout this volume), we can conclude that U.S. manufacturing is more integrated now than at any time in the past century.[1] The integration of the U.S. economy can also be viewed from the perspective of outsourcing, an activity whereby aspects of the production process are accomplished abroad and then combined with domestic production activity. This disintegration of the formerly domestically centered production process has increased considerably in the United States.[2]

The impact of free trade, now and historically, is a ready source of public debate.[3] The terms of that debate differ enormously between participants at the national level (professional economists and politicians) and participants at the local level. Professional economists highlight the net benefits of free trade: gains to consumers from lower prices, gains to the overall economy in efficiency, and higher aggregate welfare. As a group, economists are in broad agreement on the net benefits of trade to national economies. Similarly, economists agree that liberalized trade reduces incomes to some producers and workers—in other words, the distribution of the benefits from free trade, across industries, occupations, regions, and ultimately individuals, is uneven. Industries such as automobiles, steel, textiles, footwear, and consumer electronics have experienced employment declines as imported goods increasingly compete with domestically produced goods. Growth of foreign markets through exports has conveyed benefits on other industries, including aircraft, computers, entertainment, and finance.

Economists generally are in agreement with these descriptions and other broad-brush statements. For example, most economists acknowledge the existence of costs associated with moving workers and capital from import-competing sectors to other parts of the economy. After all, open trade is about shifting resources toward their most productive uses, and these shifts can be costly. Yet, individual standards of living and people's lives are in the details, and it is in the details where economists find less agreement and even outright division. Some economists, by focusing on the national level, find the costs of reallocating workers and capital across sectors and regions to be small. With large aggregate benefits and small aggregate losses, this side of the debate is "pro–free trade."

Individuals, unions, small firms, and state and local governments make up the other side of the debate. Where the pro–free trade side emphasizes the benefits, this group highlights the costs of free trade. This side was once less visible at the national level (with election years raising its visibility through the campaigns of political office seekers such as Ross Perot and Patrick Buchanan). As the 1990s ended, the "globalization backlash," first seen on a visible scale during the street demonstrations in Seattle during the November 1999 World Trade Organization Ministerial meetings, was widely recognized and a potent political force. The strength, and ultimately political clout, of this group is that the workers and communities who experience the costly dislocations from freer trade are on this side.

Scores of articles have appeared on the two sides of the debate, in the popular and academic arenas, and each side makes legitimate points. Trade of goods and services across borders is beneficial for individuals and firms that obtain what they want at lower prices and/or reach new markets. Such trade is not beneficial for those whose firms lose market share and cease production (or continue only at lower pay and profits), despite the overall gains to the economy. Ross Perot provided the debate's most visible and memorable phrase when he claimed that ratification of the North American Free Trade Agreement (NAFTA) would create "a giant sucking sound" with high-paying jobs leaving the United States for Mexico.

The ground appears to be shifting under the two sides. After much progress in unilateral and multilateral trade and investment policy liberalization, there is currently a policy stalemate on questions of further trade liberalization. One causal interpretation of the stalemate is the ascendancy of the forces highlighting the domestic labor market costs of freer trade. Even with a policy stalemate, however, the process of global economic integration will continue. Yet, it seems most important to remember that free trade is about net benefits; some will win and others will lose. In that light, understanding some of the magnitudes of costs and benefits may contribute to more educated public discourse. This book attempts to do that. Several questions frame the analysis. Is there any validity to the claim that increasing trade is associated with American job loss? What are the theoretical underpinnings of such a claim? What do the data show? Are parts of the claim consistent with the facts and other parts inconsistent?

With my training as an economist, I understand the net benefits of liberalized trade. As a scholar of labor markets and specifically job displacement, however, I also understand the costly dislocations that occur as economies change in response to freer trade. In this book, I try to bring a better understanding of the labor market costs of freer trade into the national policy-making debate. Only by understanding the costs can the nation equitably move forward on the path of international economic integration to enjoy the benefits. Balanced advocacy of free trade by economists requires full recognition that economy-wide positive net benefits do not preclude localized negative net benefits. Economic theory suggests that not everyone benefits from free trade; positive economy-wide benefits result from the gains of the winners exceeding the losses of the losers. Economy-wide, freer trade is only welfare-enhancing if the winners compensate the losers through a transfer of resources by policy. This book aims to measure some of the losses in the hope that future policy making will address them and the people who bear the burden.

OUTLINE, OBJECTIVES, AND FINDINGS

A number of recent studies of the impact of international trade on the domestic labor market have revealed potentially important links between increased foreign competition and reductions in employment and relative earnings, particularly for less-skilled manufacturing workers. This book seeks to add to that research and contribute to future policy debate by providing a detailed examination of the relationship between changes in international trade, employment, and job displacement for a sample of U.S. manufacturing industries. The link between international trade and domestic jobs is explored through studies of both net and gross employment change. Bringing together a variety of measures of employment change may offer a more complete understanding of the impact of trade on domestic employment than any one approach alone. I proceed as follows.

Economists bring to the question of the impact of trade on domestic employment an extensive and informative set of insights known as international trade theory. Some of the basics of trade theory form a useful foundation of this study's empirical focus, and this is the subject of Chapter 2. Different models of international trade point to different indicators of international linkages. In this chapter, I also discuss empirical measures of the intensity of foreign competition.

This study of trade and the domestic labor market builds on a substantial body of earlier research. In Chapter 3, I review the relevant literature in the areas of trade, employment, wages, and job loss. The review is not comprehensive; instead, it establishes basic methodologies and reviews findings. Taken as a group, these studies point to internationalization, particularly expansions of international trade, as a source of declining manufacturing employment and increasing wage inequality but not the most important source.

The real empirical work begins in Chapter 4, where the data on manufacturing employment and job loss are first introduced. The objective of the chapter is to lay out the basic trends in manufacturing employment, job loss, trade, and domestic demand over the period of 1979–1994. This time period is dictated by data availability: the job loss data begin in 1979, and 1994 represents a significant break point in the industry definitions for the trade flows data. With these trends, we can consider several questions. Has increased import competition been an important factor behind declining employment? Are changes in exports associated with changes in employment? Do these relationships hold for many industries or for a subset of industries? From the perspective of manufacturing employment, the 15-year period from the late 1970s to the mid 1990s was a difficult one. The sector as a whole was rocked by two recessions, a deep one in the early 1980s and another, not so deep, in the early 1990s. Productivity growth was sluggish, and U.S. consumer demand continued to shift away from manufactured goods and toward services. There was also a seeming continued rise of foreign competition. Manufacturing employment has remained fairly constant over the past 25 years, yet the composition of employment within the sector has changed rather dramatically across industries and over time. Employment declined (sharply in many cases) in many manufacturing industries, particularly during the late 1970s and early 1980s. Over time, import share has risen within manufacturing, from imports accounting for an average of 0.066 of domestic supply in 1975 to an average share of 0.171 in 1994 (an increase of 159 percent). In 1994, U.S. firms exported about 12.5 percent of manufacturing shipments to foreign markets, averaged across the industries in the sample. This level represents a 50 percent increase from 1975. Export intensity grew slowly over the late 1970s and fell a bit from 1980 to 1985 with the sharp dollar appreciation of the early 1980s. From 1985 to 1994, export intensity rose 68 percent from 7.2 percent of shipments to 12.5 percent.

Bringing together, descriptively, the data on employment and trade reveals that sharply declining exports are strongly associated with employment decline, particularly in the industries accounting for the bulk of the employment loss. Rising imports are also strongly associated with employment decline but more so in the smaller traditionally import-competing industries (watches and clocks, footwear, and leather products). Apparel, a traditionally import-competing industry, was the biggest employer in the set of top 10 industries for import share gain and export decline. The iron and steel industries appear hard hit by the combination of rising import share and declining exports, as well as large employment losses.

How much employment decline was associated with the rise in import share and/or the decline in exports? Due mostly to employment size, industries with the largest increases in import share accounted for a noticeably small share of total sectoral employment decline. Of the top import share gainers (and export losers, with solid domestic demand), apparel accounted for the largest share of employment declines, at 7 percent. With apparel at number 8 in rising import share, the top 10 import share gainers accounted for 21 percent of employment decline, and they started with 12 percent of 1979 employment. Four of the industries in this group had considerable export decline. The top 10 in export decline accounted for about 25 percent of employment loss, starting from a 12 percent 1979 employment share.

Industry net employment change is a result of changes in the gross flows of new hires, recalls, quits, displacements, temporary layoffs, and retirements. Following the descriptive analysis of industry net employment change, I turn to one of the gross flows, job displacement, in an analysis that is more novel.[4] As commonly understood, job displacement is an involuntary (from the worker's perspective) termination of employment based on the employer's operating decisions—not on a worker's individual performance. The focus on job displacement is motivated by the perspective that the amount of social and private adjustment to freer trade depends importantly on gross employment changes, and it is the job loss component of employment change that most concerns workers, the general public, and policymakers. International trade theory, together with previous empirical work, provides a starting point: trade liberalization will lead to labor reallocation, with jobs moving away from import-competing industries and toward export industries. From that starting point, several questions are posed. Descriptively, how does the survey evidence on job displacement accord with standard measures of increasing foreign competition? Is displacement associated with employment losses? Is the incidence of job displacement across and within industries causally related to changes in foreign competition?

The descriptive analysis reported in Chapter 4 reveals that, with a few exceptions, all industries with above-average rates of job loss have above-average employment declines in employment. Industries with employment growth tend to have lower job loss rates. The large employment industries, all with sizeable increases in import share, all had fairly large employment declines and job loss rates at or higher than the sectoral average. Interestingly, the strongest relationship between employment change and the risk of job displacement is found amongst the set of small (in employment) traditionally import-competing industries, such as leather tanning and finishing (with a 29 percent employment decline and a 0.073 job loss rate), watches and clocks (a 69 percent employment decline and a 0.091 job loss rate), and leather products (a 78 percent employment decline and a 0.142 job loss rate).

For the most part, these high job loss rate industries had both a high import share and experienced a large (positive) change in import share (increasing import competition). In other words, the combination of "trade with job loss" appears to arise from continued, sustained import competition. Industries with lower import share yet large positive change in import share have lower rates of job loss (metalworking machinery, aircraft, and knitting mills), while industries with high import share and average or smaller changes in import share also have average or lower rates of job loss (motor vehicles, and engines and turbines).

The discernible patterns found in the descriptive analysis, while interesting and informative, require more detailed examination in an econometric model. Chapter 5 describes a straightforward empirical model relating changes in foreign trade and foreign competition and changes in industry employment and job displacement, and it is the basis for the econometric analyses that follow in Chapters 6 and 7.

Changes in industry employment are the focus of Chapter 6. Overall, the results are consistent with arguments that increasing imports reduce employment and that increasing exports (and domestic demand) enhance employment. Within an industry on a year-to-year basis, rising exports are more strongly associated with employment growth than are increases in domestic demand. A 10 percent increase in sales due to exports leads to a 7 percent increase in employment, whereas a 10 percent increase in domestic demand leads to a 3.5 percent increase in employment. A 10 percent increase in import share leads to a 4 percent reduction in employment. The employment-enhancing effect of expanding exports is significantly greater than the employment-reducing effect of expanding imports. Across industries, the effect of rising import share on employment is larger, where a 10 percent increase in imports is associated with an employment decline of approximately 5 percent. This is consistent with the more descriptive analysis of Chapter 4, which revealed a relatively strong relationship between rising import share in the traditionally import-competing industries and a much less systematic relationship in other industries. Within the "typical" manufacturing industry, developed country imports and developing country imports have equally sized effects on domestic employment.

The analysis discussed in Chapter 6 measures increasing foreign competition as changes in import price and suggests that a 10 percent increase in import price is associated with an approximately 3 percent decline in employment. A one standard deviation change in import price, 6.6 percent, implies a 1.98 percent decline in employment.

At the end of Chapter 6, the within-industry estimates of the relationship between changes in trade flows and employment are used to generate counterfactual simulations of the path of employment change, had imports and exports been "frozen" at their 1979 levels. In most industries, there would have been more employment with neutral imports and less employment with neutral exports. If import share had been frozen at its 1979 level, average industry employment would have declined by 8.8 percent. For an average industry, this 4.6 percent difference, due to the increase in imports, represents 11,693 jobs. On the other hand, if exports had been frozen at their 1979 level, employment would have fallen by 19 percent, 5.6 percent more than observed. Thus, the growth in exports "saved" an average of 14,235 jobs in manufacturing. Together, if both imports and exports had been frozen at 1979 levels, employment would have declined by 16.4 percent, or 3 percent more than observed (7,626 jobs).

The empirical focus narrows to job displacement in Chapter 7. A 10 percent increase in sales is associated with a 1-percentage-point decrease in the job loss rate. The most striking result is the large responsiveness of job loss rates to changes in exports. A 10 percent rise in exports lowers the industry displacement rate by 2.2 percent. A 10 percent rise in domestic demand lowers the industry job loss rate by 0.9 percent. The sensitivity of job loss to changes in exports has been overlooked, but it may not be surprising. The rise in exports can be interpreted as a shift in labor demand, leading to an increase in the desired level of employment. At a given level of hiring (accessions) and nondisplacement separations, employment will rise with a fall in permanent job loss.

Most notably, rising import share is associated with a higher displacement rate, but the coefficient is small and the estimate is imprecise. At standard levels of statistical significance, it cannot be rejected that the "true" effect of changes in import share on the job loss rate is zero. The within-industry effect of rising import share is notably smaller than the cross-industry effect, suggesting that the relationship between rising import share and job loss holds (perhaps strongly) for a subset of industries, but it is considerably weaker systematically or for all manufacturing industries. In other words, specific high import share industries account for the rising import share–job loss relationship, and once those industry effects are accounted for, the correlation between rising import share and job loss is much weaker. This difference is consistent with the descriptive findings (noted in Chapter 4) that high rates of job loss are found in the set of industries facing sustained import competition where large positive changes in import share occur from a starting point of a high level of import share. Differentiating imports by country of origin makes no difference in understanding changes in the rate of job loss.

Chapter 8 concludes and discusses policy implications. For policy, the inclusion of exports into the story requires a reorientation of thinking. "Trade" is not just imports. A usual starting point is that if imports are a culprit in the loss of jobs, then import restrictions can be used to protect jobs. The relatively small elasticities found here show that reducing import share will not boost employment or reduce job displacement by much, and consumers will bear the cost through higher prices. There are industries, however, where the link between job loss and increasing imports is strong. For workers displaced from these industries, losing a job can be a costly experience, with two-thirds of workers earning less on the new job than they did on the old job (see Kletzer 2001). Protecting workers can be accomplished more directly through domestic adjustment assistance policy. This approach has long had considerable support in the domestic politics of freer trade.

This study broadens our understanding of the benefits of export activity. If exports enhance employment growth and reduce job loss, then acquiring or extending access to foreign markets can be a focus of policy. Increasing foreign demand, all else the same, has a sizeable impact on employment growth and it reduces job loss. Particularly for U.S. manufacturing, foreign markets provide a way to maintain demand and employment as American consumers continue, with rising incomes, to shift from goods-oriented consumption to services-oriented consumption.

Notes

1. Feenstra (1998, p. 35) reported merchandise trade relative to merchandise value-added and found the ratio 150 percent higher in 1990 than in 1890 and 273 percent higher than in 1960.
2. Feenstra and Hanson (1997) estimated that imported inputs increased from 5.7 percent of total U.S. manufactured imports in 1972 to 11.6 percent in 1990. Outsourcing is concentrated in textiles, apparel, and footwear (see also Feenstra 1998).
3. Although Americans seem particularly taken by the growth of international trade, it can be useful to remember that the share of trade in the U.S. economy in the mid 1990s was much smaller not only than the share of trade in most other industrialized countries but also smaller than the share of trade in most other industrialized countries 30 years ago. In addition, while trade has grown in the United States, it has grown even faster in some developing countries.
4. The focus is different but not unique. See also Addison, Fox, and Ruhm (1995) and Haveman (1998).

2
Understanding the Links between Increasing Foreign Competition and Domestic Employment and Job Loss

International trade theory provides a theoretical framework for thinking about how changes in the global competitive environment affect domestic labor. In this chapter I review the basics of international trade theory, focusing on theories relevant to how "trade" affects the jobs of American workers. With the theory in place, I then turn to a discussion of available empirical measures of the intensity of foreign competition.

This study is predicated on the benefits of trade. As noted in the introduction, economists agree on the proposition that people, firms, and countries should trade with each other to raise standards of living. Trade has four main benefits: 1) it leads to efficiencies in production through the principle of comparative advantage and, relatedly, specialization; 2) it leads to efficient consumption, through lower prices for goods and services that result from the lower opportunity costs of producing at comparative advantage; 3) it opens up a more competitive environment, with domestic producers competing with foreign producers, leading to lower prices both statically and dynamically as competition spurs innovation; and 4) it brings about an increased variety of available products. Readers interested in a more complete presentation are directed to Burtless et al. (1998) for a particularly clear and concise discussion.

A BRIEF EXCURSION THROUGH INTERNATIONAL TRADE THEORY: THE EFFECTS OF TRADE ON WAGES AND EMPLOYMENT

Loosely speaking, two trends appear to line up, providing the link between trade and a deteriorating labor market for manufacturing workers: 1) trade with the rest of the world has increased and 2) wages and employment of production workers have fallen. As consumers buy more foreign-produced goods, they buy fewer domestically produced goods, and American workers lose jobs and/or see their wages fall. This section discusses the theoretical foundations of such claims.

Differences in prices across countries, reflecting differences in the costs of production, are the most basic cause of trade. With these differences in prices, trade serves to minimize the resource costs of (worldwide) production. By minimizing the resource costs of production, trade maximizes the real value of production from world resources. This happens because, with trade, producers in each country can specialize in those economic activities that make the best use of their country's resources.

Restated, these international differences in the relative costs of production constitute the notion of comparative advantage, the mainstay of international trade theory (the analysis of why nations trade). Comparative advantage was introduced by David Ricardo in his *Principles of Political Economy* and extended and refined by Eli Heckscher and Bertil Ohlin.[1] At its simplest, a nation's comparative advantage in some goods and comparative disadvantage in others is a result of that nation's endowment of natural resources, weather, technology, and labor force productivity. The basic prediction of the model of international trade with comparative advantage is that countries will tend to export those goods where their endowment of land, labor, capital, and technology allows expansion of output with the smallest sacrifice of other domestic goods. Conversely, countries will import goods whose production is relatively more costly in terms of alternative domestic output. Ricardo used differences in technology to create opportunities for trade. The Heckscher–Ohlin theory is based on country differences in factor endowments. Countries will tend to export goods whose production is intensive in factors with which they are abundantly endowed and will tend to import goods whose production is intensive in factors with which they are scarcely endowed. This result, and its implications for wages and employment, can be illustrated quite clearly in the context of the two-factor, two-good Heckscher–Ohlin–Samuelson model, the standard or "textbook" model.

Each of the two countries in this basic setup is able to produce two goods, the production of which requires the use of two factors of production. These two inputs, capital and labor, are available in fixed supply in both countries. Both economies share the same technology. One of the two goods requires a higher ratio of capital to labor than does the other and is hence capital intensive. The other is labor intensive.

Each economy will tend to be relatively efficient at producing the good that is intensive in the factor with which it is relatively well endowed. The country/producer with the smaller opportunity cost of producing a good has comparative advantage in the production of that good. In this framework, comparative advantage is based on the interaction between the resources a country possesses and the existing technology of production. When trade opens up between these two countries, each one will tend to specialize in and export the good for which it has comparative advantage, the good whose production is intensive in the factor with which it is abundantly endowed. The capital-rich country will tend to specialize in and export the capital intensive good and import the labor-intensive good and vice-versa for the labor abundant country.[2]

International trade in this model will cause the export sector to expand production and the import sector to contract production as each country focuses their production on the good in which they have comparative advantage. With trade, as the two countries specialize according to their respective comparative advantages, both benefit in that their total consumption will be greater with trade than in the absence of trade. Free trade benefits both countries because it allows all resources to be used most productively.

With an assumption of full employment, the capital and labor that is "released" from the import sector is "absorbed" instantaneously by the export sector. The production of both goods is assumed to be characterized by perfect competition, in both the output market and the factor market. Therefore, the price of each good is exactly equal to the cost of producing it and prices automatically adjust so that supply equals demand. This assumption rules out market imperfections, such as monopoly pricing, long-term trade imbalances, and chronic unemployment. With the assumption of flexible prices and wages and full employment, all the effects of trade on the demand for labor are reflected in wage changes. As long as both goods are produced, there is a direct relationship between global goods prices and domestic factor prices. In other words, when world goods prices change, so do home factor prices. So, in order to find out how international trade affects wages in this model, we need to examine what happens to the relative prices of the goods.

Given that there are no barriers to trade, international trade in this model leads to a global convergence in the relative prices of the two goods. Without trade, the relative price of the capital intensive good is lower in the capital abundant country because it is produced relatively more efficiently. The relative price of the labor intensive good is lower in the labor abundant country because it is produced relatively more efficiently there. The new relative price of the capital intensive good will settle somewhere between the autarky (no-trade) levels of the relative prices in both countries. Thus, with trade, the relative price of the labor intensive good increases in the labor abundant country and falls in the capital abundant country. Given that the relative price of the goods has changed in each country, so will the relative factor prices. The Stolper–Samuelson theorem discusses how relative factor prices change in response to a change in the relative price of goods.

Stolper–Samuelson theorem

The analysis of the effect of changes in relative goods prices on factor prices, in the context of the two-factor, two-good Heckscher–Ohlin framework, first appeared in Stolper and Samuelson (1941). Generalized beyond the 2 × 2 case, this analysis now stands as the origin of the "Stolper–Samuelson effect," and it is the foundation for most studies of the effect of "trade" on wages. Stolper and Samuelson showed that there is a magnified effect of goods prices on factor prices. When, as a result of trade liberalization, the relative price of the capital intensive good increases in the capital abundant country, it will cause an increase in the rental price of capital and a fall in the wage rate (the return to labor). Since the wage rate falls, the increase in the rental price of capital must be proportionately higher than the increase in the price of the capital intensive good. In the labor abundant country, the relative price of the labor intensive good has risen which causes an increase in the wage rate and a fall in the rental price of capital. Thus, the Stolper–Samuelson effect predicts that trade liberalization will cause the wage rate to fall in the capital abundant country and to increase in the labor abundant country.[3] Note that these factor price changes are real; the real wage will fall in the capital abundant country and rise in the labor abundant country.

This analysis reveals that the benefits from trade liberalization are uneven. To fix ideas, we will focus on the U.S. perspective, where we can consider capital to be abundant and labor scarce. This is certainly true for the United States relative to other countries. The owners of the two factors of production, capital and labor, will be affected differently (in opposite directions). In the Heckscher–Ohlin–Samuelson model, the owners of the relatively scarce factor will be made worse off by freer trade, and the owners of the abundant factor will be made better off. The way this works is that the scarce factor becomes less scarce in an open economy, so its price (the wage rate) falls. Then, workers will be made worse off by falling wages with freer trade, and capital owners will be made better off. The loss to labor is more than offset by the gains to capital, leading to the net national gains from trade.[4]

In the face of these distributional questions, it is often claimed that income can be redistributed after a trade liberalization so that every individual is better off under free trade. Such a redistribution is theoretically possible, taking from the gainers to compensate the losers. If gross gains exceeds the gross losses, the redistribution will yield net benefits. A problem for the theory is that such a redistribution is not a required, or automatic, part of trade liberalization. At a minimum, some political will is required to create legislation that compels the winners, through government transfer and assistance programs, to compensate the losers.

If we expand the basic model, the two factors of production can be seen as skilled and unskilled labor, as in Wood (1994). Alternatively, the model can work with three factors of production, capital, skilled labor, and unskilled labor, as in Leamer (1993). Then, the model predicts increased wage inequality with liberalized trade, as the wages of high skilled labor (the abundant factor in the United States) rise, and the wages of low skilled labor (the scarce factor) fall.

Factor price equalization (FPE)

A second theorem relates to the distributional impact of free trade. In the context of the simple Heckscher–Ohlin–Samuelson model, perfectly free trade will cause the factor prices in the two countries to equalize. Without trade, different relative goods prices and correspondingly, different relative factor prices, will prevail in the labor abundant and capital abundant countries. With free trade, the two countries will face the same relative prices for goods, and with that, the relative factor prices they face must also be the same. This implies, for example, that wages in the United States and Mexico (and/or China) would be equalized if trade barriers were completely removed.

The conditions under which the FPE theorem holds are stringent. Both countries must produce all goods, both countries must employ identical technology, and there must be constant returns to scale (no economies or diseconomies of large-scale production). Factors must be able to move freely between sectors within each country, there can be no transport costs or other barriers to trade, and the quality of the factors of production must be identical in the two countries.[5] Given these stringent conditions, it is not surprising that the empirical evidence shows that not all factor prices are equalized internationally.

This basic model and its assumptions should not be accepted literally. Most of the model assumptions are violated, at least most of the time: there is not always full employment nor balanced trade; there are often economies of scale; technologies differ across countries; endowments of factors are not fixed; countries do specialize completely (e.g., the United States produces no bananas); and institutional and market factors do influence prices, wages, supply, and demand.

With the assumption of fully flexible, market-clearing wages and full employment, the standard model points to wage changes as the key outcome for influence by free trade. In a standard Heckscher–Ohlin–Samuelson model, if the price of an imported (substitutable) good falls, labor's marginal revenue product falls. This drop in the derived demand for labor reduces employment (on an upward sloping labor supply curve). Flexible wages dampen the fall in employment. If wages adjust fully to equate labor demand and labor supply (a competitive labor market), employment falls to desired levels through (employee-initiated) quits. How much wages and employment change will depend on supply and demand elasticities. With market-clearing wages, labor leaving the import sector will be reallocated to the export sector, and full employment will be sustained.

With the full employment assumption, conventional trade models focus their predictive power on changes in goods and factor prices.

(These prices must be flexible to ensure full employment.) The data (and reality) often reveal price and wage inflexibility and unemployment. Where wages differ from market-clearing, the likely consequences of increasing import competition differ from the conventional models. If wages are inflexible downward, the reduction in labor demand will produce a fall in employment and no wage change. Thus, the impact of trade will be felt (much) more on employment and (much) less so on wages. The distribution of employment change may also be affected. For example, in unionized labor markets where wages are set by collective bargaining, senior union members may prefer to maintain wages (and their jobs), with layoffs reducing the employment of junior workers.[6] In a limited number of cases, unions may even push for higher wages as labor demand falls, with an "endgame" bargaining strategy that tries to get as much for the union as possible before the industry disappears. Wage inflexibility does not require collective bargaining. If wages diverge from market-clearing for efficiency wage reasons, firms may be reluctant to impose wage reductions if they anticipate negative productivity consequences.

As we will see in the next chapter, the conventional model assumption of flexible wages and full employment is often not borne out in the data. Empirical studies find more evidence of negative employment effects of trade than of negative wage effects. These findings motivate the further analysis of trade-induced employment changes and job loss.

INTRA-INDUSTRY TRADE AND "NEW" TRADE THEORY

The discussion above focused on so-called "conventional" or "traditional" trade theory, where industries are characterized by constant returns to scale and perfect competition. While no longer literally new, "new" trade theory addresses the role of increasing returns to scale and imperfect competition in the world economy.[7] New trade theory offers explanations for empirical observations that cannot be adequately explained through conventional trade theory. Two empirical observations stand out: the first is the volume of trade between countries. The Heckscher–Ohlin model explains trade entirely by differences across countries in factor endowments. These differences suggest that the volume of trade between countries will be inversely related to their similarity in relative factor endowments. The data reveal, however, that most of the world's trade occurs between industrialized countries that are very similar in technology and factor proportions (e.g., trade between the United States and Canada or trade within the European Union). Second, differences between countries' relative factor endowments should generate a pattern of trade in which countries export goods whose production is intensive in their abundant factor (e.g, the United States exports cars and imports apparel). This is the case, but only for countries' net exports (exports minus imports). Again, the data reveal clear patterns of substantial two-way trade in goods of similar factor intensity (e.g., the United States exports and imports cars). This type of two-way trade within an industry is called intra-industry trade. This second empirical observation is most relevant to this study, where many industries can be characterized as both importers and exporters.

In new trade theory, trade between similar countries is explained by product differentiation and country-specific economies of scale, in particular increasing returns to scale. Increasing returns to scale refers to a production situation where output of a differentiated good grows proportionately more than the increase in inputs (factors of production). With increasing returns to scale, unit production costs of a particular variety of a good fall as the firm's output expands. Increasing returns to scale may develop as a firm grows because a larger scale of operation allows a greater division of labor and more specialization. More specialized and efficient machinery might be introduced, or there might be a fuller use of capacity or a more detailed division of worker tasks, all of which could increase worker productivity. In addition, fixed overhead costs will make a smaller contribution to average costs as they will be spread out over a larger volume of output.[8] Trade allows similarly endowed countries to specialize in the production of different varieties of a good or even different goods. They realize the lower unit costs of increasing returns to scale and trade for other goods. The production efficiencies yield a higher global level of output.

Scale economies can explain trade between countries in goods that are produced using identical proportions, which the Heckscher–Ohlin theory cannot. For example, a great deal of international trade involves imports and exports of similar, but differentiated, products (such as Chevrolet, Volvo, Toyota, and Volkswagen cars, or Californian, Chilean, French, or Italian wine). This type of trade is called intra-industry trade. Producer goods can be differentiated also, including capital goods (e.g., machine tools, photocopiers, and computers) and intermediate inputs (e.g., steel and microprocessors).

The logic of the model is straightforward. Consider an industry where the product is differentiated, and let each variety of the good be produced with increasing returns to scale. Allow these economies of scale to occur at a relatively low levels of output so that, under free entry, the industry can accommodate many producers in a monopolistically competitive equilibrium. Each firm will produce a different variety of the good, under increasing returns to scale at the level of the firm. Each firm in an industry (where industry means "product") chooses a variety of the product and an output level to maximize profits. We need to assume that industry demand displays a demand for variety. People can either like variety in their consumption bundles or different people can prefer different varieties of a product. Then, for a pair of countries that produce varieties of a product, the model predicts intra-industry trade. In this simplest form, both countries will produce different varieties of a product under trade, and every variety will be demanded in both countries. Thus, the production of and demand for differentiated products generates intra-industry trade.

Differentiated products are the key point of contrast with conventional trade theory, where products are assumed homogeneous. In the Heckscher–Ohlin two-country, two-good, two-factor model, a capital abundant country will export the capital intensive good and import the labor intensive good. This type of trade is inter-industry and is driven by comparative advantage. If goods within an industry are differentiated (there are different varieties of both the capital intensive good and the labor intensive good), then the capital abundant country will still be a net exporter of the capital intensive good, but it will also import some varieties of that good. The capital abundant country will continue to be a net importer of the labor intensive good, but it will export some varieties of that good. The two-way trade in capital and labor intensive products is intra-industry trade. Gross exports of capital intensive goods will exceed net exports from that industry.

To sum up, when products are homogeneous, all trade is inter-industry. When products are differentiated, both inter- and intra-industry trade will occur. With differentiated products and increasing returns to scale, there are gains from trade beyond the gains from comparative advantage. Product differentiation helps explain the large volume of trade among developed countries, the relative importance of intra-industry trade over inter-industry trade within these countries, and the relative importance of inter-industry trade between developed and developing countries.[9] Product differentiation also suggests higher trade volumes between advanced industrial countries than is suggested by a model of factor endowments.

Increasing returns may have different implications for the distribution of income than conventional (comparative advantage) trade models. Because economies of scale offer potential gains from trade beyond the gains from comparative advantage, the traditional impact of trade on factor returns, following Stolper and Samuelson (1941), may be reversed. As discussed above, in the conventional model with constant returns to scale, the Stolper–Samuelson theorem implies that owners of factors of production that are scarcer in a particular country than they are in the world overall are likely to lose from free trade. In the context of the United States, if unskilled labor is the scarce factor, the theorem implies that unskilled real wages will decrease, in terms of all goods, as a result of trade. In short, unskilled labor in the United States will be worse off from trade.

Conclusions can be different with scale economies, because the increasing returns provide additional benefits to trade. Bypassing the technical details (which are provided in Helpman and Krugman [1985]), if countries are sufficiently similar in relative factor endowments, so that the changes in relative factor rewards are not too big, and if economies of scale are sufficiently important, then all factors of production can gain from trade. These universal gains depend upon the degree to which different product varieties within an industry are substitutable for one another. If varieties are highly substitutable and factor abundance ratios are not very similar between countries, the Stolper–Samuelson effect can dominate, implying losses from trade for owners of the scarce factor of production.

This discussion is meant to provide only the basics of international trade theory. A far more in-depth review of trade theory and the empirical evidence is found in Leamer and Levinsohn (1995). For a comprehensive discussion of the structure of international trade that integrates conventional and new trade theory, see Helpman (1999).

MEASURING INDUSTRY TRADE SENSITIVITY

What is the best indicator of how changes in international trade affect domestic labor? As we will see in the next chapter, the trade and employment literature is divided on the answer to this question, with some studies measuring trade changes and increasing foreign competition as changes in global prices and other studies using "quantities," such as changes in import share or net imports (imports less exports). There is no unique "best" measure in the sense that the choice of a proxy for an exogenous shock in the foreign sector is model-specific (more on this point below). Causality aside, there is also a question in the literature about how to classify industries as "trade-sensitive" or "trade-impacted." In this section I take a somewhat agnostic approach and discuss the various measures available and how the measures may (or may not) be related to changes in employment and job loss.

Import penetration ratios (or import shares) provide an intuitively appealing way to categorize industries facing significant foreign competition. An import penetration ratio is calculated by dividing industry imports by the sum of industry output plus imports (the denominator is industry supply). An export penetration ratio is calculated by dividing industry exports by industry output. More generally, industries with a large (or rising) share of output (or supply) internationally traded are often labeled "trade-sensitive" (or import/export-sensitive) on the basis of calculated import (and export) penetration ratios. If the flow of imports reduces domestic employment, industries with high import penetration ratios are where that result is most likely to be found.[10]

In some quarters, a quantity-based categorization of industries has intuitive appeal. Yet from a theoretical perspective, there is no simple causal link between the volume of trade and employment changes because the rise in import share could indicate a number of foreign or domestic developments. One simple example may be illustrative of the complexity. Take the case of perfect competition, increasing but different marginal costs of production for both domestic and foreign firms, with substitutability between domestic and foreign goods. Let foreign supply expand, perhaps from technological diffusion (or an export promotion scheme) that lowers foreign costs while domestic costs remain unchanged. This reduces the foreign good price and imports rise. With constant demand, the rise in imports reduces price, domestic output, and domestic employment. With declining domestic output, import share also rises. How much import share rises depends on the elasticity of domestic supply. As domestic supply becomes more elastic, a given increase in imports produces a bigger reduction in domestic quantity (and presumably employment) and import share rises.

When trade is measured as quantity flows, it is important also to consider (or control for) demand. In the perfectly competitive case, imports may also rise if domestic demand increases. Price moves accordingly and, if foreign supply is more elastic than domestic supply, import share will also rise because the increase in imports will exceed the increase in domestic output. Alternatively, if domestic supply is more elastic than foreign supply, the rise in imports will be accompanied by a decline in import share. Here, the use of quantities reveals an ambiguity: rising imports and import share are associated with increased domestic employment and presumably less displacement, and rising imports may not be associated with rising import share. These two cases imply that, over time, industry import shares will differ as a result of differences in supply elasticities as well as differences in the competitiveness of domestic firms relative to foreign firms.

Reliance on changes in trade flows may understate the impact of foreign competition on wages and employment if the mechanism is slightly different than that described by conventional theoretical models. If employers exercise a threat, either implicit or explicit, of relocating production facilities or outsourcing some part of production, workers may feel that wage reductions are necessary to save jobs or that some thinning of payrolls is necessary to save most jobs. This threat effect will produce either wage or employment changes without actual changes in observed trade flows. Changes in industry import price might be associated with the wage and/or employment changes, but not necessarily, as it is the perception of future foreign competition that may produce the employer threat. This mechanism does assume that wages are not set in competitive markets and that a process of labor-management bargaining produces a wage agreement. The threat of production relocation and/or outsourcing changes reduce the relative bargaining power of labor.

The most immediate appeal of a "price" measure is the standard Heckscher–Ohlin model, where industries face increasing import price competition when import prices fall. The link between import price competition and industry employment is fairly straightforward. If the price of an imported (substitutable) good falls, labor's marginal revenue product falls. This drop in the derived demand for labor reduces employment (on an upward sloping labor supply curve). Flexible wages dampen the fall in employment. If wages adjust fully to equate labor demand and labor supply (a competitive labor market), employment falls to desired levels through (employee-initiated) quits. How much wages and employment change will depend on supply and demand elasticities, but there will be no displacement. Only if prices fall enough that firms find it more profitable to shut down than to continue to operate will displacements occur (through plant closings).

There are at least two reasons to think that price, conceivably the preferred measure, is not completely informative about the effect of changes in trade policy or foreign supply. The first is that during the late 1970s and early 1980s some industries had quota protection (apparel, footwear, and radio and television). Import price changes will not necessarily reflect these quantity restraints. More importantly, these quota restraints imply that market share (import share) is likely to be a determinant of foreign and domestic supply.

The second difficulty with price alone is more fundamental. Using a monopolistically competitive dominant/fringe model, Mann (1988) showed how market share is likely to be a determinant of both foreign and domestic supply. First, quantity is a key variable in monopolistic competition with heterogeneous outputs (see Spence 1976). Second, she noted that in a three-factor Cobb–Douglas production function, with no restrictions on returns to scale and with capital fixed in the short run, increasing returns to scale are an important determinant of price. In her empirical analysis, Mann found that foreign competition, measured as both import prices and import share, plays a small role in determining employment relative to the role played by domestic demand and prices.

This discussion of the basics of international trade theory and measures of foreign competition will serve as a foundation for the detailed empirical examination that follows. These basics will also be useful in our next step, when we turn to the insights of earlier studies. We can take several themes from this chapter. The first is that different models of international trade point to different indicators of international linkages. Economists differ in their views about which model and indicator is most appropriate. This diversity of opinion is reflected in existing empirical work. For that empirical work and my own analysis that follows, it is also important to be clear that both quantity and price measures are likely to be endogenous, at least in some degree, to the overall process that produces changes in domestic employment and job loss. Similarly, both indicators, or certainly their proxies, are subject to data issues, such as measurement and aggregation concerns.

Notes

1. For a more in-depth discussion of international trade theory, the interested reader can consult any college-level textbook on international economics. Salvatore (1998) provides an accessible presentation, with an emphasis on graphs rather than formal mathematics.
2. Well beyond the scope of this study, we note that neither endowments nor comparative advantage are fixed over time. Technology, productivity, and capital investments are not immutable, as they are functions of institutional factors.
3. Allowing for more than two factors weakens the Stolper–Samuelson theorem, although it still implies a weak relationship between factor abundance and the effects of protection on factor prices. See Deardorff (1993).
4. Leamer and Levinsohn (1995, p. 1348) offer a "winners and losers corollary" interpretation of the Stolper–Samuelson theorem: "When a relative price changes, there is at least one winner and one loser." They consider this corollary to be the main message of the Stolper–Samuelson paper: that free trade is not good for everyone.
5. There is one additional technical assumption of a unique relation between commodity prices and techniques of production. This assumption rules out factor intensity (of production) reversals.
6. Unionized firms most often operate with inverse seniority layoff rules. These rules are also common in the nonunion sector (see Abraham and Medoff 1984).
7. For an integrated and much-cited presentation of "new" trade theory, see Helpman and Krugman (1985). Krugman (1995) offers a condensed version of Helpman and Krugman.
8. Increasing returns to scale need to be distinguished from external economies. External economies are the reduction in each firm's unit production costs as the *industry's* output expands. External economies arise when a larger (and perhaps more geographically concentrated) industry is likely to provide more specialized labor and other factors, which leads to higher productivity and lower average costs for all the firms in the industry. The pattern of international trade and the gains from trade are not as clear with external economies as they are for internal economies.

9. It is the existence of economies of scale that matters for intra-industry trade, not their size (see Helpman 1999).
10. Davis, Haltiwanger, and Schuh (1996) found high rates of job destruction for plants in industries with very high import penetration ratios over the period of 1972–1988. Plants in the top quintile of industries ranked by import penetration ratios had average annual employment reductions of 2.8 percent.

3
Evidence from Earlier Studies

How does increasing international economic integration affect the domestic labor market? Standard theories of international trade predict that internationalization will widen the wage gap between skilled and unskilled workers in the United States. The presence of both growing internationalization and declining relative wages of low skilled workers continues to fuel an active and often heated debate over how much "globalization" is to "blame" for U.S. labor market outcomes. While the "trade and wages" research debate has become well-known for its heat, it has also generated considerable light. This chapter is designed to serve as a starting point into this large and growing literature. Interested readers will find useful reviews in Belman and Lee (1996), Burtless (1995), Richardson (1995), Cline (1997), Blanchflower and Slaughter (1999), and Blanchflower (2000).[1]

My primary goal for this chapter is to develop some perspective from the "trades and wages" literature for the analysis that follows. To that end, I will review the basic methodologies and findings of key aspects of the literature and discuss implications for my own analysis. I will also note disagreements, weaknesses, and gaps. My discussion of this large literature is not comprehensive; I include only empirical studies, not theoretical. I highlight those studies relevant either to understanding the general direction of the literature or to my interest in employment and wage change and job loss.

As in any academic research area, scholars participating in this literature have their disagreements. Unsurprisingly, a literature that is called "trade and wages" involves economists in the two fields of international trade and labor. Their disagreements tend to be methodological, although not uniformly so. I will use a simple statement of the methodological dispute as an organizational tool for reviewing the literature. That is, I will discuss the set of "product-price" studies, written mostly from the perspective of international trade, followed by the set of "factor-content" studies, written mostly from the perspective of labor economics. As Collins (1998) notes, this distinction is now a bit forced. At this point in the development of the literature, field no longer strongly determines approach, and the two approaches are seen by many as being complementary rather than substitutes or opposites.

This chapter is a way station, albeit an important one, in the presentation of my analysis of changes in employment and job loss in U.S. manufacturing. My focus on changes in employment and job loss creates a particular lens through which I see the literature, and it represents a different contribution in the sense that it focuses on an aspect of the domestic labor market that is either secondary (changes in employment) or virtually overlooked (job loss) in the rest of the literature. The vast majority of studies examine the empirical relationship between changes in "trade," variously measured, and changes in wages, thus the topic title "trade and wages." Studies of "trade and employment" or "trade and job loss" constitute a much smaller share of the literature. The focus on wages, either relative or in levels, as the primary domestic labor market outcome can be explained as a derivative of the Stolper–Samuelson theorem: in a two-factor, two-good model, trade liberalization changes the relative price of goods, leading to an increase in the real return to the factor used intensively in the production of that good and a decrease in the real return to the other factor. As such, this focus can be seen as derivative of an international trade economist's perspective. But, in all fairness, it is also a focus motivated by the observation of declining real and relative wages of lesser skilled workers and rising skill-based earnings inequality, and it is thus a focus shared by both trade and labor economists.

There is one last, largely uncontested, overview point. International trade does not affect the level of employment in the U.S. economy, rather its distribution across sectors. The level of employment in the economy is determined more by macroeconomic events and policy than by changes in global prices and trade flows. These events can change the allocation of resources (employment) and their pecuniary returns (pay). The trade and wages debate reviewed here (and my analysis more generally) addresses this type of distributional question. The largely misguided debate over the number of jobs created and destroyed by increased economic integration has created an incorrect association in the public mind: that "trade" determines the total level of jobs in the economy.[2]

THE METHODOLOGICAL DISAGREEMENT, IN A NUTSHELL

In a dynamic and open economy, resource allocations between industries and sectors can have a number of structural causes, among them differences in the income elasticities of demand across goods, differences in rates of technological advance across sectors, differences in rates of accumulation of alternative factors of production, and shifts of comparative advantage ("trade"). Macroeconomic events may also play a role.

The key (but perhaps not sole) methodological dispute is over how to measure "trade." One perspective, typically but not uniformly that of international trade economists, starts with the Heckscher–Ohlin model and in particular the Stolper–Samuelson theorem. From the Stolper–Samuelson theorem, a liberalization of trade (also known as a trade "shock") is communicated to the domestic labor market through a change in relative goods prices. Thus, this theorem offers a theoretical link between "trade" and the domestic labor market: a relative goods price change leads to a relative factor price (wage) response.[3] This view offers researchers (at least) one clear place to look for "trade" to have an effect on the domestic labor market: product prices should change. For this reason, these studies can be called "product-price" studies. The appeal of this perspective is its grounding in the standard model of international trade. Its key drawback is the treatment of changes in the prices of goods (for goods traded by the United States) as exogenous measures of foreign competition. As we will see, not all studies share this weakness, but addressing the weakness introduces other complications.

Although not solely the domain of labor economists, the alternative perspective involves measuring the impact of "trade" as changes in the effective supply and demand of domestic factors of production resulting from changes in imports and/or exports. More specifically, in the "factor content of trade" approach, imports raise the effective supply of domestic labor while exports raise the effective demand for domestic labor. This approach also considers changes in trade flows or volumes directly (and occasionally the trade deficit). It is based on a simple model of labor demand and labor supply and thus seems quite intuitive and appealing. Its key drawback is the treatment of changes in trade flows as exogenous. Trade flows change for some reasons; changes in tastes, trade liberalization that changes the prices of traded goods (as in product price studies), and technological change are three key reasons.

PRODUCT-PRICE STUDIES

Papers in the product-price category vary, somewhat narrowly, around the theme of whether changes in wages (sometimes employment) across industries are consistent with changes in industry prices and/or changes in industry productivity. Changes in prices are seen as due to international forces, and changes in productivity are seen as due to (sector-specific) technological change. In this context, the question about changes in the relative wages of American workers is taken as a question of whether wage changes are due to "trade" or "technology."

There are a vast number of papers in this category. Many of the key papers address the question of rising U.S. wage inequality. I will briefly discuss a few of these papers from the set using disaggregated industry data. For readers interested in more detail, Slaughter (2000) provides a comprehensive review of empirical product-price studies. Richardson (1995) and Blanchflower (2000) provide assessments of the state of knowledge in the area of trade, globalization, and inequality, and Cline (1997) offers a detailed and comprehensive survey of papers on the specific question of rising wage inequality in the United States.

To investigate the role of international trade in rising wage inequality, (early) researchers turned to the Stolper–Samuelson theorem and Heckscher–Ohlin model. One can draw the implication from the Stolper–Samuelson theorem that a decrease in the relative price of a good (say an unskilled labor intensive good) will decrease the real wage of the (unskilled) labor used intensively in producing such goods and will increase the real wage of the scarce factor (here skilled labor). In the end, many papers end up investigating whether factors employed intensively in industries with falling goods prices experience relative wage declines. The goods price declines are treated as though they are internationally induced (that is, due to foreign competition).

From this framework, Lawrence and Slaughter (1993) found no clear evidence of lower relative prices for unskilled labor intensive goods for the 1980s. They interpreted this result as evidence against the hypothesis that international trade contributed to rising wage inequality by lowering the price of unskilled labor intensive goods. Sachs and Shatz (1994) treated the computer industry as a special case (arguing the extraordinary productivity increases make output price calculations very difficult) and concluded that, for a non-computer sample in the 1980s, there were relative price declines in unskilled labor intensive industries.[4] The Sachs and Shatz results can be interpreted as leaning toward a "trade" explanation of rising wage inequality. Yet Leamer (1998) found relative goods price declines in unskilled labor intensive sectors in the 1970s, but not for the 1960s or 1980s, and it was the 1980s that saw a rise in U.S. wage inequality. Krueger (1997) reported similar evidence on relative price declines in unskilled labor intensive industries for the first half of the 1990s.

From this product-price sketch, what should we conclude? A safe conclusion would be that the forces of international trade have played a small role in the rise of wage inequality in the United States and that other factors, including technological change, are important. Methodologically, we learn about the importance of using disaggregated industry data and addressing the implicit and unrealistic assumption that the United States does not affect world prices. We also learn that results may be sensitive to the time frame. Another lesson is that analyzing product prices is a difficult task due to the variations in products, prices, and quality. This complexity makes the necessary data aggregation difficult.

These studies are useful for my analysis in their methodology and findings. Methodologically, they contribute ways to measure and specify the role of trade: that is, international forces influence domestic industry relative wages and employment through changes in global product prices. Conclusions vary, but overall trade has a role in rising U.S. wage inequality, but that role is secondary to (skill-biased) technological change.

Fully within the product-price categorization, but from a Ricardian perspective (country differences in technology rather than the Heckscher–Ohlin country differences in factor endowments), Feenstra and Hanson (1997, 1999) and Feenstra, Hanson, and Swenson (2000) concluded more strongly in favor of a role for international trade in increasing U.S. wage inequality. The approach in these three papers is particularly interesting, by itself and for my analysis, because they use outsourcing as the vehicle for the influence of international trade. The model, as explained in Feenstra and Hanson, uses country differences in technology and associated differences in products to create opportunities for outsourcing, with an impact on the demands of skilled and unskilled labor in both origin and recipient countries. Outsourcing raises the skilled–unskilled wage gap in both countries. For example, if the United States outsources to Mexico, it will relocate those aspects of production that are relatively unskilled, from a U.S. perspective. This reduction in the demand for U.S. unskilled labor reduces the relative wage of unskilled workers. Relative demand for unskilled labor is also reduced in Mexico, as the relocated production stage uses relatively more skilled labor, from the Mexican perspective. That is, labor that is unskilled in the United States is relatively skilled in Mexico. The skilled–unskilled wage gap will rise in Mexico. Using data from the Offshore Assembly Program (OAP), which allows direct observation of foreign outsourcing, Feenstra, Hanson, and Swenson (2000) found some evidence that the U.S. content of OAP imports (goods exported abroad for further processing) is relatively intensive in the use of skilled labor (measured as nonproduction labor) and that increases in OAP imports shift demand away from unskilled (production) labor in the United States.

One appeal of this approach is that it directly models one way for trade and technological advance to influence product prices, the location of production, and relative wages. For a set of U.S. manufacturing industries in the 1980s, Feenstra and Hanson (1999) concluded that foreign outsourcing accounted for 15 percent of the rise in the skilled–unskilled wage gap and technological upgrading accounted for 35 percent of the rise.

While not exactly product-price studies (defined as strictly derivative of the Stolper–Samuelson theorem), there are other "price" studies, ones that directly use changes in industry relative import prices to explain changes in industry employment and wages. These studies asked a slightly modified question: what is the effect of import competition on manufacturing employment and wages and what other factors play a role? Many of these studies predate the product-price studies noted above and, in popularity of approach, have, in fact, been displaced by them. Similar in spirit to the product-price findings, papers in this part of the literature found that import competition caused only a small fraction of employment and wage changes and that other factors, in particular changes in domestic demand and technology, accounted for most change.[5]

A few select industry and industry-level studies are notable and indicative of general findings. Grossman (1987) examined nine manufacturing industries over the 1969–1979 period and found a significant effect of declining import prices on employment in only one, the steel industry. In a separate study of the steel industry, Grossman (1986) concluded that most of the employment reduction over the period of 1976–1983 was due to the appreciation of the dollar and not increasing international competition. For a small sample of manufacturing industries, Mann (1988) found that foreign competition, measured as both import prices and import share, played a small role in determining employment relative to the role played by domestic demand and prices.[6] Revenga (1992) showed, for a sample of manufacturing industries over the period of 1977–1987, changes in import prices had a sizeable effect on employment and a smaller yet significant effect on wages. Her estimated employment elasticity is in the range of a 2.5–4 percent reduction in industry employment with a 10 percent fall in the industry relative import price. The 10 percent reduction in industry import price is associated with a 0.5–1 percent fall in the wage. She concluded that most of the adjustment in an industry to an adverse trade shock occurs through employment. With somewhat inflexible wages (consistent with her finding that the elasticity of industry wages with respect to import prices is smaller than the employment elasticity), these employment reductions must be occurring through involuntary separations (unless industry quits are high). Revenga took these results to suggest that workers are mobile across industries. This mobility implies that the effects of trade on the manufacturing sector are not limited to that sector, as workers seek new jobs in nonmanufacturing (and nontraded) industries.

FACTOR CONTENT OF TRADE (AND OTHER TRADE FLOWS) STUDIES

The essence of the factor-content approach is an implicit comparison of (often low skill) employment and wages in import-intensive industries to what employment and wages would be if imports were produced domestically (in autarky, a closed and isolated economy). At given wages, one can estimate the domestic and foreign labor inputs used to produce a bundle of goods. The United States tends to import goods that are low skill labor intensive, and its exports are goods that are high skill labor intensive. Therefore, trade (particularly imports from less developed countries) increases the relative supply of low-skilled labor in the United States. With estimates of the labor skills used in various sectors, it is possible to estimate how changes in imports and exports change the balance of demand and supply for high skill and low skill labor, again at given wages and prices. With estimates of labor supply and demand elasticities, these changes in labor supply and demand can be associated with estimated wage changes and, thus, estimates of changes in wage inequality. Freeman (1995, p. 23) offers a simple example:

> For example, if the United States imported 10 additional children's toys, which could be produced by five American workers, the effective supply of unskilled workers would increase by five (or alternatively, domestic demand for such workers would fall by five), compared with the alternative in which those 10 toys were produced domestically. This five-worker shift in the supply–demand balance would put pressure on unskilled wages to fall, causing those wages to fall in accord with the relevant elasticity. Any trade-balancing flow of exports would, contrarily, reduce the effective endowment of skilled workers (raise their demand) and thus increase their pay.

There are a few illustrative studies.[7] In a detailed study of employment changes over the period 1964–1987 using the March income supplements to the Current Population Survey (CPS), Murphy and Welch (1991) calculated the effect of trade on product demand in four broad sectors (traded durable goods, traded nondurable goods, traded services, and nontraded goods) and then calculated the labor content of the product demand shifts.[8] They found that the increase in trade (more specifically, the increase in the trade deficit) between 1979 and 1986 caused employment in durable goods to decline by 14.7 percent and employment in nondurable goods to decline by 1.8 percent. Trade increased employment in traded services by 1.4 percent and in nontraded goods by 4.1 percent. The concentration of the trade-induced employment reductions in manufacturing produced large effects on less-educated male workers. They calculated that trade reduced employment of men with less than a high school diploma by 2 to 3.5 percent. For male high school graduates, employment fell by 1.25 to 2.3 percent. Trade was associated with an increase in employment between 0.66 and 1.5 percent for college-educated men. For women, only those with less than a high school diploma experienced a reduction in labor demand (on the order of 0.6 to 2.2 percent). Demand for college-educated women increased by 3.3 to 4.3 percent due to trade. Although Murphy and Welch did not explicitly link these trade-induced labor demand changes to wage changes, they noted that groups facing declining demand also had declining wages, while groups in increasing demand experienced rising real wages.

Borjas, Freeman, and Katz (1992) found that trade increased the nation's effective labor supply of male high school dropouts by 5 to 9 percent in 1985–1986; for female high school dropouts, the increase in effective labor supply was from 9 to 14 percent. The increase in effective labor supply of high school graduates was smaller, around 2 percent. Trade had virtually no effect on the effective supply of college educated workers. Employing other researchers' estimates of the wage elasticity of labor supply, Borjas, Freeman, and Katz estimated that from 15 to 25 percent of the increase in the college graduate/high school graduate wage premium over the period of 1980–1985 can be attributed to large trade deficits (net imports). The effects of trade through increases in effective labor supply were smaller in the late 1980s.

Sachs and Shatz (1994) estimated the impact of the change in trade flows over the 1978–1990 period on the employment of high skilled (nonproduction) and low skilled (production) workers. For 51 manufacturing sectors, they calculated the effect of the increase or decrease in net exports (exports minus imports) on the level of output, assuming that both types of labor change in the same proportion as output. Summing across manufacturing sectors, they found that trade from developing countries reduced employment, particularly of low skilled workers, because the main output declines were in sectors where low skilled workers dominated. Compared to the counterfactual situation without trade, Sachs and Shatz estimated that trade reduced the employment of low skilled workers by 6.2 percent and the employment of higher skilled workers by 4.3 percent.

In an update, Borjas, Freeman, and Katz (1997) focused on imports from developing countries and considered immigration along with trade as an aspect of globalization. They reported that the growth of U.S. imports of less developed (developing) country manufacturing goods has increased the effective supply of less skilled labor, lowering relative earnings of low wage workers. They concluded, however, that increased trade has a substantially smaller effect on relative wages than increased immigration.

Wood (1994, 1995) reached the strongest conclusion, that trade accounts for a major part of the rise in earnings inequality. At the start of his 1995 paper (p. 57) he wrote, "This paper will argue for what is still a minority view among economists: that the main cause of the deteriorating situation of unskilled workers in developed countries has been expansion of trade with developing countries." Wood's criticism of other factor-content studies centers on the choice of labor input coefficients. Standard factor-content analyses use developed country labor input coefficients: that is, the mix of labor (of various skills) used to produce a good in developed countries. That mix of labor is very likely different in the developing country, the source of the import. For example, it was once the case that the United States made high-end men's leather shoes while the Chinese made low-end synthetic shoes. The imports of Chinese shoes, unless treated at a quite disaggregated level, would be treated as a "shoe" import and thus be multiplied by the mix of skilled labor used in the U.S. production of "shoes," that is, high-end leather shoes. If plastic shoes were made in the United States, they would likely be made with more less skilled labor than observed in the production of high-end shoes and thus the displacement of low skilled labor would be greater than that estimated in the standard treatment. Wood used an adjustment, based on labor input coefficients from developing countries at higher developed country wages. With his adjustments, Wood found a much larger impact of trade on the employment of less skilled workers (about three times larger than the impact found in Sachs and Shatz [1994]).

Trade between the United States and developing countries is the most recent focus of research activity, in part due to 1980s trade liberalization in these countries. To date, there is an emerging consensus, both theoretical and empirical, that trade between the United States and developing countries lowers the employment and wages of low skilled workers in the United States.

The decline in low skilled manufacturing employment was examined in some detail by Sachs and Shatz (1998). Using trade data by industry and by trading partner country, they found that the increase in net imports between 1978 and 1990 is associated with a 7.2 percent decline in manufacturing production employment and a 2.1 percent decline in nonproduction employment. They reported reductions in production worker employment across manufacturing, with the largest declines in "low skill" sectors. The intensity of "low skill" production is measured by the ratio of production workers to total workers in each manufacturing sector in 1978. "High" skill–intensive industries include periodicals and office and computing machines. "Low" skill–intensive industries include girls' and children's outerwear and footwear. Production employment fell by 4.1 percent in the highest skill intensive sector and by 29.1 percent in the lowest skill–intensive sector. Arguing that production jobs are lower skilled overall than are nonproduction jobs, they concluded that trade contributed to the observed rise in wage inequality between unskilled and low and high skill workers.[9] They emphasized skill differences between the manufacturing and nontraded sectors, noting that a reduction in manufacturing employment, particularly import-competing manufacturing, will release relatively unskilled workers into the nontraded (service) sector, leading to a fall in the relative wage of unskilled workers.

A number of criticisms can be directed toward factor-content studies. The one most often voiced is that factor-content calculations take the increase in imports as an exogenous event for the receiving country. While trade economists, particularly those who study the pattern of trade, found this assumption troublesome from the outset, it is not always unreasonable. If imports to the United States rise because of trade liberalization, or because skills improve in other countries or if technological diffusion enhances the productivity and competitiveness of production in other countries, then the link from these factors to trade and on to domestic employment and wages is reasonably clear and clean. The change in trade will not be exogenous if domestic events, such as wage increases, changes in innovation or technology, the health of the macroeconomy, or tastes, produce the change in trade and it will not be reasonable to infer that the link is from trade to domestic wages and employment.

Factor-content calculations also consider changes in import exports at existing wages. If wages adjust, by falling, to an in imports, then the competitive advantage of foreign workers will fall and this will put a brake on the flow of imports. The observed rise in imports will understate the pressures from foreign suppliers because it misses the feedback mechanism from imports to domestic wages and back to imports. In the extreme, perhaps even the threat of imports reduces domestic wages, and those wage reductions feedback to reduce import flows. This means that observed imports will understate the extent of foreign competition, and thus factor-content studies will understate the effects of trade on domestic relative pay. Freeman (1995) used the comparison of U.S. to European studies to assess this possibility because low skill wages are more downwardly rigid in Europe than they are in the United States due to different labor market institutions (centralized bargaining, minimum wages, and unionization). With more rigid wages, European factor-content studies should produce more accurate estimates of trade-induced pay change than U.S. studies. European trade displacement effects are not larger than those estimated for the United States, and thus the U.S. studies seem not to be downwardly biased (by the falling wages of less skilled U.S. workers).

There is an interesting additional concern about labor input coefficients. The use of skilled versus unskilled labor and the mix with capital is a choice, not a given. These ratios are choice variables influenced by a number of factors, including foreign competition and trade. If the relevant counterfactual question is, "What would labor demand look like without expansions of trade?" then the correct labor/output ratios for the calculations are the ones that existed before the trade expansions, not the contemporary ratios.

MORE FACTOR-CONTENT STUDIES, BROADLY DEFINED

Other studies use measures of trade flows more directly to explain changes in employment and wages, without the intermediate step of labor input–output coefficients. These studies share the weakness of taking trade flows as exogenous, but they avoid the pitfalls of choosing labor-output coefficients. Measuring disaggregated industry trade sensitivity through import penetration ratios and export shares, Freeman and Katz (1991) found that a 10 percent increase in imports reduces industry wages by 0 to 0.64 percent and industry employment by 5 to 6 percent. Exports raise industry wages and employment by slightly smaller magnitudes than those found for imports. The relationship between trade (imports) and wages changes over time. Freeman and Katz reported that increases in import share are negatively related to wage changes between 1958 and 1970 and after 1980, but not between 1970 and 1980.

Using similar trade sensitivity measures, Davis, Haltiwanger, and Schuh (1996) found high rates of job destruction for plants in industries with very high import penetration ratios over the period of 1972–1988. Plants in the top quintile of industries ranked by import penetration ratios had average annual employment reductions of 2.8 percent. There is little difference in job reallocation or net employment change when industries are ranked by export share.[10]

OTHER LABOR DEMAND FACTORS

With respect to earnings inequality, technological change gets the nod from many economists as the most important single cause. Technological change helps explain changes that international trade cannot: for example, the observed decline in the relative wage of low skilled labor should have been associated with an increase in its usage, as firms substituted away from the relatively higher priced skilled labor. Instead, the relative employment of skilled labor has increased in virtually all industries, traded and nontraded, and in all countries. Technical change, biased toward higher skilled workers, can explain this trend. While this can be a convincing piece of logic, there are still few studies that directly show the role of technological change because of the difficulty in measuring that change. Technological change is often the residual in the sense that if international trade measures cannot explain rising inequality or changes in employment or wages, then it must be what is not well-measured, technological change.

There are a few papers with technological change proxies. Berman, Bound, and Griliches (1994) documented technological changes in a few U.S. industries with shifts toward skilled workers, and Berman, Bound, and Machin (1998) considered a similar set of indus-

40 Evidence from Earlier Studies

tries for a broader range of Organization for Economic Cooperation and Development countries. Autor, Katz, and Krueger (1997) used computer investment as a proxy for technical change and found a high and positive correlation, across industries, between this measure and the skilled labor share of the wage bill.[11] Feenstra and Hanson (1999) modeled how trade and technology upgrading affect product prices and productivity and examined direct and indirect effects on wages. They concluded that, for U.S. manufacturing industries during the 1980s, foreign outsourcing accounted for 15 percent of the observed rise in the skilled/unskilled wage gap and that technological upgrading accounted for 35 percent of the rise.

WHAT ABOUT EXPORTS?

From the perspective of employment and job loss, increasing foreign competition is always interpreted as increasing imports (or falling import prices). To a general audience, imports are a palpable threat— they can be seen on store shelves (or car lots), and their mere presence suggests an American good, and therefore worker, displaced. Exports are much less visible, except to the workers who produce them. With transport, these goods leave the country and are more elusive to the general public. Yet, without exports, the analysis of increasing economic integration is incomplete. Rising imports means rising exports, and increasing foreign competition is more generally increasing global participation, with U.S. firms entering foreign markets as foreign firms enter U.S. markets.

As I noted previously, a number of studies have examined the role of net imports or exports (that is, the difference between the two flows), so that it is not the case that exports are overlooked in the research literature. But, it can be useful to explicitly examine export activity. How should we think about exports and employment? At the aggregate level, the role of exports as an engine of growth is widely acclaimed. Richardson (1993) reported that export growth created more than 40 percent of overall U.S. output growth between 1985 and 1992. Through this channel, the influence of exports in job creation is recognized. In addition, exports are the *quid pro quo* in the traditional accounting of the gains from trade. Exports are the means of obtaining imports.

Until recently, little attention has been paid to the specifics of exports as an "engine of growth." With the increasing availability of plant- and firm-level data, the behavior of exporters is receiving long-overdue attention. Richardson and Rindal (1995, 1996) provided insightful summary analyses of exports and exporting firms, based in large part on the research of Bernard and Jensen (1995, 1997). Briefly, good firms become exporters. Firms that become exporters have faster employment growth. Productivity and wages are higher. The line of causality seems to run from being a good firm to becoming an exporter, in the sense that successful firms (in a variety of dimensions) become exporters, rather than exports causing firms to become successful. Export activity does convey one note of success in that once firms become exporters, they have lower failure rates than do nonexporters with similar characteristics.

At the same time, exporters face risks different from the risks faced by domestic producers. Exporting activities are volatile, with substantial entry and exit of firms to and from exporting. Bernard and Jensen (1995, 1997) reported that 10 percent of manufacturing plants enter or exit exporting each year. Their study also revealed that those plants that begin or continue exporting are also 10 percent less likely to go out of business entirely. While entry is associated with growth and improved performance, exit from exporting is associated with poor firm performance.[12]

More broadly, in a highly readable critical synthesis of recent research based on longitudinal establishment as well as firm and worker data, Lewis and Richardson (2001) emphasized the widespread benefits to workers, firms, and communities of global engagement (which takes the form of export and import activity, investment, outsourcing, and technology licensing). These benefits include higher wages, better job-related benefits, more job security, more rapid sales growth, and faster productivity growth.

SUMMARY

Taken as a group, these studies point to internationalization, particularly expansions of international trade, as a source of declining manufacturing employment and increasing wage inequality but not the most important source. This conclusion does not imply that increasing economic integration across borders is the major explanation for declining manufacturing employment and rising wage inequality. The debate over how large a role trade plays in changing employment patterns and relative wages, and whether trade or technological change is more important, will continue. At this point, technological change is seen as the main culprit in the declining economic status of lower skilled workers, although, as we will see, there are industries where trade plays a larger role than it does in the aggregate.

Notes

1. The edited conference volumes of Collins (1998) and Feenstra (2000) provide focused points of entry to the literature.
2. NAFTA, starting with its negotiations in the early 1990s and continuing through its current outcomes, has been a prime source for the heated jobs debate. For an early view, see Hufbauer and Schott (1993). For a recent contribution, see Economic Policy Institute (2001).
3. Some scholars contributing to this literature have expressed strong preferences for the correct primary domestic labor market outcome and the correct measure of trade. See Leamer and Levinsohn (1995).
4. The computer industry could complicate the investigation because the relative prices of computers fell sharply over the 1980s, while productivity increased dramatically. The industry is also skilled labor intensive.
5. See Dickens (1988) for a review of this earlier literature; also see Belman and Lee (1996).
6. For footwear and radio and television, Mann did find that competition in both import price and import share is important for employment determination.
7. For early factor-content studies, see Aho and Orr (1980) and U.S. International Trade Commission (1986).
8. Their "industry" groupings were created to match trade data available in the 1988 *Economic Report of the President.*
9. The use of this limited skill classification by Sachs and Shatz (and, as noted above, by authors of other studies) is data driven to some extent. Readily available data sets with trade, employment, and wage information by industry are based on the Annual Survey of Manufactures (ASM), and the ASM occupations are limited to production and nonproduction.
10. See also Schoepfle (1982) and Bednarzik (1993). MacPherson and Stewart (1990), using CPS data on male production workers in manufacturing for the period 1975–1981, found that a 10 percent rise in industry import share lowered the union wage differential by 2 percent, with no statistically significant effect on nonunion wages.

11. For other studies that address the role of technological change, see Krugman and Lawrence (1993), Lawrence and Slaughter (1993), Leamer (1994), and Sachs and Shatz (1994).
12. Bernard and Jensen found that employment in export "stoppers" falls relative to steady nonexporters, as well as relative to export starters and steady exporters.

4
Inside Manufacturing
Trends in International Trade, Employment and Job Loss

This study seeks to bring a broader understanding of the labor market changes associated with increased trade into the national policy-making debate. One key aspect of this broader perspective is the focus on job displacement. Job loss is at the heart of the emotionally charged assertion that, "trade costs jobs." The traditional approach, built on studies of changes in net industry employment, can investigate the "trade and jobs" link only indirectly. With data on the incidence of job displacement, I can more directly examine the association between changes in trade flows and the widespread permanent job loss experienced in manufacturing from the late 1970s to the mid 1990s.

With a theoretical framework and earlier studies as a foundation, this chapter examines the descriptive evidence on changes in industry employment and involuntary job loss and their possible link to the increasing volume of trade and foreign competition. The manufacturing sector is diverse, with a wide range of activity that has changed over time. Some detail is required to do justice to the range of outcomes and changes. An up-front summary provides a roadmap to the detail that follows. The chapter begins with an overview of the manufacturing sector, followed by a brief description of the data and its sources. The bulk of the chapter then establishes basic trends and shows simple correlations.

MANUFACTURING: CHANGES IN EMPLOYMENT AND TRADE, IN BRIEF

This study examines changes in manufacturing that took place during a 16-year period, 1979–1994, that was very difficult for the sector as a whole. Employment declined steadily, by nearly 13 percent, and manufacturing's share of employment declined to 16 percent, a 31.2 percent decline from 1979. There was widespread involuntary job loss, with manufacturing accounting for 35.5 percent of total job loss (10.2 million workers).

Against this overall view of a shrinking manufacturing sector in terms of output and employment share, trade flows increased considerably. Import share rose for the sector overall, from imports accounting for an average of 6.6 percent of domestic supply in 1975 to an average of 17.1 percent in 1994 (an increase of 159 percent). Using a standard definition of "high" import competition, we get a set of industries with few surprises: apparel, footwear, leather products, toys and sporting goods, electrical machinery, (parts of) steel, motor vehicles, and textiles.

By 1994, U.S. firms exported about 12.5 percent of manufacturing shipments to foreign markets, averaged across the industries in the sample. This level represents a 50 percent increase from 1975. While sizeable, this increase, is smaller than the 159 percent increase in import share over the same time period.

Two-way, or intra-industry, trade is an important aspect of the increased trade volumes noted here. For a number of industries, the flows of both exports and imports are considerable. Almost all industries were more balanced in trade at the end of the period than they were at the start. Even where there was far more trade in one direction than the other (unbalanced trade), the smaller of the flows increased over the study period.

When the basic trends in employment, job loss, and trade flows are brought together, some basic patterns emerge. There is an association between employment decline, import share gain, export loss, and weak domestic demand for the handful of small, traditionally import-competing industries. Sharply declining exports are strongly associated with employment decline, particularly in the industries accounting for the bulk of the employment loss. Rising imports are also strongly associated with employment decline but more so in the smaller traditionally import-competing industries. Industries with high rates of job loss had both a high import share and experienced a large (positive) change in import share (increasing import competition).

We turn next to the details behind this summary.

THE STATE OF U.S. MANUFACTURING, 1975–1995

From the perspective of manufacturing employment, the 15-year period from the late 1970s to the mid 1990s was a difficult one. The sector as a whole was rocked by two recessions, a deep one in the early 1980s and another, not so deep, in the early 1990s; sluggish productivity growth; continued shifts in U.S. consumer demand away from manufactured goods and toward services; and the rise of foreign competition.

Manufacturing sector employment, from 1975 through 1995, is shown in Figure 4.1. After climbing steadily through the recovery from the 1974–1975 recession, manufacturing employment peaked, at 21 million, in 1979. Employment declined through the trough of the 1981–1982 recession, rose during the recovery and growth years of the late 1980s, declined again during the early 1990s recession, and grew slowly in the "no jobs" recovery from 1992–1995. It is clear that employment in this sector is highly pro-cyclical, and the level has declined

Figure 4.1 Manufacturing Sector Employment and Manufacturing Employment as a Share of Total Employment, 1975–1995

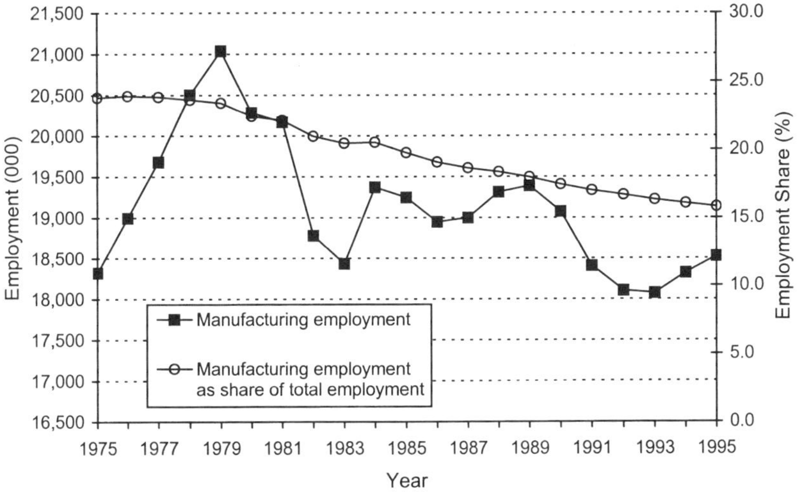

SOURCE: Data from Council of Economic Advisors (2001), Table B 46.

progressively since the late 1970s. Overall, from 1979–1994, sectoral employment fell by 12.9 percent.

While manufacturing employment declined, service-producing industries grew, both in output and employment. Manufacturing's share of GDP is shown in Figure 4.2. America's shift from manufacturing to services has been ongoing for decades, as we can see through the slow decline in share of GDP. The progressive decline in output share has been accompanied by a steeper decline in employment share. Manufacturing's share of employment fell by 31.2 percent over this period, from 23.4 percent of total employment in 1979 to 16 percent in 1994 (see Figure 4.1).

Against this overall view of a shrinking manufacturing sector in terms of output and employment share, trade flows have increased considerably. Figure 4.3 shows the increased volume of goods trade from 1975–1995, in nominal dollars. The greater dollar volume of imports over exports can be seen more clearly in Table 4.1, where information on U.S. international trade in goods and services is reported for the period of 1975–1995. In merchandise (goods) trade, 1975 was the last

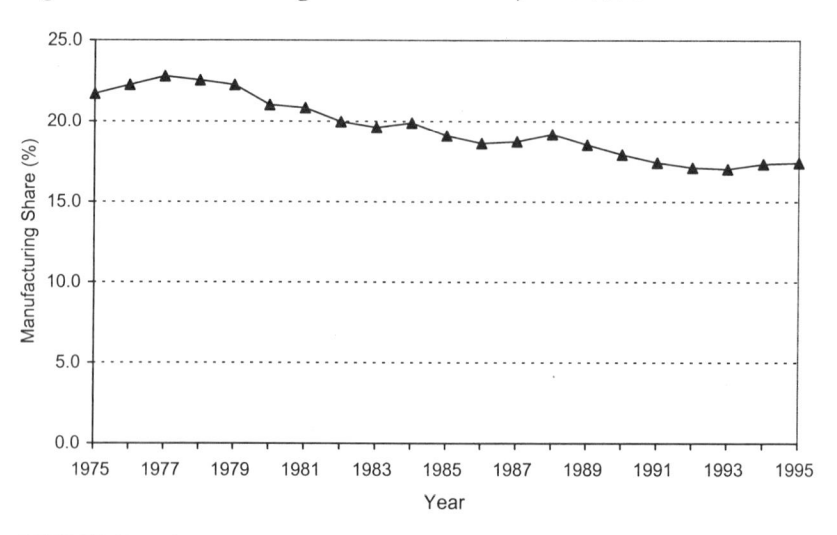

Figure 4.2 Manufacturing as a Share of GDP, 1975–1995

SOURCE: Data from Council of Economic Advisors (2001), Table B 12.

Imports, Exports, and Jobs 49

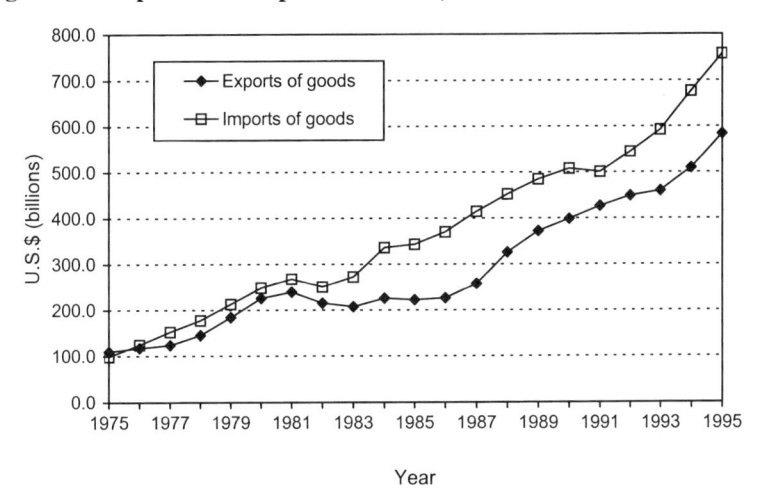

Figure 4.3 Exports and Imports of Goods, 1975–1995

[Line chart showing exports of goods and imports of goods in U.S. $ (billions) from 1975 to 1995, both rising from around 100 billion in 1975 to approximately 575 (exports) and 750 (imports) billion by 1995.]

SOURCE: Data from Council of Economic Advisors (2001), Table 24.

year for which exports exceeded imports. On the other hand, the positive trade balance in services grew steadily over the period, an accompaniment to the output and employment shift to services.

Our discussion of U.S. manufacturing over this time period would be incomplete without a word about the exchange value of the dollar. A signal event for manufacturing was the appreciation of the exchange value of the dollar, by about 50 percent against the currencies of major U.S. trading partners, from 1981 to 1985. High interest rates (from expansionary fiscal policy and tight monetary policy) and a robust U.S. recovery from the 1981–1982 recession encouraged international investment in U.S. and dollar-denominated assets, and the dollar strengthened against other industrialized currencies. The strong dollar made U.S. exports more expensive to buy and made imports cheaper. Recovery from the recession fueled U.S. demand for imports, while foreign demand for U.S. exports remained sluggish due to the slower recovery of our trading partners. The exchange value of the dollar peaked in 1985, with the September 1985 Plaza Accord that brought exchange market intervention and modified interest rates. Over 1986 to 1989, the dollar depreciated, about 30 percent, and U.S. import growth slowed and export

50 Inside Manufacturing

Table 4.1 U.S. International Trade in Goods and Services (Balance of Payments Basis, Billions $), 1975–1995

Year	Exports Total	Exports Goods	Exports Services	Imports Total	Imports Goods	Imports Services	Trade balance Total	Trade balance Goods	Trade balance Services
1975	132.6	107.1	25.5	120.2	98.2	22.0	12.4	8.9	3.5
1976	142.7	114.7	28.0	148.8	124.2	24.6	-6.1	-9.5	3.4
1977	152.3	120.8	31.5	179.5	151.9	27.6	-27.2	-31.1	3.8
1978	178.4	142.1	36.4	208.2	176.0	32.2	-29.8	-33.9	4.2
1979	224.1	184.4	39.7	248.7	212.0	36.7	-24.6	-27.6	3.0
1980	271.8	224.3	47.6	291.2	249.8	41.5	-19.4	-25.5	6.1
1981	294.4	237.0	57.4	310.6	265.1	45.5	-16.2	-28.0	11.9
1982	275.2	211.2	64.1	299.4	247.6	51.7	-24.2	-36.5	12.3
1983	266.0	201.8	64.2	323.8	268.9	54.9	-57.8	-67.1	9.3
1984	290.9	219.9	71.0	400.1	332.4	67.7	-109.2	-112.5	3.3
1985	288.8	215.9	72.9	410.9	338.1	72.8	-122.1	-122.2	0.1
1986	309.7	223.3	86.4	450.3	368.4	81.8	-140.6	-145.1	4.5
1987	348.8	250.2	98.6	502.1	409.8	92.3	-153.3	-159.6	6.2
1988	431.3	320.2	111.1	547.2	447.2	100.0	-115.9	-127.0	11.1
1989	489.4	362.1	127.2	581.6	477.4	104.2	-92.2	-115.2	23.0
1990	537.2	389.3	147.9	618.4	498.3	120.0	-81.1	-109.0	27.9
1991	581.3	416.9	164.3	611.9	490.7	121.2	-30.7	-73.8	43.1
1992	617.3	440.4	176.9	652.9	536.5	116.5	-35.7	-96.1	60.4
1993	642.8	456.8	185.9	711.7	589.4	122.3	-68.9	-132.6	63.7

| 1994 | 703.4 | 502.4 | 201.0 | 800.5 | 668.6 | 131.9 | −97.0 | −166.2 | 69.2 |
| 1995 | 795.1 | 575.8 | 219.2 | 891.0 | 749.6 | 141.4 | −95.9 | −173.7 | 77.8 |

NOTE: Data compiled from official statistics of the U.S. Department of Commerce, Bureau of Economic Analysis. Balance of payments basis for goods reflects adjustments for timing, coverage, and valuation to the data compiled by the Census Bureau. The major adjustments concern: military trade of U.S. defense agencies, additional nonmonetary gold transactions, and inland freight to Canada and Mexico. Goods valuation are F.A.S. (free alongside ship) for exports and customs value for imports

SOURCE: International Trade Administration, U.S. Department of Commerce, U.S. Foreign Trade Highlights. Available at http://www.ita.doc.gov/td/industry/otea/usfth/aggregate/H01t01.txt

growth quickened.[1] This turn in the exchange value of the dollar and the corresponding changes in import and exports (relative to growth in U.S. and world income) makes 1985 a important year.[2] Where appropriate, our time period will be divided into a pre-1985 period and a post-1985 period.

The growing importance of trade within manufacturing, and variations in trend growth (variations that we can understand now as influenced by macroeconomic factors) can be seen in Figure 4.4. This chart shows the time-series of export and import volumes, separately, as shares of manufacturing GDP. Both shares have grown since the late 1970s, imports more than exports. The dampening of export demand with the 1981–1982 recession, the relatively slow recovery of our trading partners from that recession, and the strong dollar of the early 1980s is clearly evident, as is the export surge that followed from 1986. We can also see the relatively smooth rise in export and import shares from 1985, as compared with the more variable path from 1975 to 1985.

Figure 4.4 Exports and Imports of Goods as Percentage of GDP in the Manufacturing Sector, 1975–1995

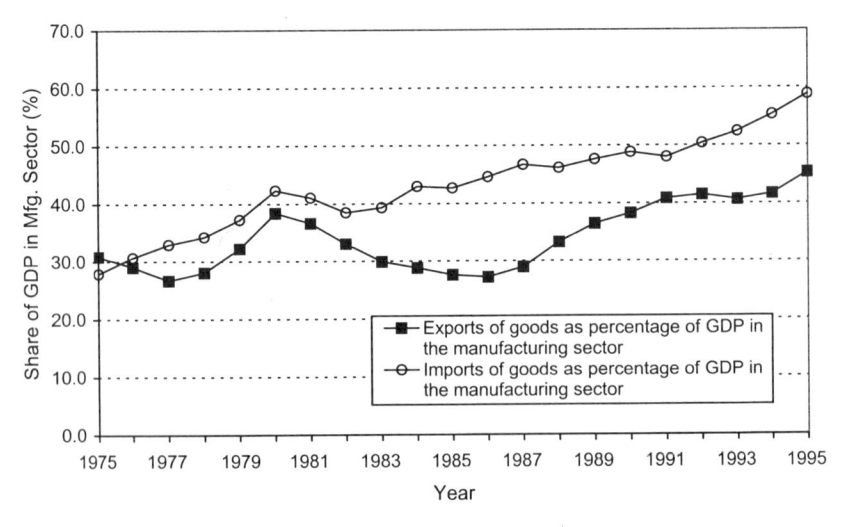

SOURCE: Council of Economic Advisors (2001), Tables B 12 and B 24.

This brief survey of the state of U.S. manufacturing reveals two trends that likely fuel American perceptions of trade: the declining level of employment in manufacturing and increased volumes of merchandise trade. Both of these trends are real, yet it is wrong to simply link trade to the number of jobs. In the standard models of international trade reviewed in Chapter 3, trade reallocates jobs according to shifting patterns of comparative advantage. In other words, we can expect trade to influence the distribution of jobs and employment. This means that we will look for employment to decline, and jobs to be lost, in some sectors, while we look for employment expansion in other sectors. Because we are concentrating on manufacturing, we will "miss" considerable employment growth in services, and some of that growth is due to foreign demand for our services exports.

We turn now to a more detailed analysis of the evidence on trade flows, employment change, and job loss. I first explain my definition of an "industry," a definition determined by data availability. Details on data sources and construction are provided in Appendix A.

DEFINING AN INDUSTRY

Data on employment levels and job loss were obtained from information in the CPS. The Displaced Worker Surveys (DWSs), biennial supplements to the CPS, are the only large-scale, nationally representative source of information on the incidence of involuntary job loss. Information on job displacement from this source is available for the period of 1979–1999. This data source dictated my definition of an "industry," because DWS-based information on job loss by industry follows the definition and classification of industry used by the CPS, a scheme called the Census of Population Industry Classification (CIC). These coding schemes have changed over time, reflecting the changing nature of the economy and improved data collection. The 1990 CIC codes are the most recent. The most detailed level of industry classification offered in the DWS is the three-digit CIC. Thus, my manufacturing industries are 1990 three-digit CIC industries.

Employment levels by (three-digit CIC) industry were constructed from the March Annual Demographic File supplements to the CPS.

Because I used CPS files dating back to the mid 1970s, I used concordances between the 1960, 1970, 1980, and 1990 three-digit CIC classification codes in order to have one uniform code, the 1990 code, for my industries.

The required three-digit CIC definition of industry affected my usage of the available data on U.S. exports, imports, and shipments. Those data are available at a more detailed level, a four-digit Standard Industrial Classification (SIC) category, from the National Bureau of Economic Research (NBER) Trade Database for the period 1958–1994. The SIC-based industry trade and shipments data were aggregated up to the three-digit 1990 CIC classification code in order to combine the trade information with CPS-based information on employment and job displacement. The last year for which the product-based trade flows data could be converted to an SIC industry format was 1994. Therefore, the availability of the trade flows data determined the end point of the study period.

Lastly, import price indices data are available for many three- and four-digit SIC manufacturing industries starting in 1982–1983, with the SIC-based series currently ending with 1992. For a smaller set of industries, the price series provides reasonable information from 1980 forward. Similar to the trade and shipments data, the price data were aggregated up to a three-digit CIC scheme. The price measure itself is a fixed weight Laspeyres index with a 1985 base period.[3] The weaknesses of the price data are several: import prices exist for relatively few industries and cover only some goods in some industries. In addition, changes in quality not captured in the price indices create measurement error.

CHANGES IN INDUSTRY EMPLOYMENT

As a companion to the discussion of overall manufacturing employment, it is useful to consider how the composition of employment changed within manufacturing over the period of 1979–1994, across industries and over time. This 16-year time period is the longest and most broadly available for the various data series. Appendix Tables A1 (1979–1985) and A2 (1985–1994) provide a quick and brief overview of the manufacturing industries in the sample, focusing on their trade and employment characteristics.[4]

Summarizing these tables briefly, employment fell 11.4 percent on average from 1979 to 1985 for the industries in the analysis sample. Employment declined sharply in a number of industries, most notably several large and visible industries, such as apparel, (non-electrical) machinery and motor vehicles. Employment losses in these industries were on the order of 11–17 percent. A number of smaller industries, particularly in traditional heavy manufacturing, experienced large percentage declines in employment: blast furnaces, 63.4 percent; iron and steel foundries, 53.2 percent; and farm machinery and equipment, 62.5 percent.[5] Among industries recording a decline in employment, employment fell by nearly 22 percent.

Very few industries saw employment rise; for the most part, growing industries started small and were not a part of traditional heavy manufacturing (printing and publishing, +18.6 percent; office and accounting machines, +26 percent; and computers, +52 percent). Amongst the employment gainers, the average increase was 20 percent. Guided missiles and ordnance benefitted from increased defense spending during the first Reagan administration, and office and accounting machines and computers were just beginning to expand.

Overall, conditions improved in manufacturing over the 1985–1994 period. Employment fell on average just 1.2 percent, with a number of industries expanding employment and just a few industries with large declines, notably electrical machinery and apparel. Over this period, employment losses were, for the most part, in a distinctly different set of industries than were losses in the earlier period. Ordnance and guided missiles saw a decline in government spending with the end of the Cold War and a related decline in employment. Employment continued to fall sharply in a number of smaller traditionally import-competing industries, such as footwear, leather products, steel and metals industries, radio and television, and toys and sporting goods. For the industries with employment declines, the average decline was 15.6 percent. With a healthier economy, more industries recorded employment gains over the late 1980s and early 1990s than for the earlier period. A number of the gains were small, and the average gain was +10 percent.

With this summarized view of manufacturing employment in place, we turn next to trends in goods trade flows.

THE EXTENT OF IMPORT COMPETITION BY INDUSTRY

The ratio of imports to domestic supply is a widely used characteristic for classifying industries as "import competing" or "high import." Consistent with the increasing trend shown in Figure 4.4, import share has also risen for the manufacturing sector overall, from imports accounting for an average of 6.6 percent of domestic supply in 1975 to an average of 17.1 percent in 1994 (an increase of 159 percent). With the exception of the food and kindred products industries, most industries experienced an increase in the share of domestically available supply that was foreign produced over the 20-year period).[6]

In which industries are imports an important or high share of domestic supply? Any discussion of high-import industries has a bit of arbitrariness in the cutoff point for high. Using the top 25 percent (top quartile) of industries ranked by mean import share, we can define the high-import industries (industries with mean annual import share of 13 percent or higher) over the full 1975–1994 period (Table 4.2).[7] The list contains few surprises, and it is fully inclusive of the group of industries traditionally considered import competing: apparel, footwear, leather products, toys and sporting goods, electrical machinery, (parts of) steel, motor vehicles, and textiles. Table 4.2 also reports import shares over time. In some industries, increases in import share are quite large (watches and clocks, footwear, leather products, and toys and sporting goods), while in other industries, import share has changed very little (textiles, and pulp and paper). Appendix Table A3 reports the full ranking of industries in the sample, from highest mean import share to lowest for the period of 1975–1994.

The group with a high import share was fairly constant over time, as industries with high import shares at a point in time retained their rankings with above-average increases in import shares over time.[8] Many of the high-import industries in 1975[9] remained the high-import industries in 1994, and similarly for the low-import industries.

The cross-time correlations of industry quartile rankings by import share shown in Table 4.3 reveal that, at 5-year intervals, the ranking of industries by import share is fairly stable. At 10- to 15-year intervals, there is considerable change in the relative sensitivity of industries to import competition. Thus, although we can consider a fairly constant

Table 4.2 Import Shares of High-Import Industries, 1975–1994

Industry	1975–94 (Mean)	1994	1990	1985	1980	1975
Watches, clocks	0.405	0.800	0.571	0.613	0.436	0.265
Footwear, ex. rubber & plastic	0.377	0.707	0.641	0.567	0.313	0.252
Leather products, ex. footwear	0.320	0.660	0.505	0.464	0.283	0.165
Pottery & related products	0.316	0.445	0.421	0.418	0.329	0.247
Toys & sporting goods	0.265	0.507	0.472	0.377	0.236	0.134
Cycles & misc. transport. equip.	0.264	0.227	0.234	0.268	0.328	0.278
Misc. manuf. industries	0.209	0.376	0.336	0.296	0.190	0.121
Motor vehicles	0.191	0.275	0.291	0.259	0.220	0.161
Electronic computing equipment	0.188	0.487	0.377	0.189	0.101	0.110
Leather tanning & finishing	0.172	0.277	0.303	0.233	0.128	0.089
Apparel & accessories	0.167	0.382	0.328	0.236	0.135	0.086
Radio, TV, & communication	0.158	0.298	0.217	0.197	0.143	0.121
Office & accounting machines	0.157	0.451	0.335	0.162	0.074	0.075
Other primary metal industries	0.156	0.191	0.176	0.211	0.244	0.106
Pulp, paper & paperboard mills	0.153	0.168	0.175	0.159	0.153	0.145
Electrical machinery, equip.	0.133	0.313	0.264	0.178	0.120	0.074
Blast furnaces, steelworks	0.130	0.190	0.154	0.193	0.125	0.117
Photographic equipment	0.129	0.260	0.214	0.172	0.116	0.075
Misc. textile mill products	0.128	0.133	0.131	0.133	0.131	0.124
Mean (column)	0.096	0.171	0.148	0.126	0.090	0.066
Std. deviation	0.086	0.164	0.136	0.122	0.088	0.063

NOTE: Import share = imports/(imports + domestic supply).
SOURCE: Author's calculations from NBER Trade Database.

58 Inside Manufacturing

Table 4.3 Cross-Time Correlation of Industry Quartile Rankings, by Import Share

Quartile ranking in:	1975	1980	1985	1990
1975	1.0			
1980	0.903*			
1985	0.871*	0.892*		
1990	0.795*	0.838*	0.881*	
1994	0.763*	0.795*	0.859*	0.935*

NOTE: * = statistical significance at the 0.05 level

set of industries as "high" import competing, we should also take note of some fluidity in relative degree of import competition.

Although descriptive tradition uses import share as a measure of foreign competition, clearly it is the change in import share that can proxy, *ex post*, a change in an industry's foreign competitive environment. Several industries experienced notable increases in import share, especially among the high import competing. The import share of computers increased by 346 percent, apparel and accessories by 344 percent, leather products by 300 percent, and toys and sporting goods by 278 percent.

As I noted above, the longest overlapping time period of the various data series is 1980–1994. Also, the dollar appreciation of the early 1980s, with a peak in 1985 and subsequent sharp depreciation, suggests a division of the 1980–1994 period into two subperiods, 1980–1985 and 1985–1994. Over the 1980–1985 period, average import share rose from 0.089 to 0.126 (a 41.5 percent increase). A number of industries experienced sharp increases in import share during the strong dollar period: construction and material handling equipment (+147 percent, from a 0.060 1980 share), knitting mills (+130 percent, from a 0.068 1980 share), primary aluminum (+129 percent, from a 0.040 1980 share), and office and accounting machines (+118 percent, from a 0.074 1980 share). In 1985, the high-import industries (top 25 percent, with import share of 0.167 or higher) included most of the industries listed in Table 4.2, with a small number of additions: tires and inner

Imports, Exports, and Jobs 59

tubes (import share of 0.167), other primary metal (0.211), farm machinery and equipment (0.195), and metalworking machinery (0.168).

The dollar peaked in 1985 and declined by 21 percent by 1986 and 39 percent by 1992.[10] From 1985-1994, average industry import share rose from 0.125 to 0.171 (an increase of 36.8 percent). Import share fell in 13 of the 75 industries in the full sample. Most of the declines were less than 1 percentage point and occurred from a small 1985 base import share, with the exception of sugar and confectionary products (-28.3 percent, from a 0.108 1985 import share) and cycles and misc. transport equipment (-15.2 percent, from a 0.268 1985 import share). Both of these industries had some protection from foreign competition during this period. Import share increased notably in a number of industries: other rubber products (+229 percent, from a 0.073 1985 import share); office and accounting machines (+178 percent, from a 0.162 1985 share); and aircraft and parts (+123 percent, from a 0.078 1985 share).

By 1994, the last year for which trade volume data is currently available at a CIC-conformable level, average industry import share was 0.171, and the high-import industries (top 25 percent) had an import share of 0.227 or higher. There were 19 high-import industries: of these 19 industries, 16 were in the top quartile by import share in 1985, 11 were in the 1980 top quartile, and 13 were in the top quartile for the full period.

This discussion of import share reveals industries where foreign-produced goods account for a sizeable share of domestic supply. In this way, these industries are import competing. It is important to understand that the industries used here are highly aggregated across goods, and import share can vary considerably across goods within an industry. Domestic firms within these industries face varying import competition depending on the goods they produce. The footwear industry defined here, CIC 221, represents (nearly) all shoes, from the detailed industry "men's dress shoes" to another detailed industry "ballet slippers and athletic shoes." The level of foreign competition, measured as import share, appears to differ between the two detailed industries. The four-digit SIC industry that includes men's dress shoes, 3143 (men's footwear, except athlctic), had an average import share of 0.326 for the 1979-1994 period. SIC industry 3149 (footwear, except rubber, nec[11]), with ballet slippers and athletic shoes, had an average import share of

0.781 for the period. Imports represent far more of the ballet and athletic shoe market than they do for men's shoes. Over the period, however, the two four-digit industries faced similar increases in import share, with an increase in import share of 76 percent for 3143 (men's footwear), from 0.203 in 1979 to 0.453 in 1994, as compared to an increase of 56 percent for 3149 (ballet and athletic), from 0.571 in 1979 to 0.889 in 1994. This example illustrates the heterogeneity within an "industry." Footwear is a broad category, one where ballet and athletic shoes do not compete with men's dress shoes. On the other hand, some industry aggregation is necessary, and this example also illustrates some of the common characteristics within a broad industry.

TRENDS IN IMPORT PRICES

As discussed in Chapter 3, changes in import prices are a more commonly used measure of competitive pressure. When import prices fall (and all else stays the same), imported goods become relatively cheaper and consumers may substitute imported goods for domestically produced goods, leading to a rise in import share. Alternatively, if domestic producers respond to changes in import prices with their own price reductions, relative prices remain constant and presumably import share remains constant. This thinking reveals that changes in the import share measure depend on the response of domestic producers to changes in import price. In this way, changes in import prices represent an alternative measure of the competitive pressures faced by domestic producers. Unfortunately, the time-series and industry coverage of import prices is more limited than it is for trade volumes. In addition, the price data involve considerable industry aggregation and measurement concerns. Appendix Table A4 lists industries, in order of mean import share as in Appendix Table A3, with their changes in import prices for the period of 1980–1992. Import prices fell sharply during the strong dollar period of 1980–1985, when import shares were also rising sharply. The price declines were considerable (in excess of 20 percent) in a number of durable goods industries, the same industries discussed above with large increases in import share. As the dollar depreciated from its 1985 level, many of these declines were reversed. From 1985 to 1992, import prices rose an average of 14 percent, having fallen nearly 15 percent from 1980 to 1985. On balance, import prices fell slightly over the 1980–1992 period.[12]

To sum up, foreign-produced goods represent an important share of domestically available output in a number of manufacturing industries. The foreign share of domestically available goods has increased considerably over the past 20 years. For consumers, this has meant a wider array of goods, often at lower prices. To even out our understanding of the extent of trade, we turn to exports, where foreigners are on the demand side instead of the supply side.

INDUSTRY EXPORT ACTIVITY

Measured by dollar value, U.S. exports are concentrated in a small number of industries, industries that are dominated by large firms for the most part. In 1994, the top export industries (and their shares of total manufacturing exports) were: electrical machinery and equipment (0.114), motor vehicles (0.108), aircraft and parts (0.083), computers (0.070), and non-electrical machinery (0.058).[13] These "large" exporters are also large in terms of shipments. The computer industry was the only newcomer to the list; computers accounted for a very small share of manufacturing shipments and exports in 1980 (ranked 52 and 7, respectively), but the industry's shipments share ranking was 11 and export share ranking was 3 by 1987.[14]

One measure of the foreign market orientation of an industry is its "export intensity," calculated as the ratio of exports to shipments. Export intensity is a composition measure, in the sense that it yields the share of an industry's output that goes to foreign markets. Foreign markets constitute an important part of output demand for industries with high export intensity. Thus, industry export intensity can also be interpreted as a measure of industry exposure to world markets.

In 1994, U.S. firms exported about 12.5 percent of manufacturing shipments to foreign markets, averaged across the industries in the sample. This level represents a 50 percent increase from 1975. This increase, while sizeable, is smaller than the 159 percent increase in import share over the same time period. Export intensity grew slowly over the late 1970s and fell a bit from 1980 to 1985.[15] From 1985 to 1994, export intensity rose 68 percent from 7.2 percent of shipments to 12.5 percent.

Average export intensity masks wide variation across industries and over time. Table 4.4 lists the top 25 percent of manufacturing industries, ranked by mean export intensity, for the period 1975–1994, with their mean export intensity and export intensities at five-year intervals between 1975 and 1994. These industries had a mean export intensity of 0.13 or higher. Appendix Table A6 reports the full set of industries. Some industries stand out as considerable exporters; in 1994, the top eight industries had export intensities exceeding 25 percent, twice the cross-industry average. The computer industry stands out for its very high, but declining, export intensity over the time period. Other industries have virtually no exports and are entirely domestically oriented (e.g., newspaper publishing and printing, cement, concrete and gypsum, and paperboard containers and boxes). Durable goods industries are far more export-oriented than nondurable goods industries, with export intensities in the range of 13–44 percent. Most industries saw an increase in export intensity.

Similar to the discussion of imports, membership in the "high-export" group was fairly constant over time. Many of the high export industries in 1994 were the high-export industries in 1975 and similarly for low-export industries. Compared to import share, there is more mobility in the rankings of high export, in the sense that high export in an earlier period is a weaker predictor of high export in a later period (Table 4.5). The correlation is strong at a 10-year interval, and it is considerably weaker at 15 years and beyond.

The early 1980s, from 1980–1985, were a very difficult time for exporters, with weak global demand due to the 1981–1982 recession and the dollar appreciation from 1981 to 1985. Most industries saw a reduction in exports and in export intensity. Sample average export intensity fell nearly 20 percent, from 0.092 to 0.074. A number of industries experienced sharp decreases in export intensity from 1980 to 1985, with a mean change of –20.2 percent. Twenty industries saw decreases in export intensity of 40 percent or more. In 5 of the 14 industries where export intensity increased, it did so because exports fell by a smaller percentage than did shipments. By 1985, the top quartile of

Table 4.4 Export Intensities of Top Exporting Industries, 1975-1994

Industry	Mean (1975-94)	1994	1990	1985	1980	1975
Electronic computing equipment	0.615	0.167	0.271	0.319	0.811	0.842
Metal forgings	0.345	0.173	0.352	0.408	0.251	0.279
Aircraft & parts	0.304	0.449	0.379	0.263	0.246	0.282
Construction & material handling machines	0.303	0.344	0.302	0.264	0.319	0.343
Engines & turbines	0.244	0.394	0.264	0.200	0.229	0.213
Scientific & controlling instrmnts	0.233	0.295	0.273	0.199	0.213	0.226
Logging	0.210	0.266	0.278	0.140	0.199	0.205
Office & accounting machines	0.192	0.249	0.232	0.123	0.190	0.207
Cycles & misc. transport. equip.	0.183	0.265	0.189	0.186	0.149	0.140
Leather tanning & finishing	0.176	0.246	0.343	0.143	0.126	0.085
Electrical machinery, equip.	0.163	0.197	0.215	0.129	0.154	0.141
Industrial & misc. chemicals	0.160	0.208	0.174	0.147	0.162	0.133
Machinery, exc. electrical	0.155	0.199	0.178	0.121	0.150	0.158
Other primary metal industries	0.146	0.215	0.178	0.085	0.226	0.076
Ordnance	0.146	0.227	0.153	0.104	0.142	0.191
Plastics, synthetics & resins	0.144	0.191	0.178	0.116	0.173	0.098
Farm machinery & equipment	0.143	0.175	0.167	0.119	0.125	0.140
Photographic equipment	0.136	0.133	0.146	0.111	0.153	0.147
Mean (across industries)	0.096	0.125	0.112	0.074	0.093	0.084
Std. deviation	0.095	0.090	0.090	0.071	0.090	0.100

NOTE: Export Intensity = (Exports/Shipments). Across-industry mean and standard deviation are weighted using industry share of total value of shipments.
SOURCE: Author's calculations from NBER Trade Database.

64 Inside Manufacturing

Table 4.5 Cross-Time Correlation of Industry Quartile Rankings, by Export Intensity

Quartile ranking in	1975	1980	1985	1990
1975	1.0			
1980	0.926**			
1985	0.635**	0.806**		
1990	0.476**	0.709**	0.888**	
1994	0.323**	0.577**	0.743**	0.902**

NOTE: ** = statistical significance at the 0.05 level

industry exporters had an average export intensity of 0.104, as compared with 0.131 in 1980.

The period after the dollar peak in 1985 and continuing to 1994 was nearly a reversal of the early 1980s. From 1985 to 1990, average export intensity rose 51 percent, from 0.074 to 0.112. In the two years from 1992 to 1994, the share of shipments exported rose 11.1 percent to 0.125. Just two industries had a decline in the value of exports (metal forgings at −80.1 percent and misc. petroleum at −0.5 percent), and three others experienced a fall in export intensity despite a rise in exports.[16] Exports (and export intensity) grew tremendously in a number of industries, particularly in those having a low starting export intensity (industries with little previous export activity): bakery products (+572 percent, from a 0.0017 1985 share), apparel and accessories (+562 percent, from a 0.012 1985 share), and footwear (+431 percent, from a 0.024 1985 share). Mean percentage change in export intensity was 132 percent.

Export intensity, useful as a measure of the foreign outlook or orientation of an industry, can change for a variety of reasons and those changes must be interpreted with some caution. For almost all industries, export volumes are much smaller than shipments, so an equal (by dollar volume) increase in exports and shipments yields a larger percentage increase in exports than in shipments and therefore an increase in export intensity. Similarly, the growth of foreign demand can be expected to exceed the growth in domestic demand in percentage terms, since the domestic market is much bigger than the foreign market for most industries.[17] Differences in the size of the foreign and domestic markets will be incorporated into the econometric analysis.

As a composition measure, a change in export intensity is not necessarily informative about changes in the level of demand for an industry's output. Export intensity can increase if domestic demand is replaced by foreign demand, with overall shipments constant. This route to an increase in export intensity should yield no change in industry employment. Alternatively, if exports grow at the same rate as shipments, export intensity will remain constant, while the industry, overall, has experienced an increase in demand for output and possibly an increase in employment.

To summarize the separate trends in imports and exports, albeit very briefly and simply, there is now vastly more trade in many, if not most, manufacturing industries. The greater flow of imports is widely acknowledged; it is important to recognize that the flow of U.S. produced goods to foreign markets is also much greater. In a considerable number of industries, both goods flows have increased.

INTRA-INDUSTRY TRADE

A simple view of trade is that the United States imports watches and apparel and exports airplanes and bulldozers. A more realistic view is that the United States imports and exports all four of these goods, either as intermediate goods or as final goods. The simple characterization of industries as either importers or exporters ignores the observation that there are significant trade flows within industries, across national borders. Intra-industry trade is a very general and rising trend. Helpman (1999, p. 134) noted that, ". . . the industrialized countries trade with each other much more than they trade with less developed countries."

Lovely and Richardson (2000) presented a useful characterization of intra-industry trade. Between industrialized countries (North–North), trade flows within an industry are differentiated, skill-intensive intermediate or final goods. Between industrialized countries and newly industrialized (North–South), the North exports skill-intensive intermediates or final goods, and the South exports labor intensive intermediates. Southern production of labor intensive intermediates (or the labor intensive assembly component of final goods), is also known as Northern "outsourcing," the import of intermediate inputs.

At the level of aggregation in this data set, it is not surprising that industries are both importers and exporters. In motor vehicles (CIC 351), for example, where finished cars are included with parts, firms located in the United States import parts for production in the United States (e.g. Honda, Toyota, and the NUMMI plant in Fremont, CA), and parts are exported for Canadian production. Of course, finished cars are also imported and exported.

An industry's import share and export intensity provide a rough understanding of intra-industry trade, in the sense that high import share teamed with high export intensity suggests that the industry is actively importing and exporting. A more precise, and now established, method for measuring intra-industry trade was offered by Grubel and Lloyd (1975). That measure is:

$$IIT = 1 - \frac{|X - M|}{X + M}$$

where X and M represent, respectively, the value of exports and imports of an industry and the vertical bars in the numerator denote the absolute value. The value of IIT ranges from 0, when an industry exports or imports (but not both), to 1, when an industry's exports and imports are equal. Thus, the higher the value of IIT, the greater the degree of trade overlap, or intra-industry trade.

This measure, and other similar measures, reveal significant trade overlap within industries, especially for the industrialized countries. Helpman (1999) reported that 65 percent of European Union trade was within the Union in 1996. Intra-industry trade can also be quite high in particular sectors, such as pharmaceuticals and electrical machinery.

Table 4.6, which reports the Grubel-Lloyd measure of trade overlap, along with import share and export intensity, provides a basic picture of the extent to which industries were both importers and exporters in 1994. Industries are listed in rank order of trade overlap, from the lowest degree of overlap (unbalanced, or little intra-industry, trade) to the highest degree of trade overlap. At low values of intra-industry trade, industries have far more trade on one side than the other. Import-

Table 4.6 Industry Trade Overlap, Import Share, and Export Intensity, 1994

	Trade overlap	Import share	Export intensity
Logging	0.113	0.020	0.266
Footwear, ex. rubber & plastic	0.118	0.707	0.127
Watches, clocks	0.149	0.800	0.237
Leather products, ex. footwear	0.182	0.660	0.152
Newspaper publishing & printing	0.246	0.000	0.001
Apparel & accessories	0.262	0.382	0.082
Tobacco manufactures	0.296	0.008	0.252
Structural clay products	0.322	0.179	0.039
Blast furnaces, steelworks	0.330	0.190	0.045
Knitting mills	0.337	0.219	0.052
Misc. manuf. industries	0.341	0.376	0.111
Pottery & related products	0.351	0.445	0.146
Grain mill products	0.362	0.018	0.080
Toys & sporting goods	0.396	0.507	0.195
Paints, varnishes	0.397	0.016	0.057
Aircraft & parts	0.429	0.176	0.449
Petroleum refining	0.462	0.085	0.039
Misc. fabricated textile products	0.473	0.148	0.048
Misc. petroleum & coal products	0.505	0.072	0.038
Furniture & fixtures	0.519	0.133	0.048
Wood bldgs. & mobile homes	0.520	0.035	0.012
Other rubber products	0.526	0.243	0.101
Engines & turbines	0.535	0.189	0.394
Beverage industries	0.594	0.068	0.029
Fabricated structural metal	0.597	0.016	0.036
Tires & inner tubes	0.616	0.225	0.116
Misc. paper & pulp products	0.617	0.025	0.050
Iron & steel foundries	0.634	0.046	0.022
Cement, concrete, gypsum	0.637	0.012	0.005
Paperboard containers & boxes	0.641	0.013	0.025
Misc. wood products	0.645	0.101	0.045
Office & accounting machines	0.645	0.451	0.249
Ship & boat building & repair	0.651	0.040	0.076
Motor vehicles	0.653	0.275	0.146
Meat products	0.655	0.034	0.065

Table 4.6 (continued)

	Trade overlap	Import share	Export intensity
Plastics, synthetics & resins	0.658	0.104	0.191
Soaps & cosmetics	0.660	0.039	0.072
Sawmills, planning mills	0.664	0.144	0.075
Photographic equipment	0.677	0.260	0.133
Metal forgings	0.679	0.042	0.173
Screw machine products	0.683	0.156	0.087
Printing, publishing	0.688	0.021	0.033
Misc. food preparations	0.696	0.066	0.114
Construction & material handling machines	0.725	0.237	0.344
Industrial & misc. chemicals	0.726	0.132	0.208
Radio, TV, & communication	0.744	0.298	0.193
Electronic computing equipment	0.763	0.487	0.167
Drugs	0.765	0.093	0.126
Ordnance	0.773	0.153	0.227
Yarn, thread & fabric mills	0.778	0.108	0.067
Primary aluminum industries	0.779	0.157	0.102
Railroad locomotives	0.783	0.141	0.096
Optical & health supplies	0.795	0.115	0.162
Household appliances	0.801	0.168	0.117
Cutlery, handtools	0.816	0.176	0.135
Scientific & controlling instrmnts	0.826	0.228	0.295
Metalworking machinery	0.839	0.236	0.176
Electrical machinery, equip.	0.863	0.313	0.197
Cycles & misc. transport. equip.	0.864	0.227	0.265
Glass & glass products	0.882	0.129	0.096
Pulp, paper & paperboard mills	0.883	0.168	0.126
Misc. plastics products	0.904	0.076	0.059
Floor coverings	0.911	0.070	0.056
Leather tanning & finishing	0.929	0.277	0.246
Misc. textile mill products	0.944	0.133	0.151
Farm machinery & equipment	0.944	0.158	0.175
Misc. nonmetallic mineral & stone products	0.944	0.112	0.100
Misc. fabricated metal products	0.960	0.085	0.076
Bakery products	0.962	0.014	0.012
Other primary metal industries	0.965	0.191	0.215
Machinery, ex. electrical	0.977	0.187	0.199

Table 4.6 (continued)

	Trade overlap	Import share	Export intensity
Dairy products	0.981	0.017	0.017
Canned & preserved fruits	0.983	0.054	0.050
Sugar & confectionary products	0.988	0.078	0.074
Guided missiles, space vehicles	0.989	0.057	0.048
Mean (unweighted)	0.653	0.171	0.124
Std. deviation (unweighted)	0.237	0.164	0.093

NOTE: Import share is calculated as imports divided by the sum of imports and domestic supply; export intensity is calculated as exports divided by shipments. Trade overlap (IIT) is defined in the text.
SOURCE: Author's calculations from the NBER Trade Database.

competing industries have export activity, but it is swamped by imports. These industries include apparel, footwear, leather products, structural clay products, and watches and clocks. The unbalanced and high export industries are logging, tobacco, and grain mill products. Trade flows are more balanced in durable goods than in nondurable goods. There is considerable balanced trade in leather tanning and finishing, miscellaneous textile mill products, machinery, farm equipment, and cycles and miscellaneous transport, where high import share is combined with high export intensity. A few industries are balanced with very little trade (high domestic orientation), such as dairy products; bakery products; paperboard containers; printing and publishing; cement, concrete, and gypsum; and fabricated structural metal.

In sum, corresponding to the overall increase in trade flows noted throughout this chapter, virtually all industries were more balanced in trade at the end of the period than they were at the start. Even where there is far more trade in one direction than the other (unbalanced trade), the smaller of the flows increased over the study period. Exports represent a small, although far from trivial, share of domestic shipments in traditionally import-competing industries, such as footwear, watches and clocks, leather products, pottery, and toys and sporting goods. Other traditionally import-competing industries have more

70 Inside Manufacturing

balanced trade, such as leather tanning and finishing and cycles and miscellaneous transport.[18]

We now have in place basic trends in employment, trade flows, and foreign competition. Employment has declined, and in many cases sharply, for most manufacturing industries. Trade volumes have increased. To get at the questions raised in the introductory chapter, we need to consider the variation across industries in changes in trade flows, foreign competition, and employment. Has increased import competition been an important factor behind declining employment? Are changes in exports associated with changes in employment? Do these relationships hold for many industries, or for a subset of industries?

CHANGES IN INDUSTRY EMPLOYMENT: THE ROLE OF TRADE AND FOREIGN COMPETITION

As a first take on these ideas, Table 4.7 reports summary information on changes in employment, trade flows, and domestic demand for our subset of high-import industries for 1979–1985 and 1985–1994. The full set of industries are reported in Appendix Tables A8 and A9 for 1979–1985 and 1985–1994, respectively.[19] To establish the importance of an industry to sector employment gains or losses, the table also reports each industry's share of total manufacturing employment loss, if that industry lost employment, or the share of total manufacturing employment gain, if that industry gained employment over the period.

In the 1979–1985 period, apparel (representing 5 percent of manufacturing employment in 1979) accounted for 7 percent of employment losses, while it was in the top 10 of industries in terms of import share gain and export losses. Non-electrical machinery, 5 percent of beginning period employment and 4 percent of employment losses, saw a more modest increase in import share and export decline. Blast furnaces accounted for just under 3 percent of 1979 manufacturing employment but, with a 63 percent decline in employment, accounted for almost 11 percent of manufacturing employment loss. It saw a rise in import share of 7 percentage points (61 percent) and a 106 percent decline in exports. Domestic demand was also very weak, falling 55 percent. Construction and material moving machinery, accounting for just under 2 percent of 1979 employment, produced 5 percent of manufacturing employment loss, associated with a 9-percentage-point increase in import share (152 percent increase) together with a nearly 48 percent decline in exports. Domestic demand was also very weak, declining 33 percent.

There is also an association between employment decline, import share gain, export loss, and weak domestic demand for the handful of small traditionally import-competing industries. Watches and clocks, with a 0.1 percent employment share and accounting for 0.6 percent of employment losses (with a 81 percent employment decline), experienced the largest percentage-point increase in import share (22.6 percentage points, a 58 percent increase) and an 84 percent decline in exports, along with a 41 percent decline in domestic demand. Footwear, with a 40 percent decline in employment, accounted for just under 2 percent of employment losses from a 0.7 percent employment share. The rise in import share in that industry was 22 percentage points, a 63 percent increase. Unlike other import-competing industries, exports rose in footwear over the period. Leather products saw a large rise in import share and a sizeable decline in exports. Toys and sporting goods experienced similar changes.

Several general points can be made from this table (bringing in observations from Appendix Table A8 as well). Sharply declining exports are strongly associated with employment decline, particularly in the industries accounting for the bulk of the employment loss. Rising imports are also strongly associated with employment decline but more so in smaller, traditionally import-competing industries (watches and clocks, footwear, and leather products). Apparel, a traditionally import-competing industry, was the biggest employer in the top 10 set of industries for import share gain and export decline. The iron and steel industries appear hard hit by the combination of rising import share and declining exports, as well as by large employment losses. Of the top export losers, blast furnaces was the biggest employer, experiencing a 63 percent decline in employment. Other primary metals also experienced a large decline in exports, a modest rise in import share, and a 20 percent decline in employment.

How much employment decline was associated with the rise in import share and/or the decline in exports? Due mostly to employment

Table 4.7 Long-Period Changes in Industry Employment, Import Share, Exports, and Domestic Demand for Selected High-Import Industries

	Employment share[a]	Employ. change	Share of total mfg. employment losses/gains	Import share change	Export change	Domestic demand change
1979–85						
Electrical machinery	0.062	−0.030	0.015	0.071	0.026	0.217
Apparel	0.054	−0.175	0.070	0.103	−0.621	0.060
Machinery, exc. electric	0.050	−0.113	0.043	0.052	−0.212	0.027
Motor vehicles	0.049	−0.115	0.043	0.086	−0.017	0.161
Blast furnaces	0.028	−0.634	0.107	0.074	−1.067	−0.553
Office & acct machines	0.019	0.260	0.141	0.083	−0.100	0.293
Construction machines	0.019	−0.414	0.052	0.091	−0.478	−0.334
Electronic computing eqp.	0.018	0.521	0.311	0.086	0.586	0.676
Misc. manuf industries	0.014	−0.145	0.015	0.110	−0.740	0.028
Pulp, paper	0.012	−0.057	0.005	0.004	−0.129	0.047
Footwear	0.007	−0.406	0.020	0.219	0.078	0.058
Photographic eqp.	0.007	−0.090	0.005	0.052	−0.350	0.096
Toys & sporting goods	0.006	−0.242	0.010	0.148	−0.476	0.064
Radio, TV	0.006	−0.315	0.012	0.046	0.107	0.445
Other primary metal	0.005	−0.204	0.008	0.022	−1.139	−0.248
Misc. textile	0.003	−0.237	0.006	0.014	−0.230	−0.157
Cycles & misc. transport eqp.	0.003	−0.065	0.001	−0.022	0.410	0.006
Leather products	0.003	−0.444	0.007	0.195	−0.555	−0.063
Pottery & related	0.002	−0.237	0.004	0.105	0.061	0.022

Watches, clocks	0.001	−0.812	0.006	0.226	−0.841	−0.415
Leather tanning & finish	0.001	−0.296	0.002	0.073	−0.192	−0.359
1985–94						
Electrical machinery	0.066	−0.072	0.054	0.135	1.146	0.456
Apparel	0.050	−0.222	0.118	0.146	1.965	0.223
Machinery, exc. electric	0.049	−0.000	0.000	0.050	0.757	0.302
Motor vehicles	0.048	0.029	0.032	0.016	0.800	0.323
Electronic computing eqp.	0.034	−0.285	0.099	0.298	0.595	0.475
Radio, TV	0.031	−0.297	0.094	0.101	1.205	0.014
Office & acct machines	0.027	−0.345	0.094	0.289	0.249	−0.331
Blast furnaces	0.016	−0.235	0.041	−0.003	1.084	0.187
Construction machines	0.014	−0.179	0.027	0.087	0.287	0.061
Misc. manuf industries	0.013	0.145	0.045	0.080	0.773	0.410
Pulp, paper	0.013	−0.057	0.008	0.010	0.772	0.207
Photographic eqp.	0.007	−0.329	0.022	0.088	0.378	0.174
Footwear	0.005	−0.544	0.027	0.140	1.297	0.028
Toys & sporting goods	0.005	0.194	0.025	0.130	1.495	0.512
Other primary metal	0.005	−0.119	0.006	−0.020	1.092	0.172
Misc. textile	0.003	0.006	0.000	0.000	1.017	0.308
Cycles & misc. transport	0.003	−0.006	0.000	−0.041	0.565	0.275
Pottery & related	0.002	0.043	0.002	0.027	0.693	0.317
Leather products	0.002	−0.336	0.006	0.196	1.328	0.208
Leather tanning & finish	0.001	−0.188	0.002	0.045	0.752	0.450
Watches, clocks	0.001	−0.381	0.003	0.187	0.793	0.215

NOTE: Changes are log changes. See Appendix Tables A8 and A9 for explanations.
[a] Employment share data refer to 1979 for the 1979–85 panel and 1985 for the 1985–94 panel.

size, industries with the largest increases in import share accounted for a noticeably small share of total sectoral employment decline. Of the top import share gainers (and export losers, with solid domestic demand), apparel accounted for the largest share of employment declines, at 7 percent. With apparel at number 8 in rising import share, the top 10 import share gainers accounted for 21 percent of employment decline, and they started with 12 percent of 1979 employment. Four of the industries in this group had considerable export decline. The top 10 in export decline accounted for about 25 percent of employment loss, starting from a 12 percent 1979 employment share.

On the employment gain side, advances were concentrated in computers, office and accounting machines, and printing and publishing. Computers saw an 8-percentage-point increase in import share, along with a 58 percent increase in exports and strong domestic demand. Office machines was similarly situated, although exports declined by about 10 percent. Printing and publishing has little exposure to imports or exports, and domestic demand growth was strong.

For the 1985–1994 period, we have a different set of observations. A number of the same industries appear in the top 10 of import share gainers (leather products, watches and clocks, apparel, footwear, and toys and sporting goods). The computer industry moved to number 1 from 11, and office and accounting machines moved up also, from 13 to 2. Rising imports were associated with employment decline in all these industries. The surge in exports, nearly across the board, produced some (simple) surprises, in that many of the top import share gainers had big increases in exports. Apparel accounted for almost 12 percent of employment losses, from a 5 percent 1985 employment share, while import share increased, exports surged, and domestic demand was moderately strong. Import share rose 159 percent in computers (29 percentage points), exports increased 59 percent, and employment fell 28 percent, accounting for nearly 10 percent of total sectoral employment loss from a 3 percent employment share. The story in office and accounting machines was very similar. Scientific and controlling instruments, small by employment, saw an increase in import share of 11 percentage points and a 58 percent increase in exports, with solid domestic demand, but a 16 percent decline in employment that accounted for 4 percent of employment losses.

Imports, Exports, and Jobs 75

The top 10 import share gainers accounted for 46 percent of employment losses while representing 21 percent of 1985 employment. The surge in exports appears more weakly related to employment growth. The top 10 export gainers accounted for just 5 percent of employment growth, from an 18 percent employment share. Weak domestic demand, through changed circumstances in international politics, played a larger role in this later period, particularly for aircraft and guided missiles and ordnance.

With respect to the degree of intra-industry trade (and considering data from Appendix Table A9), there is some evidence of greater employment loss in unbalanced trade industries (industries that are either importers or exporters) than in balanced trade industries. The average weighted employment change in the most unbalanced trade industries (with values of mean IIT less than 0.46) was –23 percent, and the average weighted employment change in the most balanced trade industries (with values of mean IIT greater than 0.795) was –7 percent, a difference that is statistically significant at the 0.05 level.[20]

Several conclusions emerge from these observations about changes in industry employment and trade flows. Rising import share is associated with declining employment, particularly for a few industries over the full period. Watches and clocks, footwear, leather products, apparel, and construction and material handling machines all had large to very large increases in import share and very large declines in employment. Computers and office and accounting machines saw large increases in import share and expanding employment. With respect to simple correlations, exports are more complicated. From 1979–1985, when export demand was weak, employment declined in a number of industries. Yet, when exports surged, from 1985–1992, employment continued to decline.

WHAT ABOUT IMPORT PRICES?

At this very descriptive level, it is more difficult to draw conclusions about the association between changes in employment and changes in import prices. The simple correlations between changes in log industry employment and changes in import share appear stronger than the employment/import price associations. This may be somewhat a product of timing: once import share has risen, an industry is revealed to be facing stronger import competition, whereas a decrease in import price reveals potentially more import competition, and the effect on industry employment depends on the industry response to the import price decline. In other words, rising import share is an *ex post* measure of increasing import competition, whereas declining import price is a measure of potential competition. We will return to this point in Chapter 6.

Job loss, not net changes in industry employment, is at the heart of the emotionally charged assertion that, "trade costs jobs." Having built a foundation from the traditional focus on net industry employment change, we conclude this chapter with a discussion of the incidence of job loss and how trends in job loss are associated with trends in trade flows.

JOB LOSS AND TRADE, 1979–1994

The best available measure of permanent job loss is provided by the DWSs, biennial supplements to the CPS. As CPS data, the DWSs offer the advantage of being drawn from a large-scale, nationally representative sample. In each survey, adults (aged 20 years and older) in the regular monthly CPS were asked if they had lost a job in the preceding 5-year period due to "(1) a plant closing, (2) an employer going out of business, (3) a layoff from which he/she was not recalled, or (4) other similar reasons." If the answer was yes, a series of questions followed concerning the old job and period of joblessness. By drawing a sample of workers who responded that their job loss was due to the first three reasons, we obtain a reasonable and sound measure of involuntary permanent job loss. A key disadvantage of the DWSs is their retrospective nature—respondents are asked to recall events 3–5 years in the past. I discuss the DWS and its advantages and disadvantages in more detail in Appendix A.

Based on calculations from a sample drawn from the DWSs, 32 million nonagricultural workers reported experiencing at least one permanent job loss over the 1979–1994 period (Appendix A reports sample construction details). Manufacturing accounted for 35.5 percent of total job loss, with 10.2 million workers reporting a job loss from that sector. Manufacturing accounted for an average of 18–19 percent of total nonagricultural employment over the 16-year period, starting with 23.4 percent in 1979 and ending at 16.0 percent in 1994.

Figure 4.5 plots the total and manufacturing displacement rates over the 1979–1994 period. The rate of job loss from manufacturing is considerably higher than the overall rate for all industries. The manufacturing displacement rate rose to 8 percent in the early 1980s recession and then fell sharply until the late 1980s. It rose steadily through the prolonged early 1990s recession and then fell as the economy recovered from the recession. By 1994, the rate of job loss was down from its 1992 peak, but it remained high for a recovery phase. The total displacement rate follows a similar, although dampened, pattern. The overall rate of job loss was high in 1994, given the strength of the

Figure 4.5 Manufacturing and Total Displacement Rates, by Year (1979–94)

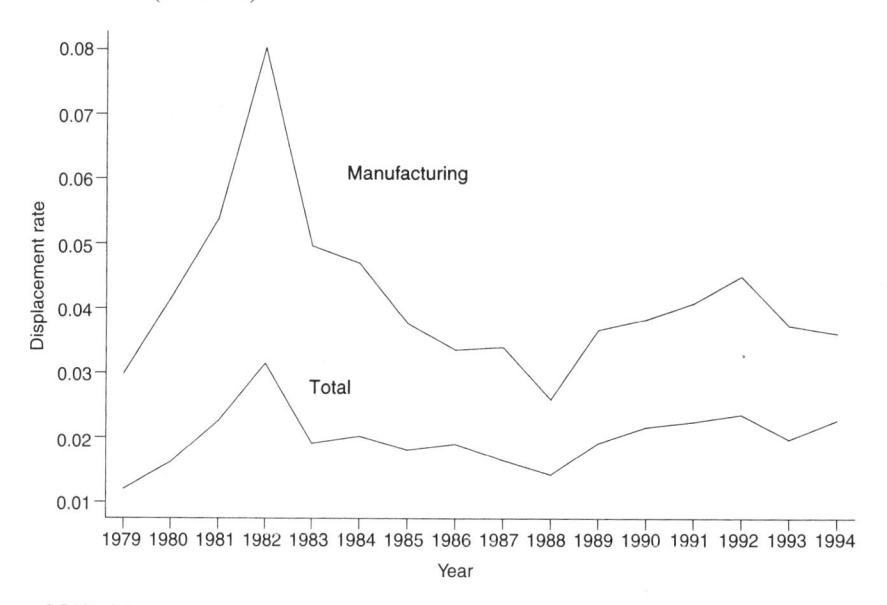

SOURCE: Kletzer (2000, Figure 10.1).

economy (for more on the pattern of job loss over the 1980s and 1990s, see Farber 1997).[21]

TRADE AND JOB LOSS BY INDUSTRY

The years 1979–1994 were characterized by widespread job loss in manufacturing. Table 4.8 presents the top job loss manufacturing industries. In part, these industries accounted for much job loss because they are large industries in terms of employment. By adjusting for employment, the displacement rate offers a proxy for the "risk of job loss." All these industries were near or below the average job loss rate for manufacturing industries.

Is displacement associated with employment losses? Appendix Table A10 reports information at a more detailed level on employment change, displacement, and changes in trade flows, ranking industries by 1979 employment levels. With a few exceptions, all industries with above-average rates of job loss have above-average declines in employment. Industries with employment growth tend to have lower job loss rates. The large employment industries, all with sizeable increases

Table 4.8 Top Job Loss Manufacturing Industries, Measured by Total Workers Displaced, 1979–1994

Industry	Workers displaced (000s)	Average annual displacement rate
Electrical machinery	822.9	0.042
Apparel	748.3	0.052
Motor vehicles	675.5	0.051
Machinery, exc. electric	633.3	0.044
Printing & publishing	580.8	0.037
Electronic computing equipment	394.9	0.045
Fabricated structural metals	386.3	0.056
All manufacturing industries	11,380	0.051

in import share, all had fairly large employment declines and job loss rates at or higher than the sector average. Notably, electrical machinery, apparel, motor vehicles, and blast furnaces accounted for larger shares of displacement than their corresponding employment share. Interestingly, the strongest relationship between employment change and the risk of job displacement is found amongst the set of small (in employment), traditionally import-competing industries, such as leather tanning and finishing (with a 29 percent employment decline and a 0.073 job loss rate), watches and clocks (a 69 percent employment decline and a 0.091 job loss rate), and leather products (a 78 percent employment decline and a 0.142 job loss rate).

For the most part, industries experiencing high job loss rates started with a high import share and experienced a large (positive) change in import share (increasing import competition). Industries with lower import share yet large positive change in import share had lower rates of job loss (metalworking machinery, aircraft, and knitting mills), while industries with high import share and average or smaller changes in import share also had average or lower rates of job loss (motor vehicles, and engines and turbines). Exports appear important: while four of the top 10 job loss rate industries had large increases in import share, five of the top 10 had small increases in exports or even a decline in exports. At the same time, the top three job loss industries had large increases in exports. Over this long period, export change may be deceiving. Exports surged strongly after 1985, and it is likely that the long-period change is driven by the 1985–1994 period. The econometric analysis of annual changes in the next chapter will provide a better perspective on export change.

Table 4.9 reports additional summary univariate classifications of trade volumes and job loss. Panel I reports the mean annual displacement rate for each quartile of the industry mean import share distribution. The highest import share industries have, on average, the highest job loss rate, but job loss rates are relatively uniform below the top quartile. Within each quartile, the distribution of job loss rates is fairly similar. Panel II reports mean job loss rates by the long-period change in import share. In this panel, job loss rates are higher for industries with large positive changes in import share. Panel III reports the mean annual displacement rate for each quartile of the distribution of the long-period change in exports. Here, we might expect declining job

Table 4.9 Industry Displacement, Import Share, and Exports

	Lowest quartile	2nd quartile	3rd quartile	Top quartile
I.				
By mean import share	<0.043	0.043–0.076	0.079–0.140	>0.140
Mean annual displacement rate	0.042	0.052	0.041	0.066
(min, max)	(0.024, 0.080)	(0.021, 0.126)	(0.020, 0.083)	(0.008, 0.142)
II.				
By change in import share, 1979–94	<0.0131	0.0131–0.0614	0.0615–0.1170	>0.1172
Mean annual displacement rate	0.044	0.049	0.051	0.058
(min, max)	(0.021, 0.098)	(0.021, 0.126)	(0.024, 0.108)	(0.008, 0.142)
III.				
By change in ln(exports), 1979–94	<0.149	0.149–0.709	0.709–1.043	>1.044
Mean annual displacement rate	0.059	0.042	0.053	0.047
(min, max)	(0.008, 0.107)	(0.023, 0.074)	(0.026, 0.142)	(0.020, 0.126)
IV.				
By mean annual displacement rate	<0.031	0.032–0.043	0.044–0.061	>0.065
Mean import share	0.077	0.074	0.096	0.184
(min, max)	(0.002, 0.181)	(0.009, 0.154)	(0.006, 0.234)	(0.023, 0.458)

SOURCE: Author's calculations from the Displaced Worker Surveys and the NBER Trade Database.

loss with more growth of exports, so that from the bottom quartile to the top, job loss rates would fall. This is the overall pattern found in Panel III, although the decline in job loss as exports rise is not smooth, and the range of job loss rates within each quartile is fairly similar. Lastly, Panel IV reports mean import share for the full job loss industry distribution. Similar to what can be seen in Appendix Table A10, import share is highest among the high job loss rate industries, and the top half of the job loss rate distribution has distinctly higher import share than the lower half of the distribution.[22]

One suggestion from these univariate classifications is that the combination of "trade with job loss" arises from continued, sustained import competition. That is, high rates of job loss are found for industries with high import share and large (positive) changes in import share. For the most part, increasing import competition (positive changes in import share), from a lower level of import share, is associated with below-average job loss (photographic equipment, scientific and controlling instruments, and pulp and paper).

A few general observations emerge from Appendix Table A10 and Table 4.9. There is a set of industries facing sustained import competition, those with both high levels of import share and positive changes in import share where the rate of job loss is high. At the same time, there is a considerable amount of variation in job displacement across industries, and the risk of job loss can be high in the absence of changes in foreign competition. Thus "trade" itself can explain only a small share of the variation in job displacement.

SUMMARY

When the basic trends in employment, job loss, and trade flows are brought together, some basic patterns emerge. There is an association between employment decline, import share gain, export loss, and weak domestic demand for the handful of small traditionally import-competing industries. Sharply declining exports are strongly associated with employment decline, particularly in the industries accounting for the bulk of the employment loss. Rising imports are also strongly associated with employment decline but more so in smaller, traditionally im-

82 Inside Manufacturing

port-competing industries. High job loss rate industries were both high import share and experienced a large (positive) change in import share (increasing import competition). From this descriptive background, the next step is the estimation of an econometric model that allows for the inclusion of other factors in the determination of employment change and job loss. Chapter 5 presents such a model, with estimates following in Chapters 6 and 7.

Notes

1. This brief discussion owes its clarity to the more complete discussion in Mann (1999).
2. This is not to say that trade flows are solely determined by exchange rates and other macroeconomic factors such as differential country growth rates. Chapter 2 discussed how trade flows are also a function of price competitiveness, from a microeconomic perspective. What we can see now is that microeconomic decisions and broad macroeconomic factors affect global price competitiveness and trade flows.
3. These indices are described in more detail in U.S. Bureau of Labor Statistics (1992). They are based on a survey of actual transactions prices, and to the degree possible, they reflect c.i.f. (cost, insurance, freight) prices. When aggregation was needed, the SIC indices were weighted by their relative shares in total imports, using the NBER Trade Database.
4. Because attention is often, although not always, paid according to the size of an industry, industries are listed in the two tables in descending order of beginning-of-period employment.
5. In the case of farm machinery and equipment, and for all small employment industries, it is worth noting that arithmetically, when a given number is divided by a small base, it yields a larger percentage change than the same number divided by a larger base.
6. Import share fell in just four industries over the 1975–1994 period. These industries are newspaper printing and publishing (import share fell by 82.5 percent), sugar and confectionary products (a drop of 54.2 percent), cycles and miscellaneous transport (–18.3 percent), and petroleum refining (–16.1 percent). Note that sugar and motorcycles had trade protection during some or all of the period.
7. Table 4.2 lists two additional industries, with import shares of 0.129, very close to the 0.13 cutoff.
8. See Schoepfle (1982) for classifications over the period 1972–1979 and Bednarzik (1993) for the period 1982–1987.
9. Import share of 0.089 or higher.
10. As measured by the multilateral trade-weighted value of the dollar, in Council of Economic Advisers (1999).

11. Nec stands for "Not elsewhere classified."
12. Import prices are not available for all industries. Mean price changes are reported in the last rows of the table. These means are simple means, not weighted by industry output, nor corrected for the use of two-digit import prices for a number of three-digit industries.
13. These industries correspond to a lineup of the top exporting firms General Motors, Boeing, Ford Motor, General Electric, Chrysler, IBM, Motorola, and Hewlett-Packard (reported in Richardson and Rindal, 1995).
14. More detail on industry shipments shares and export shares is contained in Appendix Table A5.
15. As discussed below, the slight average decline in export intensity from 1980 to 1985 masks a wide variation, with exports falling dramatically in a number of industries.
16. The three (computers, railroad locomotives, and petroleum) all had shipments growth exceeding export growth.
17. Computers are an exception here, as export intensity fell over the 1980–1994 period (by –0.643), due to faster growth in shipments and domestic demand than in exports (all three positive). The other industries where exports, shipments, and domestic demand all grew, and export intensity fell due to the growth in shipments (and domestic demand) exceeding the growth in exports are grain mill products, misc. fabricated textile products, guided missiles, photographic equipment, and misc. manufacturing industries.
18. Appendix Table A7 reports mean trade overlap, import share, and export intensity separately for 1980, 1987, and 1994.
19. Appendix Tables A8 and A9 list industries in descending order of beginning year employment share (i.e., largest employment industries first) and reports changes in employment, import share, exports, and domestic demand. A ranking of industries is also provided for each of the four changes, where a ranking of "1" denotes largest percentage employment loss, largest import share gain, largest export loss, and largest domestic demand loss. The ranks provide some evidence of the rank-order correlations between the changes. If an industry's rank numbers are all small, then that industry had large employment declines, large increases in import share, large decreases in exports, and large reductions in domestic demand.
20. The weights are 1979 industry employment.
21. My estimates of the rate of job loss are lower than Farber's due to differences in sample construction. Farber corrects the DWS numbers for an undercount of job loss that results from a change in the recall period. I do not follow his procedure and therefore my count of manufacturing job loss should be considered a conservative one.
22. In results not reported, there is little suggestion of a simple, univariate, relationship between intra-industry trade and job loss rates. More balanced trade industries have similar job loss rates as unbalanced trade industries.

5
Modeling Labor Market Responses to Changes in Trade and Import Competition

In the previous chapter, I examined the descriptive evidence on changes in industry employment and job loss and the possible link to the increasing volume of trade and foreign competition. I noted a number of discernible patterns. I also noted a number of issues likely to affect estimates of the relationship between foreign competition, trade, and changes in employment. In this chapter I discuss these issues more formally and present an empirical strategy for estimating these relationships.

The very basic question I seek to answer is, "How is trade associated with employment change and job loss?" As such, my goal is not a model of why industries trade or more generally a model of the determinants of trade. My question fits into an approach with a long tradition in labor economics: it is partial equilibrium, not general equilibrium, in that I examine employment changes and job loss in an industry in relation to changes in trade flows and/or foreign competition in that industry, with no explicit allowance for spillover effects. This partial equilibrium approach stands in contrast to the perspective of international trade economists, who study the determinants of trade and trade patterns in interrelated markets. My partial equilibrium modeling is not unique: often-cited examples include Grossman (1987), Freeman and Katz (1991), and Revenga (1992).

Even as the analysis gains econometric structure and a bit of formalism, it remains descriptive, not causal. By choice, I want to assess how changes in employment and job loss have been associated with changes in trade flows and prices, controlling for other factors that influence employment and job loss. I acknowledge, although I do not address in depth, the important (and correct) view that trade flows and prices are jointly determined with other variables, including production, domestic demand, and employment. This joint determination makes trade flows and prices endogenous to the process I am modeling.

I do not attempt to uncover the underlying causes of changes in either trade flows or prices. Thus, my analysis is not truly causal; it is descriptive and meant to reveal the associations between U.S. jobs and increasing economic integration that concern policymakers, workers, the general public, and academics.

The basic empirical specification is presented in the following section. I also discuss some of the qualifications of the estimation, along with econometric issues that arise. For the reader less interested in the technical details, the first section contains all the essential points. A more technically complete presentation of the model follows. Reading the more technical presentation is not essential for understanding the discussion of econometric results presented in Chapters 6 and 7.

THE BASIC EMPIRICAL FRAMEWORK

I use a fairly simple empirical framework for examining the associations between changes in product demand, import (price) competition, employment change, and job displacement. The framework is developed from a straightforward industry model of employment determination.

The model begins with the labor market. Using first differences, the demand for labor in industry i in year t (N_{it}) can be written as:

(1) $d\ln N_{it} = -kd\ln W_{it} + d\ln Z_{it}$,

where W_{it} is the industry wage, Z_{it} is the shift in the derived labor demand curve due to shifts in product demand, k is the wage elasticity of labor demand, ln is the natural logarithm, and d is the difference operator.

Also in first differences, labor supply can be written as:

(2) $d\ln N_{it} = ed\ln W_{it} + d\ln H_{it}$,

where e is the wage elasticity of labor supply, H_{it} is a vector of factors that shift labor supply. Labor market clearing, where wages in an industry adjust to equate labor supply and labor demand) implies:

(3) $d\ln N_{it} = (ed\ln X_{it} - kd\ln H_{it})/(k + e)$, and

(4) $d\ln W_{it} = (d\ln X_{it} + d\ln H_{it})/(k + e)$.

With respect of changes in product demand, the coefficient of interest is $e/(k + e)$, which we will call h.

This model highlights the relationship between changes in employment (and wages) and (exogenous) shifts in demand (and supply). Taking this framework to the data requires empirical measures of these shifts and, in particular, the relationship between changes in our measures of trade and changes in product demand. It is precisely this aspect where my approach is descriptive rather than causal because I use measures of industry sales, decomposed into domestic market demand, exports, and imports or industry (import) price as measures of exogenous shifts in product demand. Realistically, these measures are not exogenous; they depend on industry supply as well as demand and are further influenced by wages and employment and the factors that determine them. The more technical derivation in the section that follows discusses this point in more detail. That section shows how changes in sales can be used to proxy for changes in product demand.

With these qualifications in mind, we can isolate the trade-related components of product demand. Data on industry shipments (sales) is available from the NBER Productivity data set, and data on exports and imports from the NBER Trade Database (the Trade Database contains information on all three variables—shipments, exports, and imports). Following Freeman and Katz (1991), we can decompose sales into its component parts. Define D (= domestic) as gross domestic market sales, where D = sales − exports + imports ($D = S − X + M$). A first-order approximation gives:

(5) $d\ln S = w_1 d\ln D - w_2 d\text{Mshare} + w_3 d\ln X$,

where Mshare is import share, defined as M/D. The w's are various weights: $w_1 = [(S − X)/S]$, $w_2 = (X/S)$, and $w_3 = (D/S)$. The weights adjust changes in the three components for the difference in the absolute magnitude of sales generated by the domestic side as compared to exports and imports.

Allowing changes in sales to proxy changes in product demand (explained more fully in the section that follows), we get a specification relating changes in sales (decomposed) to changes in employment:

(6) $d\ln N = Bw_1 d\ln D + Bw_2 d\ln X - Bw_3 d$Mshare,

where B, a coefficient to be estimated, is a combination of various structural parameters explained more fully below in the following section. Note that from Equation 4, labor supply factors (H) are being ignored for now. These factors reappear in a more complete specification below.

Note that this model makes an implicit assumption that changes in industry employment due to (weighted) changes in trade-related sales are similar to changes in industry employment due to changes in domestic sales. This assumption appears as the same "B" on the three different components of sales. In the long run, there seems little reason to expect industry labor markets to react differently to changes in sales from different sources. An export-related shift in demand is a shift in demand. In the short run, we may have less confidence about this assumption. If trade-generated shifts are perceived to be temporary, say because of exchange rate volatility, then there may be different responses by industry labor markets to shifts in demand.

Note also that the underlying approach in Equation 6 is a consideration of shifts in demand, shifts that allow us to consider whether domestic employment is more or less sensitive to changes in imports or exports than to changes in domestic demand. As an economy becomes more open (trade flows rising as a share of GDP), industry labor markets will be subject to shifts that are trade generated, along with the domestic demand shifts that prevailed (alone) in a closed economy. This perspective allows us to ask how much of the observed changes in employment can be related to changes in trade flows.

More technically, in the regression context, Equation 6 considers the domestic employment change associated with a change in one of the components of sales ($S = D + X - M$), holding the other two components constant. Each one of these demand shifts cannot be viewed in isolation, due to the sales (or demand, $D = S - X + M$) identity that defines them. Take changes in import share, for example. Let imports rise, producing a rise in import share. The rise in import share is correspondingly a reduction in the domestically produced *share* of domestic

Imports, Exports, and Jobs 89

demand, through a decline in shipments that will hold constant the level of domestic demand. The decline in shipments will be one-for-one with the increase in imports. Thus, the rise in import share is a change in the composition of total domestic demand, holding the level constant.

In the case of a shift in export demand, exports can only rise if industry sales/shipments rise. This again follows from the domestic demand identity. If exports rise and imports are held constant, a rise in shipments is required to hold domestic demand constant. Another way of stating this is that an increase in weighted exports, where the weight is the share of exports in sales, represents an increase in overall sales due to exports, holding the other components constant.

Domestic demand is the last, and biggest, component. Averaged over time and the industries in this sample, domestic demand represents 91 percent of sales. Examining an increase in domestic demand, holding import share and exports constant, is complicated a bit by the fact that domestic demand is part of (the denominator of) import share. This complication means that when domestic demand increases, imports must also increase, to hold import share constant. Thus, the rise in shipments that spurs a domestic demand increase is accompanied by an increase in imports. For example, domestic demand for cars is satisfied by domestic producers and foreign producers. When domestic demand increases, with no change in the foreign share, there will be more imports, to meet the increased (absolute) demand for foreign cars, and more domestic car shipments, to meet the increased (absolute) demand for domestically produced cars. In an open economy, some of the increase in domestic demand is satisfied by foreign producers.

These interactions highlight the partial equilibrium nature of my approach. The introduction of trade flows takes the level of domestic demand as a given, without a feedback mechanism that would allow for economic growth. There is also no provision for spillover employment effects from goods trade to other sectors of the economy.

In this framework, these relationships imply that the correlation between import share increases and employment declines will be overstated, due to the effect of falling shipments. The association between export growth and employment growth will also be overstated, due to the effect of rising shipments. The (employment-stimulating) effect of a rise in domestic demand will be understated due to the accompanying rise in imports. Given the size of the domestic market, we expect this understatement to be small. We will return to this point in Chapter 6.

Returning to our modeling strategy, an alternative specification relates changes in industry employment and changes in industry relative prices, using these price changes as a proxy for changes in sales:

(7) $d\ln N_{it} = B[(1-f^1)d\ln(P_i/P_a)_t + f^2 d\ln(P_m/P_a)_t + d\ln X_{it}]$,

where P_i is the price of the domestically produced good; P_m is the dollar price of the foreign good; P_a is the dollar price of all other goods; f^1 is the domestic price elasticity of demand; f^2 is the foreign price elasticity of demand; and X is shifts in product demand.

Equations 6 and 7 will become estimable below with the addition of error terms. The error terms that will be added reflect measurement issues and the stochastic nature of changes in employment. There are, however, other error terms relevant to these equations. Turning first to Equation 6, sales (decomposed) are being used as an estimate of product demand. The following section explains how this is done through demand, price, and employment determination equations that link product demand to shipments/sales. These links mean that our measure of sales (decomposed into trade flows) is determined, in part, by domestic demand, production, and employment. These interrelationships mean that sales is not a variable exogenous to the determination of employment. Technically speaking, this means that the error terms we add to Equation 6 will very likely be correlated with (some of) the determinants of sales. If sales are correlated with any of the components of the error term, ordinary least squares (OLS) parameter estimates will be biased and inconsistent.

Similar issues arise for the treatment of industry prices in Equation 7. As noted by Revenga (1992), several factors may induce correlation between the import price measure and the stochastic errors in changes in employment, such as unmeasured worldwide shocks to materials costs or unobserved and unmeasured taste or demand shifts in the United States that influence import prices due to the size of the U.S. market. In addition, as in the model in Mann (1988), import prices may be set specifically for the U.S. market, and this price setting will produce a correlation between import price and the disturbance terms. The direction of the bias is ambiguous. For example, a worldwide oil price shock will increase import prices and (separately) depress U.S. employment, inducing a negative correlation between import price and employment change. Alternatively, if foreign producers price to the U.S. market, they may reduce prices when U.S. demand is slack, inducing a positive correlation as import prices fall while domestic employment falls. On balance, it is not clear whether the OLS estimates of the employment change elasticities will be understated or overstated.

In principle, these endogeneity concerns are most properly addressed with a system of equations for domestic demand, exports, imports, and industry prices, changes in employment and job loss. In practice, such a system presents a very difficult and complex estimation task. Since my goal is to inform the policy debate, I do not take that approach here. In what follows, I do explore instrumental variables estimation of industry import prices but with limited success. Given that limited success, I do not extend the instrumental variables analysis to trade flows. My method for instrumenting industry import prices is discussed in Appendix B.

Most importantly, the endogeneity of changes in trade flows and changes in prices constrains our interpretation of the regression analyses that follow. The regressions are descriptive; they will enable us to assess how changes in employment and job loss have been associated with changes in trade flows and import prices. I cannot conclude that changes in "trade" *cause* changes in employment and job loss because my chosen trade measures are themselves determined, at least in part, by some of the factors that influence changes in employment.

With these caveats stated clearly, we can return to Equations 6 and 7 as the basis for our econometric specifications for changes in industry employment. These specifications, however, make provisions only for trade-related factors and not the other factors that were noted in previous chapters and are likely to influence resource allocations (e.g., technological change, other factor prices and factor usage, supply, and macroeconomic influences). In what follows, these other factors will enter as the vector X^2_{it}.

The nature of the questions asked (within an industry, how are changes in trade flows and import competition associated with employment change and job loss) and the available panel structure of the data (observations on a cross section of industries over several time periods) suggest the following error term structure:

(8) $d\ln N_{it} = Bw_1 d\ln D_{it} + Bw_2 d\ln X_{it} - Bw_3 d\text{Mshare}_{it} + G_1 X^2_{it} + u^1_{it}$, and

(9) $d\ln N_{it} = B[(1-f^1)d\ln(P_i/P_a)_t + f^2 d\ln(P_m/P_a)_t + d\ln X_{it}] + G_2 X^2_{it} + u^2_{it}$,

where $B(1-f^1)$, Bf^2, G_1, and G_2 are coefficients to be estimated and u^1_{it} and u^2_{it} are error terms. We will utilize a two-way error component model, with

(10) $u^j_{it} = \mu_i + \lambda_t + v^j_{it}$, $j = 1,2$,

where μ_i denotes an unobservable industry-specific effect, λ_t denotes an unobservable time effect that is industry invariant, and v_{it} is the stochastic disturbance. We note that μ_i is time-invariant and accounts for any industry-specific effect that is not included in the regression. The term λ_t is industry-invariant and accounts for any time-specific effect that is not included in the regression. For example, it can account for macroeconomic influences that are not otherwise captured by the economy-wide proxies. The remainder disturbance, v_{it}, varies with industries and time and should be considered as the usual disturbance term in the regression.

With this type of error structure, a "fixed effects" model is the appropriate specification, as we are focusing on a specific set of manufacturing industries, and our statistical inference will be limited to the behavior of these industries. It is important to recognize that the industries in the data set are not a random sampling of the population of industries.[1] In the fixed effects model, the μ_i and λ_t are assumed to be fixed parameters to be estimated. With industries differing in size and scale, the stochastic remainder disturbances (v_{it}) are assumed to be zero mean with nonconstant, heteroscedastic variances.[2]

Estimation will first proceed assuming that the explanatory variables are independent of the disturbance terms, for all industries and time periods. Given this assumption, and the above assumptions about the disturbance terms, feasible generalized least squares (FGLS) is a standard estimation technique. With more cross-section variation (number of industries) than time variation (number of time periods), however, FGLS variance-covariance estimates are anti-conservative (unduly optimistic in the simple sense of being too small). An alternative is OLS, with an adjustment for autocorrelation and panel-corrected standard errors (PCSE).[3] Most of the panel estimates that follow will be from OLS/PCSE estimation.

Job loss is the last component of the basic empirical framework. Starting from changes in net industry employment, a simple model of turnover can be used to modify and narrow the focus to just one of the gross flows, job displacement.[4] Firms implement net employment reductions through the use of displacements and unreplaced attritions. Attritions are separations due to quits, discharges (for cause), retirements, and deaths. Attritions that are not replaced by employers are called unreplaced attritions. For an industry, net employment change in year t can be written as:

(11) $DIS + UA = -\Delta N$,

where DIS is displacements, and UA is unreplaced attritions (other nondisplacement separations minus accessions).[5] This net change in employment can be expressed as a proportion of total employment:

(12) DIS/N_{t-1} = Displacement rate = $-(N_t - N_{t-1})/N_{t-1} - UA/N_{t-1}$.

Relying on the approximation of the rate of change of employment, $(N_t - N_{t-1})/N_{t-1}$, to the change in log employment, $(\ln N_t - \ln N_{t-1})$, for small changes, Equation 9 is approximately equal to:

(13) Displacement rate$_t = -d\ln N_t -$ UA rate,

where UA rate = UA/N_{t-1}. Rearranging yields:

(14) $-$(Displacement Rate$_t$ + UA rate) = $d\ln N_t$.

Equations 8 and 14, and separately Equations 9 and 14, can be combined to yield reduced-form equations for industry i displacement:

(15) Displacement rate$_{it}$ = $B_2 w_1 d\ln D_{it} + B_2 w_2 d\ln X_{it} - B_2 w_3 d$Mshare$_{it}$
$+ G_3 X^2_{it} + u^3_{it}$, and

(16) Displacement rate$_{it}$ = $B_2[(1 - f^1) d\ln(P_i/P_a)_t + f^2 d\ln(P_m/P_a)_t + d\ln X_{it}]$
$+ G_4 X^2_{it} + u^4_{it}$,

where B_2, G_3, and G_4 are coefficients to be estimated and $u^3{}_{it}$ and $u^4{}_{it}$ are error terms. We will continue to utilize a two-way error component model, with fixed effects as discussed above.

The specifications in Equations 15 and 16 acknowledge that the dependent variable will be measured with error because information is not available on industry UA rates. Appropriate for dependent variable measurement error, the omission is subsumed in the error terms, u^3 and u^4.[6] Even with information on UA rates, moving that variable to the right-hand side of Equations 15 or 16 is inappropriate because that would treat quits, discharges, and accessions (the components of the UA rate) as independent variables in a displacement relationship. Quits are very likely to be influenced by conditions within the industry.[7] Firms and industries are likely to differ in their use of the various components of turnover to implement desired changes in employment.

Other factors: technological change

The vector X^2 provides room in the empirical model for other factors influencing changes in industry employment. Technological change is the most prominent factor revealed in the "trade and wages" literature, and that literature points clearly in the direction of technological change as a key explanation to declining unskilled employment in manufacturing and increasing wage inequality (see the references in Chapter 3). The challenges of proxying technological change are clear, and there is the additional issue of potential endogeneity in this case. Industries facing increasing foreign competition may be driven toward technological change as a response (see Lawrence 2000). That is, technological change can be seen as both a driving force in increasing economic integration, as well as a force driven by increasing economic integration. This interaction is complicated, and any separation of trade and technology is beyond the scope of this study. In what follows, I use two measures of technological change: changes in the output intensity of research and development spending and changes in total factor productivity (TFP). Following a number of studies (Bartel and Lichtenberg 1987; Mincer 1991), research and development intensity is measured as the ratio of research and development expenditures to sales. Research and development expenditures are available at the two- and three-digit SIC industry level from the National Science Foundation (1981, 1989, 1999). The use of TFP, my second measure, as a proxy for technological change has a considerable history in economics, dating back to Robert Solow's work in the 1950s. Total factor productivity is the portion of output growth unexplained by labor, capital, or energy input growth. It is a residual, a combination of all the unmeasured factors contributing to output growth.

Briefly, other variables are included to control for effects known to influence employment change. These variables are important to include but of less interest to the main discussion. The change in the index of manufacturing industrial production is included to capture cyclical fluctuations in labor demand. Average hourly earnings in services is included as a measure of an alternative wage. Production function characteristics are proxied by the capital intensity of shipments (the natural logarithm of the ratio of the capital stock to shipments).

Readers most interested in the empirical results can now proceed directly to Chapter 6, where estimates of the employment change specifications, Equations 8 and 9, are reported. Chapter 7 reports estimates of the displacement specifications, Equations 15 and 16. Readers interested in the more technical issues involved in deriving the basic framework should continue through to the end of this chapter.

THE BASIC EMPIRICAL MODEL, IN MORE DETAIL

Even in full detail, the empirical framework for examining the relationship between changes in product demand, import (price) competition, employment change, and job displacement is fairly simple and straightforward. I specify a simple structural model and estimate the reduced-form equations that result from solving out for employment (and the other dependent variables) in terms of the exogenous variables. The basic setup borrows from models of import competition and employment change developed in Mann (1988), Freeman and Katz (1991), and Revenga (1992).

The description of the labor market remains as previously stated, and I repeat Equations 1–4, renumbered for this section as Equations

17–20. Using first differences, the demand for labor in industry i in year t (N_{it}) can be written as:

(17) $d\ln N_{it} = -kd\ln W_{it} + d\ln Z_{it}$,

where W_{it} is the industry wage, Z_{it} is the shift in the derived labor demand curve due to shifts in product demand (discussed in more detail below), k is the wage elasticity of labor demand, ln is the natural logarithm, and d is the difference operator.

Also in first differences, labor supply can be written as:

(18) $d\ln N_{it} = ed\ln W_{it} + d\ln H_{it}$,

where e is the wage elasticity of labor supply, H_{it} is a vector of factors that shift labor supply. Labor market clearing, where wages in an industry adjust to equate labor supply and labor demand) implies:

(19) $d\ln N_{it} = (ed\ln Z_{it} - kd\ln H_{it})/(k + e)$, and

(20) $d\ln W_{it} = (d\ln Z_{it} + d\ln H_{it})/(k + e)$.

With respect of changes in product demand, the coefficient of interest is $e/(k + e)$.

In the data, industry product demand is represented by 1) industry shipments, decomposed into domestic market demand, exports, and imports (more on this below), or 2) industry price. Both shipments and prices depend on industry supply as well as demand; therefore, replacing Z with shipments in Equations 19 and 20 fails to recognize the simultaneity that arises from the effect of wages/employment on industry price and shipments.

Product demand can be represented as:

(21) $d\ln Q = -fd\ln P + d\ln Z$,

where Q is industry output; P is industry price, f is the price elasticity of product demand, and Z is shifts in product demand. The industry (i) and time (t) subscripts have been omitted. Following Freeman and Katz (1991), assume that industry i's price at time t depends only on production costs. Industry price is determined by wages,

Imports, Exports, and Jobs   97

(22) $d\ln P = g d\ln W$,

where g is labor's share of total cost.
Wage and employment determination (ignoring H for now):

(23) $d\ln W = q d\ln Z$,

where $q = 1/(k + e)$.

(24) $d\ln N = h d\ln Z$,

where $h = e/(k + e)$. Both wages and employment depend on exogenous shifts in product demand.
Substituting Equation 22 into 21 yields

(25) $d\ln Q = -fg d\ln W + d\ln Z$

Using the identity $d\ln S$ (Sales) $= d\ln P + d\ln Q$ and substituting,

(26) $d\ln S = -fg d\ln W + d\ln P + d\ln Z$

Substituting Equation 22 into 26

(27) $d\ln S = (1 - f)g d\ln W + d\ln Z$

Solve for $d\ln Z$,

(28) $d\ln Z = d\ln S - (1 - f)g d\ln W$

Use Equation 23 to substitute for $d\ln W$

(29) $d\ln Z = \{1/[1 + g(1 - f)q]\} d\ln S$

To write an equation between changes in employment and changes in sales (shipments), use Equation 24 for employment determination and substitute Equation 29 for $d\ln Z$:

(30) $d\ln N = \{h/[1 + g(1 - f)q]\} d\ln S = (h/C) d\ln S = B d\ln S$,

where $C = \{1/[1 + g(1-f)q]\}$. With the addition of an error term, Equation 30 can be estimated using OLS, producing an estimate of B. The coefficient of interest, however, is h, not B, where h is the response of industry employment to changes in product demand. With an estimate of B, h can be determined from Equation 14, rearranging terms,

$$h = B(1 - g(1-f)q),$$

where f is the (absolute value of the) price elasticity of product demand, g is labor's share of total cost, and q is the wage elasticity of product demand.

The difference between B and h depends on the term $\{g(1-f)q\}$. B equals h only if: 1) $f = 1$ (unitary price elasticity), $g = 0$ (labor share equals zero), or q equals 0. At plausible values of g and q, if $f < 1$, B will overstate h; if $f > 1$, B will understate h. The bias is small; for example, using an estimate for q of 0.04 (a quick consensus across the estimates in Freeman and Katz [1991]), and g of 0.25 (from the NBER Productivity file), if goods are elastically demanded (f in the range of 1.2 to 2.5), h will differ from B by at most 1.5 percent. If goods are inelastically demanded (f ranges from 0 to 1), h differs from B by less than 1 percent.[8] Even at "large" price elasticities, for example if f equals 5, h will differ from B by about 4 percent.

As I discussed above, there are error terms in Equations 22 and 24 that get carried into Equation 30, because we are using shipments as an estimate of product demand and a price determination and employment determination equation to link product demand to shipments. This leaves $d\ln S$ in Equation 30 correlated with the error terms. As a result, $d\ln S$ should be instrumented to obtain consistent estimates of B.

Changes in trade flows

To isolate the trade-related components of sales, we return to the information on exports, imports, and shipments from the NBER Trade Database. Following Freeman and Katz (1991), define D (= domestic) as gross domestic market sales, where D = sales − exports + imports ($D = S - X + M$).

Define import share as Mshare, or M/D (imports as a share of domestically available product). Then

$(S - X)/D = 1 - \text{Mshare}$

Substituting,

$S = (1 - \text{Mshare})D + X$

(31) $dS = d[(1 - \text{Mshare})D] + dX$,

where d is the difference operator. Time subscripts help clarify the derivation,

$dS_t = (1 - \text{Mshare}_t)D_t - (1 - \text{Mshare}_{t-1})D_{t-1} + dX_t$,

$\quad = (1 - \text{Mshare}_t)dD_t + (1 - \text{Mshare}_t)D_{t-1} - (1 - \text{Mshare}_{t-1})D_{t-1} + dX_t$,

$\quad = (1 - \text{Mshare}_t)dD_t - D_t d\text{Mshare}_t + D_t d\text{Mshare}_t - d\text{Mshare}_t D_{t-1} + dX_t$,

(32) $\quad = (1 - \text{Mshare}_t)dD_t - D_t d\text{Mshare}_t + dD_t d\text{Mshare}_t + dX_t$.

If the interaction term, $dD_t d\text{Mshare}_t$, is ignored,[9]

(33) $dS/S = [(S - X)/S]dD/D - (D/S)d\text{Mshare} + (X/S)dX/X$.

Using ln changes as approximate percentage changes yields:

(34) $d\ln S = [(S - X)/S]d\ln D - (D/S)d\text{Mshare} + (X/S)d\ln X$.

Substituting this last equation in Equation 30 yields:

(35) $d\ln N = Bw_1 d\ln D + Bw_2 d\ln X - Bw_3 d\text{Mshare}$.[10]

The w's are the various weights: $w_1 = [(S - X)/S]$, $w_2 = (X/S)$, and $w_3 = (D/S)$. Given the derivation above, we note that the weights are more accurate for small changes than for large changes.

Note that this model assumes, implicitly, that changes in employment respond similarly to weighted changes in sales, whether those (weighted) changes are due to exports, import share, or domestic demand. The assumption can best be seen as a statistical hypothesis, one derived from the derivation of the empirical specification. It is not an assumption imposed by economic theory. It does seem plausible in the long run, in that we might expect industry employment to respond to a given change in demand, regardless of the source. In the short run, Freeman and Katz (1991) noted that industries may differentially assess the persistence of trade-related changes in demand, given the role of exchange rates. Alternatively, across industries, this assumption may not hold if industries differ in their export or import orientation. In their analysis, based on four-digit SIC industry data from 1958–1984, Freeman and Katz (1991) found roughly comparable effects of the three components of sales on both changes in industry wages and employment.

Changes in import competition

As discussed in Chapter 4, another strand of the literature looks at import competition, highlighting the influence of changes in industry import prices. The model of Equations 17–24 can be altered to separate industry domestic price from industry import price. Equation 21 for product demand becomes:

(36) $d\ln Q_i = -f^1 d\ln P_i + f^2 d\ln P_{im} + d\ln Z_i,$

where P_i is the price of the domestically produced good; P_m is the dollar price of the foreign good; f^1 is the domestic price elasticity of demand (f in Equation 21); f^2 is the foreign price elasticity of demand, and Z is shifts in product demand. This specification allows the domestic and foreign goods to be imperfect substitutes, with differing elasticities.[11]

Adding $d\ln P$ to $d\ln Q$ yields a different definition of $d\ln S$ (Sales):

(37) $d\ln S = (1 - f^1) d\ln P_i + f^2 d\ln P_m + d\ln Z.$

Substituting for $d\ln S$ into Equation 30,

(38) $d\ln N = B d\ln S = B[(1 - f^1) d\ln P_i + f^2 d\ln P_m + d\ln Z].$

In this form, the coefficient of interest is Bf^2, the import price elasticity of industry employment.

The discussion of the labor turnover model in the previous section was complete, and there are no additional details to be noted here.

SUMMARY

In this chapter, I developed a straightforward empirical model for estimating relationships between changes in industry employment and job loss and measures of trade flows and import competition. With estimates of the model's parameters, we can understand how changes in trade are associated with domestic labor market changes, controlling for (some of) the other factors influencing these important outcomes. The framework has a number of practical and policy benefits. Its technical simplicity eases interpretation, as will be seen in Chapters 6 and 7. The addition of job displacement to the literature's traditional focus on net employment changes allows a focus on "real" job loss, the type of event that happens to "real" workers, rather than the "summing-up" of employment gains and losses that lies behind industry net employment change. This addition has clear policy implications, as it will yield an understanding of the association between industry job loss and changes in trade and foreign competition. Chapter 6 is devoted to the employment change specifications, Equations 8 and 9. Chapter 7 reports estimates of the displacement specifications, Equations 15 and 16.

Notes

1. In this case, a random-effects model would be more appropriate.
2. The econometric estimation will also allow for the disturbances to be serially correlated within industries and contemporaneously correlated across industries.
3. The Prais–Winsten approach is used to account for serially correlated errors within industries.
4. Kletzer (1998b, 2000) contains a similar discussion in the context of an empirical model relating changes in foreign competition to job displacement.
5. Accessions are new hires and rehires. The term unreplaced attritions appears in Brechling (1978).
6. The industry fixed effects may also capture some cross-industry differences in quit rates.
7. Brechling (1978) presents a model of turnover with endogenous quits. In that

102   Labor Market Responses to Changes in Trade and Import Competition

model, quits rise and fall with industry employment growth and the state of the overall economy. In depressed industries, workers are much less likely to quit; therefore, "normal" attrition cannot be counted on to reduce employment.

8. Most estimates of price elasticities of demand are at the final goods level, not the industry level. For a number of goods where aggregation to the industry level is straightforward, demand appears to be price inelastic. See Field and Pagoulatos (1997) and Koutsoyiannis (1984). Estimates in Comanor and Wilson (1974) are more price elastic.
9. This is done for simplicity. Checks reveal that the interaction term is empirically very small (near zero) in the data.
10. This equation is the same as Equation 6.
11. This equation is in the spirit of the discussion in Mann (1988).

6
Measuring the Link between Changes in Industry Employment and Changes in Trade Flows

Chapter 4 discussed basic trends in industry employment, trade flows, and foreign competition as well as associations between the trends. A number of other factors, some related to foreign competition and others not (e.g., the overall health of the economy, wages, and technological change), are also likely related to industry employment change. Chapter 5 presented an empirical model for estimating the influences of changes in trade flows and increasing import competition on industry employment. Implementing the econometric model, I here report estimates of employment changes associated with changes in trade flows and increasing foreign competition, controlling for these other factors.

CHANGES IN EMPLOYMENT AND TRADE FLOWS

To fix ideas, we start with the within-industry, or industry fixed effects, estimates (Equation 8 from Chapter 5). With data that are pooled across industries and time, the error term in Equation 8 will include time-related and cross-section disturbances along with possible omitted explanatory variables. Industry fixed effects allow the intercepts to vary over cross-section units, in this case industry.[1] In large part, these are the preferred estimates, as they address directly the question of whether increasing trade and/or import competition, within an industry over time, is associated with declining employment. This approach fully recognizes that industries differ, in both observable and unobservable ways, in the responsiveness of employment to changes in technology, wages, foreign competition, and the overall health of the economy. This approach is also the proper way to frame the question from a policy perspective, in that a revealed link between increased trade flows and declining employment may signal some harm to workers that could be mitigated by assistance programs. Again, the empirical analysis should not be taken as causal in the sense of concluding that employment changes would have been different if trade flows had been different. Without a model of the dependence of trade flows on wages, employment, and production, the estimates must be viewed as broadly descriptive.

Table 6.1 reports the first fixed-effects estimates, on a sample period 1979–1994.[2] The table reports coefficient estimates from regressions using the change in log industry employment as the dependent variable (see Equation 8 in Chapter 5). The various explanatory variables are listed in the first column of the table. In the main body of the table, each number represents the change in log industry employment (approximately the percent change in industry employment) associated with a one-unit change in an explanatory variable. Each column of the table represents a separate and distinct regression specification. Specifications differ either by their explanatory variables or by the time period of the estimation.

From the estimates presented in Table 6.1, one can see a number of clear observations.[3] Rising sales, domestic demand, and exports are all strongly associated with rising employment. Using the column 1 estimate for changes in sales, a 10 percent increase in sales is associated with a 3.9 percent increase in employment, all else the same.[4] Given the size of the domestic market for most U.S. manufacturing industries, it is not surprising that the estimated coefficient on (weighted) changes in domestic demand in columns 2–4 closely approximates the estimated coefficient on changes in sales reported in column 1. The direction of this estimated association is reassuring—that employment moves positively with demand changes. At the same time, the estimated magnitudes reveal that domestic demand alone cannot explain changes in industry employment. With this point estimate, the average annual cross-industry weighted change in domestic demand, +5.35 percent, yields a predicted change in industry employment of +2.0 percent. The mean observed annual change in employment for this period was approximately –0.2 percent.

Foreign demand is equally important, as seen in results across the columns for changes in sales due to exports. From the estimate in column 2, a 10 percent increase in overall sales due to exports is associated with a 7.9 percent increase in employment. The average weighted annual change in sales due to exports was 0.82 percent; with this estimated elasticity, the change in exports would be associated with a 0.65 percent increase in employment, whereas the mean annual change in employment was a decline of 0.9 percent.

Note here that the point estimates for weighted changes in sales due to exports are a bit larger than the point estimates for changes in domestic demand, and the differences are statistically significant at standard levels. Our discussion in Chapter 5 anticipated an overstatement of the export–employment association and an understatement of the domestic demand–employment association. The results are consistent with that discussion. The rise in export demand is met by an increase in shipments to meet the increased foreign demand, allowing domestic demand to remain constant. On the other hand, the overall increase in domestic demand is met, in part, by an increase in imports that holds the import share of domestically available output constant. Thus, in an open economy, not all of the increase in domestic demand is met by domestic shipments (production). Given the size of the domestic market relative to imports, and the much smaller share of exports in sales, we expect the understating of the domestic demand association to be smaller in effect than the overstating of the export association.

These measurement concerns may explain why the estimated B's (coefficient of changes in sales), within each specification, are different, when the statistical maintained assumption from Chapter 5 is that changes in employment respond similarly to changes in sales, whether those (weighted) changes in sales result from domestic demand, exports, or imports. At a basic level, the statistical assumption makes sense, at least in the long run, in that there seems to be no reason to anticipate that industries would respond differently to variation in demand coming from the domestic market as compared to the foreign market.

Turning to import share, we find that employment declines are associated with a rise in import share. Holding domestic demand constant, a 10 percent rise in the import share of domestic sales is associated with a 4 percent decline in employment. The mean weighted annual change in import share was about +1 percent, associated with a 0.4 percent annual decline in employment. Again, the observed mean annual change in employment was –0.9 percent. It was anticipated that the

Table 6.1 Changes in Industry Employment, Sales, Domestic Demand, Exports, and Imports: Within-Industry Estimates, 1979–1994

	(1)	(2)	(3)	(4)
Change in ln(sales)	0.3920*** (0.0353)			
Weighted change domestic demand		0.3745*** (0.0385)#	0.3744*** (0.0385)#	0.3266*** (0.0393)#
Weighted change exports		0.7957*** (0.1324)	0.7977*** (0.1328)	0.7214*** (0.1286)
Weighted change import share		−0.4004*** (0.0811)#		−0.1981** (0.0803)#
Weighted change DC import share			−0.4865*** (0.1092)#	
Weighted change LDC import share			−0.2992*** (0.1038)#	
Change index of industrial production	0.0068*** (0.0012)	0.0031** (0.0013)	0.0031** (0.0013)	0.0031** (0.0013)
Change R&D intensity	0.0912*** (0.0207)	0.0988*** (0.0234)	0.1007*** (0.0235)	
Ln(capital stock/shipments)	−0.0183 (0.0155)	−0.0180 (0.0151)	−0.0174 (0.0150)	−0.0204 (0.0152)
Change ln(alternative wage)	−0.0055 (0.0540)	−0.0173 (0.0559)	−0.0171 (0.0559)	−0.0094 (0.0560)
Change TFP				0.1043 (0.0712)

Constant	−0.0178 (0.0273)	−0.0460 (0.0260)	−0.0449 (0.0258)	−0.0488 (0.0263)
Industry effects	Yes	Yes	Yes	Yes
Year effects	Yes	Yes	Yes	Yes
Observations	1198	1198	1198	1166
Number of industries	75	75	75	73
R^2	0.36	0.38	0.38	0.38

NOTE: Panel-corrected standard errors in parentheses. ** = significant at 5%; *** = significant at 1%; # = significantly different from export coefficient (in absolute value) at 5% level.

import share association would be overstated due to the accompanying decline in shipments. The overstatement may explain how the estimated import share association, at the mean weighted annual change in import share, more than accounts for the observed annual change in employment.

Note also that the responsiveness of employment to a change in import share is smaller than the responsiveness of employment to a change in exports, and the difference in the point estimates is statistically significant at standard levels.

What share of industry employment change is accounted for by changes in trade flows and domestic demand? For a representative industry experiencing sample mean (weighted) annual changes in domestic demand, exports, and import share, these three estimated employment elasticities yield a predicted change in employment of +1.98 percent. The mean annual change in industry employment observed in the data over the 1979–1994 percent was −1.03 percent. Thus, although the separate trade flows and domestic demand are each significantly associated with employment changes as predicted, they clearly cannot, alone, explain the average industry employment change. Trade has an effect, but the effect is small and it cannot explain the overall pattern of employment change in manufacturing.

These findings on the components of demand basically hold across the four specifications reported in Table 6.1. The specifications themselves differ in a number of ways. The first difference is the proxy for technological change. Changes in research and development (R&D) intensity are the main measure of technological change (R&D intensity is measured as the ratio of R&D spending to the value of shipments). Increases in the intensity of R&D are positively associated with employment change. This is consistent with the Rybczynski theorem, where factors, including employment, flow into sectors experiencing technological change. A similar positive relationship is found for changes in TFP in column 4, although the estimated coefficient is not statistically significant.

Imports from developing countries have received considerable recent attention. Industry import data is available by country of origin from the NBER Trade Database, allowing the disaggregation of import share into two parts: developing country (LDC) import share and developed country (DC) import share. Following Borjas, Freeman, and

Katz (1997), I classify western European countries (except Greece and Portugal), Australia, New Zealand, Japan, and Canada as developed countries and include all imports into the United States from all other countries as LDC imports. Including these two import share measures separately allows for differences in their correlations with employment change. Averaged across industries, about 40 percent of import share originated in developing countries over the 1979–1994 period. Consistent with the rise in attention to imports from developing countries, the average percentage increase in LDC import share was 5.4 percent, approximately double the percentage increase in DC import share.

Column 3 of Table 6.1 reports results for the separate import share measures. Within industries, rising import share is associated with employment decline regardless of country of origin. The larger of the point estimates indicates that, for changes in DC import share, a 10 percent increase in DC import share is associated with a 4.8 percent decline in industry employment. The difference in the estimated magnitudes for DC and LDC import share may be informative about the overstatement of the import share association. If DC imports are closer substitutes than LDC imports to domestically produced output, then the shipments response to a change in DC import share will be larger than the shipments response to LDC imports. This differential shipments response will produce a larger estimated DC import share association than a LDC import share association. The average increase in DC import share was 0.2 percent, and the average increase in LDC import share was 0.3 percent.

The remaining variables in the specifications indicate that more capital intensive industries had smaller employment growth, and as predicted, employment growth is negatively correlated with wage growth. Overall, the fit of the model to the data is modest; around one-third of the variation in industry employment growth is explained by the included explanatory variables. It is clear that the sales and trade variables alone have limited explanatory power.[5]

The relationship between import share and employment change is stronger for the 1979–1985 time period than for 1985–1994 (see columns 1–3 of Table 6.2 for 1979–1985 and columns 4–6 for 1985–1994 and columns 2–4 of Table 6.1 for 1979–1994), and it remains smaller than the responsiveness of employment to changes in exports. Thus, the employment-enhancing role of increasing exports exceeds

Table 6.2 Changes in Industry Employment, Sales, Domestic Demand, Exports, and Imports: Within-Industry Estimates, 1979–1985 and 1985–1994

	1979–1985			1985–1994		
	(1)	(2)	(3)	(4)	(5)	(6)
Change in ln(sales)	0.4458*** (0.0417)			0.1812*** (0.0557)		
Weighted change domestic demand		0.4629*** (0.0458)	0.4654*** (0.0469)		0.1604*** (0.0611)#	0.1605*** (0.0611)#
Weighted change exports		0.7259*** (0.2058)	0.7247*** (0.2064)		0.7186*** (0.1851)	0.7225*** (0.1855)
Weighted change import share		−0.5438*** (0.1984)			−0.2026** (0.0826)#	
Weighted change DC import share			−0.7224*** (0.2688)			−0.2678** (0.1137)#
Weighted change LDC import share			−0.2433 (0.2017)			−0.1348 (0.0927)
Change index of industrial production	0.0041*** (0.0015)	−0.0002 (0.0015)	−0.0002 (0.0015)	0.0051*** (0.0004)	0.0051*** (0.0005)	0.0052*** (0.0005)
Change R&D intensity	0.0251 (0.0830)	0.0538 (0.0792)	0.0633 (0.0788)	0.0430** (0.0213)	0.0523** (0.0235)	0.0544** (0.0239)
Ln(capital stock/shipments)	−0.0579*** (0.0181)	−0.0480*** (0.0185)	−0.0462** (0.0190)	−0.0755*** (0.0167)	−0.0738*** (0.0169)	−0.0728*** (0.0172)
Change ln(alternate wage)	0.0584 (0.0709)	0.0652 (0.0736)	0.0634 (0.0735)	−0.0288 (0.0376)	−0.0503 (0.0356)	−0.0498 (0.0355)

Constant	−0.0768**	−0.0892***	−0.0861***	−0.1238***	−0.1261***	−0.1245***
	(0.0326)	(0.0325)	(0.0331)	(0.0287)	(0.0289)	(0.0294)
Observations	525	525	525	748	748	748
Number of industries	75	75	75	75	75	75
R^2	0.59	0.61	0.61	0.23	0.26	0.26

NOTE: Panel-corrected standard errors in parentheses. ** = significant at 5%; *** = significant at 1%; # = significantly different from export coefficient (in absolute value) at 5% level.

the employment-reducing role of increasing import share. The effect on employment of changes in domestic demand is statistically equivalent to the effect on employment of changes in exports. Over this early part of the period, increases in DC import share are associated with declining employment, at a magnitude similar to the effect of declining exports. A 10 percent increase in DC imports, or a 10 percent decrease in sales due to exports, is associated with a 7 percent decline in employment. The effect of changes in LDC import share is imprecisely estimated.

Relative to changes in domestic demand and import share, employment change due to sales of exports emerges with strength in the 1985–1994 period. Again the estimated export elasticity is different, in absolute value, from both the domestic demand and import share elasticities. It is over this later period that a weaker import share–employment change relationship emerges. A rise in DC import share is associated with a decline in employment, and the LDC import share effect is estimated with more precision, but it is still outside the standard bounds of statistical significance.

It is interesting to note that, although the difference is not statistically significant, the estimated coefficient on DC import share is greater than the estimated coefficient on LDC import share when the analysis controls for time-invariant industry effects. The discussion above noted how the measurement issues may differ between the two sources of imports. That argument can be expanded to consider the nature of import competition induced by developing and developed countries. Within a three-digit industry, DC imports may well be goods that compete more closely with domestic supply (and domestic employment), while LDC imports are less directly competitive with domestic supply because they are different goods. For example, within the footwear industry, an increase in the import share of shoes produced in China (an increase in LDC imports), holding constant the share of domestic supply originating in Italy (DC import), may represent a broadening of the variety of goods domestically available. In other words, an increase in the imports of plastic shoes (perhaps water sandals) from China does not displace domestic production, because plastic shoes are not produced in the United States. An increase in imports of high-end Italian dress shoes, holding constant the domestic share of supply originating in China, is associated with employment decline because high-end Italian dress shoes compete more directly with American shoes.

LONG-PERIOD CHANGES IN INDUSTRY EMPLOYMENT

The changes in Tables 6.1 and 6.2 are annual, that is, year-on-year. Although the model sketched out in Chapter 5 provides no explicit room for timing, it is useful to consider the difference between changes over the long period (from 1979–1994) and changes over the short run (annual). Import competition that persists over a few years, or is steadily increasing, seems more likely to affect employment change than a short-run change. To consider a long-period change, however, we must estimate across industries, not within, because there is only one long-period change observation per industry. Table 6.3 reports a number of cross-section estimates, with the long-period change reported in column 1 and annual (but cross-section) changes in columns 2–4. The estimation is Weighted Least Squares (WLS), with 1979–1994 changes in sales, the composition of demand, and industry employment.[6]

A first observation is that, over the long period, the responsiveness of employment to changes in the three components of sales is indeed the same, as assumed in the empirical model. It is over a long period that we can reasonably expect this assumption to be valid, and the data are consistent with the assumption. With these equal estimated elasticities, a 10 percent increase in sales due to domestic demand or exports is associated with approximately an 8 percent increase in employment, and a 10 percent increase in imports is associated with a 8 percent decline in employment. For the "average" manufacturing industry, experiencing the sample mean long-period changes in domestic demand, exports, and imports, these estimates predict an increase in employment of 11.5 percent. The mean long-period change in employment observed in the data is -15 percent. It is clear that the pattern of employment change across industries cannot be explained by changes in trade flows (or the demand composition analysis more generally).

Although the industry fixed-effects estimates are preferred from a statistical perspective and offer a sharper focus on how changes in trade

Table 6.3 Changes in Industry Employment, Sales, Domestic Demand, Exports and Import Share, Cross-Section Estimates, Long-Period and Annual, 1979–1994

	Long-period (1)	Annual (2)	Annual (3)	Annual (4)
Change in ln(sales)		0.4178*** (0.0363)		
Weighted change domestic demand	0.8869*** (0.1202)		0.4058*** (0.0363)#	0.4224*** (0.0317)#
Weighted change exports	0.8092 (0.4859)		0.6983*** (0.1292)	0.7348*** (0.1332)
Weighted change import share	−0.8376*** (0.1704)		−0.5233*** (0.0699)	−0.5016*** (0.0644)
Change index of industrial production		0.0024 (0.0014)	0.0035** (0.0015)	0.0033** (0.0015)
Change R&D intensity		0.0702*** (0.0175)	0.0963*** (0.0179)	0.0994*** (0.0178)
Ln(capital stock/shipments)		−0.0052 (0.0033)	−0.0057 (0.0034)	−0.0068 (0.0036)
Change ln(alternate wage)		−0.0038 (0.0513)	−0.0169 (0.0583)	−0.0183 (0.0596)
Change ln(imported intermediate inputs)				−0.8907 (0.5781)
Constant	−0.2701*** (0.0426)	−0.0365*** (0.0078)	−0.0517*** (0.0081)	−0.0496*** (0.0083)

| Observations | 75 | 1198 | 1198 | 1194 |
| R^2 | 0.59 | 0.33 | 0.34 | 0.36 |

NOTE: Robust standard errors in parentheses. ** = significant at 5%; *** = significant at 1%; # = significantly different from export coefficient (in absolute value) at 5% level.

flows may be associated with changes in industry employment, a multivariate analysis across industries reveals a few different points as well as the robustness of the findings. For the annual changes, Table 6.3 reports estimates from WLS regressions using pooled cross-section timeseries annual data on changes in sales, the composition of demand, and industry employment. Year effects are included. Note here that, with the inclusion of year effects, the important variation is across industries in these cross-section regressions.

Rising sales, domestic demand, and exports are all strongly associated with rising employment across industries as well as within. Using the column 2 estimate for changes in sales, a 10 percent increase in sales is associated with a 4.2 percent increase in employment, all else the same. Again, given the size of the domestic market for most U.S. manufacturing industries, it is not surprising that the estimated coefficient on (weighted) changes in domestic demand in columns 3–4 closely approximates the estimated coefficient on changes in sales reported in column 2. With this point estimate, the average annual (weighted) change in domestic demand, +4.4 percent, yields a predicted change in industry employment of +1.8 percent. The mean observed annual change in employment for this period was approximately −1 percent.

Foreign demand is equally important, as seen in results across the columns for exports. From the estimate in column 2, a 10 percent increase in sales due to exports is associated with a 6.9 percent increase in employment. The mean weighted annual change in exports was 0.79 percent; with this estimated elasticity, the change in exports would produce a 0.53 percent increase in employment, slightly less than half the observed mean annual change in employment. The point estimates for (weighted) changes in exports are larger than the point estimates for changes in domestic demand, and the differences are statistically significant at standard levels.

As with the fixed-effects estimates, the estimated responsiveness of employment to changes in import share is somewhat smaller than the export response. A 1-percentage-point increase in import share is associated with an approximately 0.5 percent decline in employment. The difference between the magnitude of the import share coefficient and the estimated coefficient on exports is statistically significant. The mean weighted annual change in import share was about +1 percent, yielding a 0.5 percent annual decline in employment. Again, the observed mean annual change in employment was −1 percent.

What share of industry employment change is accounted for by changes in trade flows and domestic demand? For a representative industry experiencing sample mean (weighted) annual changes in domestic demand, exports, and import share, these three estimated employment elasticities yield a predicted change in employment of +1.97 percent. The mean annual change in industry employment observed in the data over the 1979–1994 percent was −1.03 percent. Thus, although trade flows and domestic demand are (significantly) associated with employment changes as predicted, they cannot, alone, explain the cross-industry variation in employment change. Trade has an effect, but the effect is small and it cannot explain the overall pattern of employment change in manufacturing.

Column 4 considers the question of outsourcing in an abbreviated fashion. Does the use of imported intermediate goods reduce the demand for labor and employment? The measure of outsourcing is the annualized difference in imputed imports of intermediate goods between 1979 and 1990.[7] Controlling for overall import share, industries with greater imports of intermediate goods had smaller employment growth, although the effect is measured imprecisely.

As in the industry fixed-effects estimates, more capital intensive industries had smaller employment growth, and employment growth is negatively correlated with wage growth as predicted. Technological change is positively related to employment change across industries. Overall, the fit of the model to the data is modest; about one-third of the variation in industry employment growth is explained by the included explanatory variables. It is clear that the sales and trade variables alone have limited explanatory power.

INCREASING IMPORT COMPETITION—MEASURED AS CHANGES IN IMPORT PRICE

As noted in previous chapters, changes in import prices are seen by a number of scholars to be "cleaner" measures of changes in foreign competition than are changes in trade flows. In principle, changes in import prices can be the mechanism through which changes in the trading environment affect the domestic labor market. Certainly for a small country, changes in import prices may be considered to be exogenous to changes in production and employment. For a large country like the United States, however, changes in import prices may well be related to factors that influence changes in production (and employment and demand). The analysis here will proceed first with observed import price changes and then, to illustrate some of the questions of endogeneity, turn to instrumental variables estimation.

The first set of estimates for prices are reported in Table 6.4. The time period is somewhat shorter for the price estimates because the import price series is available for a large set of industries only from 1982–1983. There are some industries with data from 1980, in the interests of using the largest possible sample, columns 1 and 2 of Table 6.4 report estimates for 1980–1992, while columns 3 and 4 use 1983–1992 estimates. The samples also vary between balanced (where every industry is represented for the same number of time periods) and unbalanced. Similar to Grossman (1987) and Mann (1988), industry relative domestic price enters separately from industry relative import price. Both price terms enter the specification contemporaneously and with a one-year lag.

Across the columns, the estimated relative import price elasticity for changes in total industry employment is in the range of 0.14 to 0.34. With this range, a 10 percent decrease in import price is associated with a 1.4 to 3.4 percent decline in employment. The mean annual change in import price was very small, –0.07 percent, with a large variation. The employment change associated with this mean annual change in import price using the middle of the estimated elasticity range, would be –0.017 percent, when the observed mean annual change in employment was –1 percent. A one standard deviation change in import price, 6.6 percent, would be associated with a 1.6 percent decline in employment.

With the dollar peaking in 1985, however, the full period analysis masks very different import price behavior. Import prices fell around 14 percent over 1980–1985. The estimates reported in column 3 indicate a 14 percent decline in import price would be associated with a predicted 3.4 percent decline in employment. Employment fell 8.5 percent over the period. In one industry, import prices fell by 45.4 percent, which would lead to a 11.1 percent reduction in employment.

As expected, increases in industry relative domestic price are negatively related to employment. Employment change is pro-cyclical, as captured as the positive coefficient on the index of industrial production. Changes in R&D intensity are negatively related to employment change. Rising capital intensity of production is associated with falling employment.

The complex question of endogenous import prices is examined in Table 6.5. To take a more straightforward approach to the question, I altered the specification of price slightly. Rather than separately including domestic price and import price, the "price" variable is relative import price, that is, import price relative to domestic price (calculated as import price divided by industry producer price index). The first three columns of Table 6.5 report the estimated relative import price elasticities for the three samples used in Table 6.4, and the estimates are very similar.

The data requirements for the instrumental variables (IV) estimation are considerable, and they reduce the sample size appreciably.[8] For the subset of industries with available data, the fixed effects estimate of the import price elasticity is 0.233 (see column 5). The IV estimate reported in column 6 is lower, at 0.053, and it is not statistically significant. Revenga finds the IV estimate to be larger in magnitude than the (in her case) OLS estimate. The discussion in Chapter 5 noted that the sign of the bias is ambiguous in theory. Revenga's analysis used a different sample of industries over a different time period, and it should not be expected that the estimated bias found here would be the same as she found.

Bringing together the range of time periods and estimation techniques, we get a range of estimates for the elasticity of industry employment to changes in import price: 0.05 (IV, fixed effect) to 0.35 (fixed effects, without instruments; Revenga). From the IV estimate reported here, one can conclude that, with small average changes in import price and small elasticities, falling import prices alone can account for only a small decline in employment. This IV estimate can reasonably be considered as a lower bound. The noninstrumented estimates and Revenga's IV estimates provide more room for the effect of changing import prices on domestic employment.

Before we turn to an assessment of the empirical model, we should note a limitation. As I stated previously, the analysis is partial equilibrium, where changes in an industry's trade environment affect only that

Table 6.4 Changes in Industry Employment, Domestic Prices, and Import Prices: Within-Industry Estimates

	(1) 1980–92	(2) 1980–92 balanced	(3) 1983–92 balanced	(4) 1983–92 col. 2 sample
Change ln(domestic price)	−0.2720 (0.1095)	−0.3420 (0.1271)	−0.4430 (0.1978)	−0.3541 (0.1830)
Change ln(import price)	0.1478 (0.0413)	0.2283 (0.0719)	0.2450 (0.0855)	0.3468 (0.9847)
Change index of industrial production	0.0063*** (0.0010)	0.0063** (0.0028)	0.0067*** (0.0009)	0.0056*** (0.0014)
Change R&D intensity	−0.0129 (0.0107)	−0.7986*** (0.2809)	−0.0082 (0.0170)	−0.5740 (0.3321)
Ln(capital stock/shipments)	−0.0927*** (0.0313)	−0.1040*** (0.0386)	−0.0951** (0.0441)	−0.0595 (0.0557)
Change ln(alternative wage)	−0.0305 (0.0407)	−0.0786 (0.1261)	−0.0438 (0.0846)	−0.0941 (0.1265)
Constant	−0.1503*** (0.0518)	−0.1789*** (0.0628)	−0.1516** (0.0744)	−0.0978 (0.0917)
Industry effects	Yes	Yes	Yes	Yes
Year effects	Yes	Yes	Yes	Yes

Observations	717	286	470	220
Number of industries	68	22	47	22
R^2	0.33	0.47	0.28	0.28

NOTE: Panel-corrected standard errors in parentheses. Specifications include one lag in the domestic price and import price. ** = significant at 5% level; *** = significant at 1% level.

Table 6.5 Changes in Industry Employment and Relative Import Prices: Within-Industry Estimates

	(1) 1980–92	(2) 1980–92 balanced	(3) 1983–92 balanced	(4) 1983–92 col. 2 sample	(5) 1983–92, IV sample	(6) 1983–92 IV estimates
Change ln relative import price	0.1674 (0.0469)	0.2553 (0.0651)	0.2766 (0.0762)	0.3590 (0.0858)	0.2334** (0.0979)	0.0530 (0.0959)
Change index of industrial production	0.0064*** (0.0009)	0.0061** (0.0029)	0.0067*** (0.0009)	0.0054*** (0.0014)	0.0081*** (0.0006)	0.0065*** (0.0006)
Change R&D intensity	−0.0133 (0.0135)	−0.7861*** (0.2844)	−0.0094 (0.0195)	−0.5398 (0.3178)	−0.0027 (0.0209)	−0.0036 (0.0102)
Ln(capital stock/shipments)	−0.0931*** (0.0355)	−0.1054*** (0.0403)	−0.0952 (0.0497)	−0.0593 (0.0566)	−0.0913 (0.0525)	−0.0934*** (0.0041)
Change ln(alternative wage)	−0.0340 (0.0385)	−0.0758 (0.1307)	−0.0428 (0.0807)	−0.0834 (0.1279)	−0.0274 (0.0543)	0.0651** (0.0224)
Constant	−0.1489** (0.0583)	−0.1777*** (0.0655)	−0.1505 (0.0837)	−0.0970 (0.0930)	−0.1444 (0.0878)	−0.1557 (0.0041)
Industry effects	Yes	Yes	Yes	Yes	Yes	Yes
Year effects	Yes	Yes	Yes	Yes	Yes	Yes
Observations	710	286	470	220	290	290
Number of industries	68	22	47	22	29	29
R^2	0.33	0.46	0.28	0.28	0.39	0.35

NOTE: Panel-corrected standard errors in parentheses. Specifications include one lag in the relative import price. IV denotes instrumental variables. ** = significant at 5% level; *** = significant at 1% level.

industry. This approach does not allow for spillover effects between industries. For example, the model does not have a mechanism for allowing an increase in the import share of cars to affect employment in industries manufacturing equipment for automobile assembly lines. Without these interaction effects, the economy-wide employment gains and losses from industry-specific increases in exports or import shares will likely be underestimated. The degree to which employment changes are underestimated is likely to differ across industries because the linkages to upstream and downstream industries differ. These spillovers are properly the subject of another analysis. They are important, however, when considering trade or employment policies that protect individual industries.

ASSESSING WHAT THE MODEL SAYS ABOUT THE "COSTS" OF TRADE FOR AMERICAN EMPLOYMENT

A number of questions remain. Industry employment fell, despite growth in exports and domestic demand. The import share elasticity and rise in import share cannot account for much of the substantial decline in employment. An even weaker assessment applies to the import price estimations. For the trade flows estimations, the statistical fit of the models can be described as, "is the glass half empty or half full?" That is, the estimates account for about 40 percent of the industry variation in employment, which is modestly respectable, but that leaves about 60 percent of the variation in employment change unexplained. It is natural to suspect technological change as a suspect whose presence is not well captured by the empirical proxies. Advancing labor-saving technological change could account for employment declines in the face of growing demand.

In the context of these estimates, how can we assess the extent to which "trade" has been responsible for changes in employment? Following the interesting approach in Grossman (1987), we can use the parameter estimates reported in Table 6.1 with a counterfactual path of exports and imports. The counterfactual path assumes that trade flows remain unchanged from their 1979 levels. The counterfactual simulations that follow take the trade flows model at face value; all the conditions and qualifications required to accept the model have been stated in the discussions above.[9] The model reported in column 2 of Table 6.1 was simulated using historical data for all of the independent variables, except for, alternately, changes in exports and imports. Thus, the simulations generated paths for changes in employment over the period 1979–1994 that correspond to the counterfactual assumption of either no import change, no export change, or no change in either imports or exports.

The simulated changes in employment are reported in Table 6.6 for the average manufacturing industry and for a selected set of "visible" industries. Here, "visible" is defined by employment size or a tradition of import competition or export history. For the average manufacturing industry, employment fell by 13.4 percent over the 1980–1994 period. Averaged across industries, the full historical model predicted an employment decline of 17.9 percent. If import share had been frozen at its 1979 level, average industry employment would have declined by 8.8 percent. For an average industry, this 4.6 percent difference, due to the increase in imports, represents 11,693 jobs. On the other hand, if exports had been frozen at their 1979 level, employment would have fallen by 19 percent, 5.6 percent more than observed. Thus, the growth in exports "saved" an average of 14,235 jobs in manufacturing. Together, if both imports and exports had been frozen at 1979 levels, employment would have declined by 16.4 percent, or 3 percent more than observed (7,626 jobs).

The domestic employment outcomes of increasing foreign competition have not been uniform across industries. In a handful of industries, there would have been less employment in 1994 than was actually observed, had trade been neutral from 1979 to 1994. In most industries, however, there would have been more employment with neutral imports and less employment with neutral exports. In footwear, for example, holding imports at their 1979 levels would have "saved" 27,695 jobs because employment would have fallen by 18.6 percent less than observed. While employment losses were very large in that industry, 34,232 additional jobs would have been lost with constant 1979 exports. The counterfactual changes in apparel are also notable. Observed employment loss would have been an employment gain if imports had been held at the 1979 level. Where observed employment fell by 39.7 percent, it would have risen by 25.3 percent with constant imports, a difference of 711,647 jobs. With constant imports and exports, employment would have increased by 18.5 percent, a difference of 636,708 jobs. For electrical machinery, the largest industry in 1979 by employment, neutral trade would have increased employment by 39.2 percent, rather than its observed decrease of 10.2 percent, a difference of 619,712 jobs.

In many industries, holding exports at their 1979 levels would have resulted in larger employment losses, sizably so in high-wage industries. Employment would have fallen by an additional 63,839 in blast furnaces, by an additional 195,288 in aircraft and parts, by an additional 206,696 in motor vehicles, and by an additional 26,044 in iron and steel foundries.

Holding imports at 1979 levels would have resulted in smaller employment losses in a number of industries: (small) leather products, 9,936 jobs would have been "saved"; tires and inner tubes, 26,030 jobs; and construction and material moving machines, 113,270 jobs. In some small employment industries, employment would have increased instead of decreased: watches and clocks, 28,556 jobs (employment would have increased by 33.4 percent, instead of falling by 69.7 percent); toys and sporting goods, 30,965 jobs (growth of 20.8 percent instead of a decline of 4.7 percent); and scientific and controlling instruments, 22,210 (growth of 20.6 percent instead of the smaller +3.3 percent).

SUMMARY

The empirical analysis reported in this chapter produced five main findings.
- Employment declines with a rise in imports and it grows with a rise in exports.
- Changes in trade (including domestic demand and the demand composition analysis) cannot account for the declining trend in overall manufacturing employment. With the strong growth in exports and domestic demand over the period, the model predicts less employment decline than observed. Other factors,

Table 6.6 The Effect of Changes in Imports and Exports on Changes in Employment

	Mean trade overlap, 1980–94	Change in employment 1979–94	Predicted change in employment	Simulated change, no import change	Simulated change, no export change	Simulated change, no export, no import change
Footwear	0.082	−0.950	−0.987	−0.764	−1.180	0.846
Leather products	0.140	−0.779	−0.730	−0.584	−0.921	0.664
Watches, clocks	0.156	−1.193	−1.157	0.334	−0.305	0.276
Apparel	0.174	−0.397	−0.383	0.253	0.104	0.185
Blast furnaces	0.321	−0.869	−0.845	−0.937	−0.981	0.963
Toys & sporting goods	0.339	−0.047	−0.074	0.208	−0.058	0.048
Aircraft & parts	0.393	−0.207	−0.141	−0.239	−0.537	0.524
Furniture & fixtures	0.412	0.013	0.018	−0.074	−0.136	0.117
Tires & inner tubes	0.494	−0.479	−0.461	−0.275	−0.403	0.380
Motor vehicles	0.540	−0.085	−0.068	−0.153	−0.294	0.268
Construction & material moving machines	0.584	−0.593	−0.579	−0.297	−0.409	0.386
Newspaper	0.595	0.065	0.067	−0.079	−0.080	0.080
Iron & Steel foundries	0.611	−0.654	−0.632	−0.737	−0.763	0.757
Fabricated structural metals	0.631	−0.233	−0.223	−0.130	−0.147	0.145
Sawmills, planing mills	0.638	−0.019	−0.009	−0.027	−0.071	0.069
Scientific & controlling	0.679	0.033	−0.241	0.206	−0.041	0.018
Printing, publishing	0.721	0.294	0.299	0.152	0.124	0.125
Yarn, thread	0.722	−0.450	−0.456	−0.263	−0.303	0.290

Industrial & misc. chem.	0.743	-0.149	-0.185	-0.256	-0.373	0.363
Office & acct. machines	0.762	-0.085	0.005	-0.020	-0.233	0.147
Other primary metal	0.782	-0.322	-0.390	-0.166	-0.293	0.291
Primary aluminum industries	0.783	-0.405	-0.358	-0.301	-0.407	0.384
Electronic computing eqp.	0.803	0.236	0.300	0.265	-0.186	0.110
Metalworking machinery	0.816	-0.203	-0.189	-0.170	-0.300	-0.273
Cycles & misc. transport	0.832	-0.071	-0.202	-0.324	-0.596	0.607
Metal forgings	0.833	-0.241	-0.238	-0.321	-0.339	0.335
Meat products	0.857	0.232	0.203	0.090	0.045	0.042
Electrical machinery	0.863	-0.102	-0.073	-0.143	-0.433	0.392
Leather tanning & finish	0.887	-0.296	-0.425	-0.510	-0.709	0.683
Means for all manufacturing industries in the sample:		-0.134	-0.179	-0.088	-0.192	-0.164

most importantly, technological change, must account for some part of the decline where demand composition changes cannot.
- Focusing on the average manufacturing industry misses striking differences across industries. For some industries, an important share of employment change can be explained by changes in the composition of demand. This point is seen most clearly in the simulations for a handful of traditionally import-competing industries, where freezing imports at their 1979 levels would have "saved" many jobs. The implied burden of worker adjustment to these changes is sizeable.
- Domestic employment appears less sensitive to changes in imports than to changes in exports or domestic demand. The word "appears" is critical here because this result appears more strongly in some specifications than in others, and it is colored a bit by the measurement issues noted above.

Allowing that the export association may be overstated, the greater responsiveness of employment to changes in exports over changes in import share is an interesting, if subtle, finding. In this data set, exports actually do represent goods produced by U.S. workers. Thus, a fall in exports is a reduction in demand that can be expected to result in a fall in employment. Imports, on the other hand, are not as closely tied to jobs for U.S. workers. Imports are goods made by foreign workers, and they may not be goods that exactly duplicate goods made by U.S. workers. For imports to displace goods made in the United States, there must be some substitutability between foreign and domestic goods. Certainly within the level of aggregation of this data set (three-digit CIC), it seems possible that imports could represent different goods (in fact different four-digit industries) than the goods produced domestically, with little substitution. For example, imports of expensive watches may not result in lower employment for U.S. watch workers if those watches are not substitutable for the more moderately priced watches made in the United States. Consider import share in this case: as U.S. incomes rise, demand for expensive watches may rise, and with expensive watches made almost exclusively outside the United States, the import share of watches will rise while demand for U.S. watches remains virtually unchanged. In this case, buyers (or owners) of expensive watches usually own more than one watch. The decision to buy an expensive (imported) watch will not mean a substitution away from a lower price watch, rather an addition to the consumption bundle. So, while we can be certain that exports are produced by U.S. workers, we cannot be certain that an industry import directly substitutes for a domestic good.

The difference between the export and import association emerges in the annual change regression but not in the long-period regression. One interpretation is that production responds with a greater lag to changes in imports than exports. This estimated difference in timing may be a result of not having inventories directly in the model. Let export growth represent a direct increase in demand, then contemporaneous changes in exports will be associated with contemporaneous changes in production and employment. Perhaps an increase in imports is associated with a contemporaneous rise in inventories, with domestic production adjusting over time if the rise in import share persists.

Manufacturing sector employment has been in decline since 1979. Up to 1994, the simulations suggest that employment decline would have been even greater, 16.4 percent instead of 13.4 percent, if both imports and exports had been frozen at 1979 levels. If exports do represent jobs more closely than imports represent the absence of a job, then the relationship between rising exports and rising employment could well be stronger than the relationship between rising imports and falling employment. Venturing into the dangerous terrain of speculating how many jobs are associated with trade, this result suggests that rising exports from manufacturing were associated with more job gains than the job losses that can be associated with rising import share.

The conclusion is clear, if a bit nuanced. Imports are associated with employment declines, and manufacturing employment is advanced with increases in exports. Given the growth in exports, there is a strong message in the empirical analysis: with growing exports over time, employment increases associated with rising exports will dominate employment declines associated with export drops. Therefore, while policymakers need be mindful of short-term volatility in export markets due to foreign country recessions and financial crises, efforts to enhance the long-run growth in exports will be beneficial to employment.

Notes

1. This specification also includes time fixed effects to capture omitted-variable bias arising from excluded time-varying variables. The estimation uses balanced panel samples (where every industry is represented for the same number of time periods).
2. A small number of observations were excluded, where the log change in industry employment exceeded 0.75 in absolute value. These observations represent 1.9 percent of otherwise-eligible industry-year observations for the 1979–1994 period. Upon inspection, these data points appear to have measurement problems when checked against an alternative employment source.
3. Standard errors are corrected for arbitrary within-panel heteroscedasticity and first-order within-panel autocorrelation, where the coefficient of first-order process is common to all panels. A Hausman test shows the fixed industry effects to be an appropriate assumption, that the industry-specific effects in the sample are fixed and estimable.
4. From Chapter 5 we know that the estimated coefficient on changes in sales (or weighted changes in domestic demand, exports, or import share), B, is not directly an estimate of the total employment change to changes in product demand. Using the point estimate of the coefficient on change in sales as an estimate of B yields an estimated elasticity of total employment change to changes in product demand, h of 0.384 to 0.416, depending on whether the own-price elasticity of demand is elastic or inelastic. A 10 percent increase in sales is associated with an approximately 4 percent increase in employment.
5. The estimated year effects are of some interest. Employment growth was stronger in 1979–1980 (relative to 1982, the excluded year), dropped in 1983, grew in each of the years 1984–1987, grew more strongly from 1988–1990, slowed in 1991, fell in 1992, and grew a bit in 1993–1994.
6. Standard errors are corrected for arbitrary heteroscedasticity and the clustering of observations by industry.
7. The data are described in Feenstra and Hanson (1997). I am grateful to Gordon Hanson for providing the imported intermediate goods data.
8. The fit of the first-stage regression is quite good ($R^2 = 0.447$), and the signs of the estimated coefficients are as predicted and statistically significant. As the industry exchange rate increases (more national currency units per U.S. dollar), the import price index increases, and as foreign production costs increase, so do import prices. The first-stage estimates are reported in Appendix B.
9. For example, if imports are kept unchanged, with domestic demand and exports evolving as they did, we assume that shipments adjusted accordingly.

7
Job Displacement and Foreign Competition

Employment expands in industries with growing exports, and it declines with a rise in import share. These results are consistent with a reallocation of labor away from industries losing comparative advantage and toward industries gaining comparative advantage. Discussions of comparative advantage aside, one aspect of the policy debate can be stated simply. Are increasing imports associated with involuntary job loss? Can rising exports forestall job loss? Chapter 4 discussed the descriptive evidence linking job loss to changes in industry foreign competition. A number of other factors, some related to foreign competition and others not, are also likely related to industry job loss, as discussed in the empirical model of Chapter 5. In this chapter, I report estimates of job loss associated with increasing foreign competition, controlling for those other factors.

It is important to turn the focus to displacement. Public perceptions of the cost of free trade rest heavily on the perception that trade costs some people their jobs. Turning the focus to permanent job loss does, however, make the empirical analysis a bit more complicated because it is more difficult to find systematic patterns in the data on job loss than it is with the data on industry employment. The difficulty is both theoretical and empirical. From theory, changes in product demand (domestic or foreign) can be fairly directly tied to changes in labor demand and employment. Less clear is the notion that changes in product demand should influence how firms change their employment levels. When the desired level of employment changes for a firm following some change in product demand (or technology), displacements (permanent layoffs) are just one mechanism firms can use to change employment. Other ways include "natural" attrition (quits, retirements, or deaths) or changing hiring and rehiring, as noted in Chapter 5. Chapter 6 concluded that firms do change the level of employment in response to changes in the composition of demand, and this chapter looks at just one of the ways firms make those changes. This chapter analyzes the data to see how changes in the composition of product demand are associated with one of the ways firms adjust employment.

I considered this question, in a similar analysis, in Kletzer (2000). Before turning to the econometric estimates, it is useful to repeat a few observations about the evidence on industry risk of job loss and changes in import share from that analysis. There are a handful of industries (footwear, leather products, apparel, and steel) where positive (negative) changes in import share are associated with a high (low) displacement rates so that casual observation suggests a relationship between increasing import share and a high risk of job loss (or a simple regression line drawn through the data has positive slope).[1] At the same time, across industries and time, there is ample evidence of considerable job loss in the absence of changes in foreign competition. We saw this variation across industries in Table 4.6 of Chapter 4, where I noted that there is a set of industries facing sustained import competition, those with both high levels of import share and positive changes in import share, where the rate of job loss is high. At the same time, the bulk of the industry observations reveal a considerable amount of variation in job displacement across industries. Thus, at the outset, it appears that trade itself can explain only a small share of the variation in job displacement.

CHANGES IN THE COMPOSITION OF DEMAND AND THE RISK OF JOB LOSS

Within industries

In a manner parallel to the discussion in the previous chapter, within-industry estimates are first reported in Table 7.1. Given the likely heterogeneity across industries in the use of layoffs, hiring, discharges, and quits to change employment levels, it is desirable to estimate the relationships in an industry fixed-effects framework. In this framework, the estimation focuses on changes over time in job loss and trade within an industry. That is, when a given industry faces increasing foreign competition, what happens to job loss?

Table 7.1 Changes in Industry Employment, Sales, Domestic Demand, Exports, and Imports: Within-Industry Estimates (1979–1994)

	(1)	(2)	(3)
Change in ln(sales)	–0.1041***		
	(0.0187)		
Weighted change domestic demand		–0.0993***	–0.0980***
		(0.0228)	(0.0227)
Weighted change exports		–0.2208***	–0.2201***
		(0.0821)	(0.0824)
Weighted change import share		0.0786	
		(0.0591)	
Weighted change DC import share			0.0992
			(0.1214)
Weighted change LDC import share			0.0680
			(0.1350)
Change index of industrial production	–0.0044***	–0.0034***	–0.0035***
	(0.0013)	(0.0010)	(0.0010)
Change R&D intensity	0.0315	0.0203	0.0225
	(0.0841)	(0.0957)	(0.0963)
Ln(capital stock/shipments)	–0.0164	–0.0172	–0.0171
	(0.0088)	(0.0117)	(0.0118)
Change ln(alternative wage)	–0.0496	–0.0472	–0.0471
	(0.0487)	(0.0464)	(0.0466)
Constant	–0.0069	0.0146	0.0147
	(0.0180)	(0.0197)	(0.0199)
Industry effects	Yes	Yes	Yes
Year effects	Yes	Yes	Yes
Observations	816	816	816
Number of industries	51	51	51
R^2	0.73	0.74	0.74

NOTE: Panel-corrected standard errors in parentheses. ** = significant at 5% level; *** = significant at 1% level.

134   Job Displacement and Foreign Competition

As in Chapter 6, the main explanatory variables of interest in Table 7.1 are changes in sales, domestic demand, import share, and exports. The table reports coefficient estimates from regressions using the industry displacement rate as the dependent variable (see Equation 15 in Chapter 5). The various explanatory variables are listed in the first column of the table. In the main body of the table, each number represents the change in the industry displacement rate associated with a one-unit change in an explanatory variable. Each column of the table represents a separate and distinct regression specification. Specifications differ either by their explanatory variables or by the time period of the estimation. The time period is 1979–1994, and the specifications are similar to those reported in the previous chapter in their proxies for technological change, alternative wages, manufacturing capacity, and capital intensity. All reported specifications include controls for year, to capture unobservable time-varying factors.[2]

Rising sales, domestic demand, and exports are all associated with lower rates of job loss. A 10 percent increase in sales (column 1) is associated with a 1.0-percentage-point reduction in the rate of job loss. With a mean job loss rate of 0.049 across industries for the 1979–1994 period, a 1-percentage-point reduction is a 22 percent decline (or slightly less than one-third of a standard deviation). Moving to the separate components of sales in column 2, the estimated coefficient on domestic demand is close in size to the estimated effect of changes in sales, at –0.09. Again, this similarity in magnitude is not surprising given the dominant size of the U.S. market for most industries. If –0.09 is used as a typical estimate for the elasticity of job loss to changes in domestic demand, the average annual (weighted) change in domestic demand of +4.4 percent yields a small change in the rate of job loss (0.39 percentage point).

The most striking result is the large responsiveness of job loss rates to changes in sales due to exports. A 10 percent rise in sales due to exports is associated with a 2.2 percent decline in the industry displacement rate. A 10 percent rise in domestic demand is associated with a 0.9 percent decline in the industry job loss rate. The export association is slightly more than twice the domestic demand association. As discussed in Chapters 5 and 6, the estimated export association may be somewhat overstated due to the associated rise in shipments along with the rise in exports. Yet, it is precisely the rise in shipments that is of interest because, when domestic demand remains constant, the increase in foreign demand will be met by an increase in shipments. The sensitivity of job loss to changes in exports has been overlooked but may not be surprising. The rise in exports can be interpreted as a shift in labor demand, leading to an increase in the desired level of employment. At a given level of hiring (accessions) and nondisplacement separations, employment will rise with a fall in permanent job loss.

Most notably, rising import share is associated with a higher displacement rate, but the coefficient is small and the estimate is imprecise. At standard levels of statistical significance, it cannot be rejected that the "true" effect of changes in import share on the job loss rate is zero. Estimates reported in column 3 of Table 7.1 show that differentiating imports by country of origin makes no difference in understanding changes in the rate of job loss. For increases in both developed and developing country import share, the coefficient estimates are very imprecise.

Changes in R&D intensity and TFP are negatively correlated with job loss rates, although the coefficient estimates are imprecise. Lower job loss rates are associated with more capital intensive industries. The sensitivity of displacement rates to the business cycle, captured in part by changes in domestic demand, is also revealed by the estimated coefficient on the change in the index of manufacturing industrial production, with the negative coefficient showing the countercyclical nature of displacement.[3]

Briefly, the level of job displacement (i.e., the number of displaced workers) is an alternative approach to measuring job loss.[4] With job loss levels sensitive to industry employment levels, a within-industry, fixed-effects specification is the most appropriate. The results are relatively unchanged, with the exception that the responsiveness of the level of job loss to changes in domestic demand is similar in magnitude to its responsiveness to changes in exports. A 1 percent increase in either sales, domestic demand, or exports (holding other factors constant) lowers the level of job loss by approximately 2 percent. Imprecisely estimated, a 1 percent increase in imports increases the level of job loss by 1.4 percent.

Across industry

Although the within-industry approach is preferred, it is also useful to briefly discuss one set of cross-industry estimates. The more descriptive evidence discussed in Chapter 4, in particular Table 4.6, revealed that industries with the highest import share have, on average, the highest rates of job loss. Below the top quartile of industries with respect to import share, job loss rates are more uniform. In addition, high rates of job loss were found for industries with high import share and large increases in import share. This evidence suggests that there may be a stronger association across industries between changes in import share and the risk of job loss than was found within industries.

Cross-industry estimates are reported in Table 7.2. For changes in sales and domestic demand, the estimated coefficients are very similar to those reported in Table 7.1 (see columns 1 and 2). There are two notable differences between the two tables. The first difference is the anticipated one for changes in import share. The cross-industry association between rising import share and the risk of job loss is considerably stronger than the estimated within-industry association. A 10 percent increase in import share is associated with a 1.4–1.6 percentage point increase in the rate of job loss, across industries. The contrast between the within-industry and cross-industry estimates suggests that specific industries with high import share account for the rising import share–job loss relationship, and once those industry effects are accounted for, the correlation between rising import share and job loss is much weaker.

The second difference between the within-industry and cross-industry estimates is the estimated correlation between changes in sales due to exports and the job loss rate. First, the cross-industry estimates are considerably smaller than the within-industry estimates, and the coefficients are estimated imprecisely. With year effects, there is not sufficient variation in changes in exports to pick up a statistically significant relationship between changes in sales due to exports and job loss, although the estimated coefficient is negative as expected (Table 7.2). In results not reported, without year effects, the estimated elasticity of displacement with respect to changes in exports is negative and statistically significant. A 10 percent rise in exports is associated with a 2-percentage-point decline in the displacement rate.

Imports, Exports, and Jobs   137

The influence of outsourcing can only be investigated in the cross section. Augmenting the specification with the annualized change in imported intermediate inputs between 1979 and 1990 reveals that the correlation between growth in imported inputs and the risk of job loss is positive but not statistically significant (column 3 of Table 7.2).

Consistent with the different import share estimates between the within- and cross-industry frameworks, there is a slight difference with respect to the separate measures of changes in import share by country of origin. Column 4 of Table 7.2 shows rising imports from both developing and developed countries are associated with higher rates of job loss; only the LDC elasticity is statistically significant. This result again suggests that certain industries, those with large increases in LDC import share, had associated high job loss rates, while the within-industry relationship is considerably weaker.

The overall fit of the displacement model to the cross-industry variation in displacement rates is modest, and, as expected, not as good as in the case with the employment change data. At best, only 13 percent of the job loss rate variation is explained by the model.

Measuring the dependent variable as the natural log of displacement produces very similar results, which are not reported here. This alternative way of specifying the dependent variable yields similar results to those discussed above. In results not reported, the point estimates imply that a 1 percent increase in industry sales reduces the level of job loss by 1.5 percent, a 1 percent increase in domestic demand reduces job loss by 1.6 percent, a 1 percent increase in exports reduce job loss by 2.1 percent (the estimated export coefficient is not statistically significant), and a 1 percent decrease in import share reduces job loss by 0.6 percent (the import share point estimate is not statistically significant).

Within industry: changes in relative import price

Estimates with time-invariant industry controls are reported in Table 7.3. In the basic sample (column 1), the estimated import price elasticity is negative as expected but small and estimated imprecisely. When year effects are omitted (results not reported), the within-industry estimated elasticity equals –0.10. This estimate implies that a 10 percent increase in relative import price is associated with a 1-percentage-point decrease in the rate of job loss.

Table 7.2 Industry Displacement Rates, Changes in Sales, Domestic Demand, Exports, and Import Share, Cross-Section Estimates (1979–1994)

	(1)	(2)	(3)	(4)
Change in ln(sales)	-0.1122***			
	(0.0253)			
Weighted change domestic demand		-0.1066***	-0.1069***	-0.1061***
		(0.0290)	(0.0291)	(0.0291)
Weighted change exports		-0.0692	-0.1021	-0.0734
		(0.0762)	(0.0828)	(0.0757)
Weighted change import share		0.1613***	0.1374***	
		(0.0410)	(0.0415)	
Weighted change DC import share				0.1079
				(0.1166)
Weighted change LDC import share				0.2760***
				(0.0914)
Change index of industrial production	-0.0036***	-0.0029**	-0.0028	-0.0029**
	(0.0014)	(0.0015)	(0.0015)	(0.0015)
Change R&D intensity	-0.0678	-0.0673	-0.0828	-0.0646
	(0.0389)	(0.0429)	(0.0467)	(0.0414)
Ln(capital stock/shipments)	-0.0171***	-0.0159***	-0.0146***	-0.0159***
	(0.0032)	(0.0032)	(0.0032)	(0.0032)
Change ln(alternative wage)	-0.0612	-0.0595	-0.0613	-0.0601
	(0.0470)	(0.0469)	(0.0483)	(0.0468)
Change imported intermed. inputs			0.8219	
			(0.4357)	

Constant	0.0364***	0.0456***	0.0437***	0.0455***
	(0.0062)	(0.0059)	(0.0061)	(0.0059)
Observations	963	963	961	963
Adjusted R^2	0.11	0.11	0.12	0.11

NOTE: Robust standard errors in parentheses. Specifications include year dummy variables. ** = significant at 5% level; *** = significant at 1% level.

Table 7.3 Changes in Industry Employment and Relative Import Prices: Within-Industry Estimates (1983–1992)

	1 OLS estimates	2 IV sample, OLS estimates	3 IV sample, IV estimates
Change ln(relative import price)	−0.0461 (0.0490)	−0.1021 (0.0965)	−0.2562*** (0.1044)
Change index of industrial production	0.0021*** (0.0004)	0.0021** (0.0009)	0.0023*** (0.0005)
Change R&D intensity	0.1100 (0.1075)	0.0791 (0.0924)	0.0859 (0.0704)
Ln(capital stock/shipments)	0.0271** (0.0125)	0.0559*** (0.0192)	0.0483*** (0.0037)
Change ln(alternative wage)	−0.0984*** (0.0327)	−0.1711** (0.0709)	−0.1592*** (0.0211)
Constant	0.0743*** (0.0217)	0.1221*** (0.0327)	0.1192*** (0.0041)
Industry effects	Yes	Yes	Yes
Year effects	Yes	Yes	Yes
Observations	300	180	180
Number of industries	30	18	18
R^2	0.70	0.71	0.70

NOTE: Panel-corrected standard errors in parentheses. Specifications include one lag in the relative import price. ** = significant at 5% level; *** = significant at 1% level. IV denotes instrumental variables.

This estimated magnitude is found, with the inclusion of year effects, in an early step of the IV approach. Again, the data requirements for the IV estimation are considerable. For the subset of industries with available data, the OLS estimate is reported in column 2, and it is small (−0.10) and statistically insignificant. The IV estimate (in column 3) is considerably larger in magnitude at −0.255 and is statistically significant. The sign of the OLS bias, here positive, is consistent with results from the employment estimation reported in the previous chapter. The bias is a result of correlation between the relative import price variable and the error term in the displacement regression. If there is an unobservable global price shock (perhaps an oil price shock) that increases domestic displacement and increases relative import price (because costs rise), then import price movements will be positively correlated with increases in the rate of displacement rate, and this will impart a positive bias to the OLS estimated coefficient. The IV technique addresses this potential bias by treating relative import price as an endogenous variable and predicting it from a set of conventional import price predictors (instruments), such as trade-weighted exchange rates and trade-weighted foreign relative factor costs. With the IV estimate, a 10 percent increase in import price reduces the rate of job loss by 2.5 percentage points.

SUMMARY

Three main findings can be distilled from this chapter:
- Rising sales, domestic demand, and exports are all associated with lower rates of job loss. The most striking result is the large responsiveness of the risk of job loss to changes in sales due to exports. The rise in sales due to exports can be associated with an increase in the desired level of employment and, with this increase, comes a fall in permanent job loss.
- Rising import share is associated with a higher displacement rate, but the coefficient is small and estimated imprecisely. Within industries, it cannot be rejected that the "true" association between changes in import share and the risk of job loss is zero.
- The cross-industry association between rising import share and the risk of job loss is considerably stronger than the estimated within-industry association. The contrast between the within-industry and cross-industry estimates suggests that specific high import share industries account for the rising import share–risk of job loss relationship. Once these industries are accounted for,

the correlation between rising import share and the risk of job loss is much weaker.

Overall, the estimates are consistent with common perceptions of the link between increasing foreign competition and job loss. Across industries, there is some weak evidence that the risk of job loss increases as import share rises. There is a weaker cross-industry relationship between falling import prices and rising job loss. This is consistent with the discussion in Chapter 4 that noted that the industries with high job loss, high import share, and increasing import share were not the ones with the largest reductions in import prices. At the same time, this simple cross-industry specification explains little of the variation in job loss rates.

Within industry, there is more evidence consistent with falling import prices leading to job loss, and the correlation between rising import share and job loss is positive, if weaker. Together, the employment change and job loss evidence show that, as relative import prices fall, consumers substitute foreign-produced goods for domestic and domestic demand falls, import share rises, and employment falls as output is scaled back. The employment reduction occurs, in part, through displacement.

Notes

1. See Kletzer (2000), Figure 10.2.
2. Similar to the employment change analysis, observations where the log change in industry employment exceeded 0.75 in absolute value were excluded.
3. The year effects work in the same way, and their estimated magnitudes are consistent with the pattern of the business cycle over the time period.
4. To be precise, the natural logarithm of the number of displaced workers in an industry. Haveman (1998) used this measure.

8
Conclusions and Policy Implications

Americans are of two minds about globalization. They recognize the benefits of lower prices and broader choices, while being fully cognizant of the worker costs. Opinion surveys note the ambivalence. In a survey conducted in 1999, 44 percent of respondents endorsed the idea that, "Free trade is a bad idea, because it can lead to lower wages and people losing their jobs" (Program on International Policy Attitudes 2000). Fifty-one percent of respondents endorsed the other option: "Free trade is a good idea, because it can lead to lower prices and the long-term growth of the economy." In the same survey, respondents were presented with the following scenario: "The U.S. makes a trade agreement that leads to a U.S. shoe factory closing. The workers have to find new jobs that pay on average $5,000 per year less, but American consumers save $20 per pair of shoes." Based on this information, 63 percent of respondents said the United States would have made a mistake by entering into the agreement (Program on International Policy Attitudes 2000).

One of the endnotes of the twentieth century was the globalization backlash. Its voices are less a backlash and more an amplification of old themes. The most prominent is the claim that "trade costs jobs," and the resulting debate over the number of jobs affected by free trade.[1] Although the level of employment in the U.S. economy is determined far more by macroeconomic events and policy than by changes in trade policy, it is important to the policy debate to understand more about the link between U.S. jobs and job loss and increasing trade flows. In this spirit, one of the goals of this book was an examination of the claim that increasing trade is associated with job loss in the United States.

The focus on job loss represents the most novel contribution of this study. Having spent the last 15 years studying the consequences of job loss, I thought it natural to examine some of the underlying causes of job displacement. Job loss is considered by many Americans to be the central domestic focus of free(r) trade, and many participants and observers of the U.S. political scene consider the domestic labor market

consequences of "trade-related" job loss to be the key political economy issue for the future of U.S. international trade policy.
The research reported here has five main findings.

- Increasing imports are associated with employment reductions. Increasing foreign competition, measured as a decline in relative import price, is associated with a decline in employment. The sensitivity of employment and job loss to fluctuations in import price and import share reported here confirms and extends the earlier work of other researchers. The relatively small magnitude of the average estimated associations between rising import share and job loss (and employment reductions) is consistent with the consensus of the "trade and wages" literature that trade plays a smaller role than technological change in accounting for rising wage inequality.
- Increasing exports (and domestic demand) enhance employment. Within industries, the employment-enhancing effect of expanding exports is significantly greater than the employment-reducing effects of increasing imports. Admittedly, this result is stronger in some specifications than in others, and there are measurement issues.
- With respect to job displacement, there is a set of industries facing sustained import competition, those with both high levels of import share and increasing import share, where the rate of job loss is high. Beyond this subset of industries, the rising import share–high rate of job loss relationship is considerably weaker. This finding means that increasing imports play a small role in aggregate economy job loss but a larger role in traditionally import-competing industries. Within a given industry, there is also evidence that more competitively priced imports (falling relative import prices) are associated with job loss.
- The steady focus on import competition and its potential role in job loss has caused the export side to be overlooked. As a mirror image to export growth associated with employment growth, it is also a counterforce against permanent job loss. As sales increase due to exports, the risk of job loss falls. Restated slightly, an open economy involves more exports along with more imports, and increasing exports reduce job loss.

- Although some jobs are lost when imports rise while others are maintained or created when exports rise, the trend in manufacturing employment from the late 1970s to the early 1990s cannot be completely explained by changes in trade flows or foreign competition. Technological change, changes in the composition of consumer demand, corporate restructuring, and downsizing have, all played a role in declining manufacturing employment. At the same time, while increasing imports have played a small role in sectoral job loss, they have played a much larger role in traditionally import-competing industries. These industries include apparel, textiles, footwear, electrical machinery, some of the metals industries, and motor vehicles. In these industries, the implied burden of worker adjustment is dramatic.

POLICY IMPLICATIONS

Import barriers are a traditional focus of trade policy analysis. Import protection is known to be costly to consumers.[2] It is also contrary to the multilateral reductions in trade barriers of the past three decades, although allowable under certain conditions. More importantly, this study finds the risk of job loss to be not very responsive to changes in import share within industries. Reducing import share through import restrictions will not reduce job loss by much, and consumers will bear the high costs.

For policy, the inclusion of exports and the strength of the findings in regard to exports, suggests a needed reorientation of thinking. Imports are half the story, not the whole story. Fluctuations in employment and job loss are more sensitive to changes in sales due to exports than to changes in the import share of domestic demand. Employment grows, and job loss is reduced, with increases in foreign demand.

Opening markets to U.S. goods is strongly supported by this study. Export promotion is currently a major item for the U.S. Department of Commerce, and this study supports continued emphasis. The United States has not concluded a multilateral trade agreement since the passage of NAFTA in 1993. The bilateral agreements (with Jordan, Chile, and Vietnam) are very small additions to open markets for U.S. exporters and are generally seen as most important for their symbolic values.

Richardson (1993) assessed the degree to which the United States' own domestic microeconomic policy impeded exports. He concluded that as much as $40 billion in exports annually were discouraged through a variety of export disincentives. He highlighted inadequate official support for export finance as a significant discouragement. On this point, strengthening the Export-Import Bank can be an important step in export promotion.

With the expected continued trend growth in exports, the vulnerability of jobs to fluctuations in foreign demand will likely gain some visibility in line with the known vulnerability of jobs to fluctuations in domestic demand. These short-run fluctuations can be addressed through the current system of unemployment compensation (UC), the primary source of income for workers unemployed due to cyclical fluctuations. Helping workers with income losses associated with export-related unemployment may present additional claims on the UC system.[3]

As I noted at the beginning of this chapter, protecting workers from import competition resonates loudly with the American public. This study has revealed that considerable employment decline and some job loss is associated with rising imports. For many industries, skill-biased technological change is a part of that association. To the workers who lose their jobs and their communities, the "trade versus technology" question is irrelevant. That question is very likely also irrelevant to the public policies that help workers adjust to job loss. This study underscores that the job losses are real and that there is some connection to trade.

In related research, I have found that workers displaced from import-competing industries face difficult adjustments following their job loss.[4] Import-competing job loss is associated with low re-employment rates because the workers vulnerable to rising import job loss experience difficulty gaining re-employment, based on their individual characteristics. It is not import competition per se; it is who gets displaced from (and is employed by) industries with rising import competition. What limits the re-employment of import-competing displaced workers? The same characteristics that limit the re-employment of all displaced workers—low educational attainment, advancing age, high tenure, minority status, and marital status. Married women, even those displaced from full-time jobs, are much less likely to be re-employed. Difficulties do not end with the transition to a new job. Difficulties continue in trying to recover earnings. For re-employed import-competing displaced workers, the average earnings loss is about 13 percent. Two-thirds earn less on their new job than they did on their old job. One-quarter reported earnings losses of 30 percent or more. The same average and distribution is found for manufacturing workers as a whole.[5]

Trade barriers are seen by some as the way to "protect" workers from import competition. An alternative perspective is that workers should be protected from undue losses associated with increasing trade. This kind of protection is accomplished through domestic policy, rather than trade policy, and it is the backdrop of the current programs of Trade Adjustment Assistance (TAA) and North American Free Trade Agreement Transitional Adjustment Assistance (NAFTA-TAA).

From this perspective, it is useful to assess the current state of domestic adjustment assistance policy as we look to the future of international trade and trade policy. The federal role in assisting "trade-displaced" workers began with the Trade Expansion Act of 1962. This Act established the TAA program. For eligible workers for whom it can be documented that increasing imports have contributed importantly to their job loss, additional assistance is available. The size and form of TAA has changed considerably in the four decades since the passage of the Trade Expansion Act. Under its current form, qualified workers may gain an additional 52 weeks of income support (called Trade Readjustment Allowances [TRA]) after they have exhausted their standard UI eligibility (26 weeks), provided they are enrolled in an approved training program. The program also provides job search and relocation assistance. Income support payments are set at the prevailing state UI benefit level. Although income support payments under TAA are an entitlement, the other benefits, including training, are limited by the availability of funds. The entire TAA program is funded out of general revenues.

Federal efforts directed toward trade-displaced workers were enhanced with the passage of the North American Free Trade Agreement Implementation Act of 1993, legislation that created the NAFTA-TAA program. The NAFTA-TAA is similar to TAA in general form, although it covers only workers who have lost jobs because of increased imports from, or shifts of production to, Mexico or Canada. Workers can be certified under both programs but must choose one from which to claim benefits. Benefits provided under NAFTA-TAA are identical to those provided under the TAA program. Under TAA, NAFTA-TAA provides benefits to secondary workers, defined as workers employed by upstream producers and/or suppliers. Similar to TAA, the federal government pays all NAFTA-TAA expenses. Over the last half of the 1990s, TAA and NAFTA-TAA service and benefit payments have been less than $300 million annually.[6]

In 1999, the latest year for which information is available, 227,650 workers were certified eligible for TAA and/or NAFTA-TAA.[7] Certifications include workers who lose jobs as well as those who are threatened with job loss. Interestingly, the number of 1999 certifications is close to a DWS estimate of the number of workers displaced from high-import industries in 1999 (295,000).[8] A much smaller number of workers received readjustment allowances (36,910), and only 32,120 received training. The General Accounting Office report discussed reasons for low training enrollment, including training waivers (allowed under TAA but not under NAFTA-TAA), funding shortfalls, and a strong labor market that allowed displaced workers to become re-employed more readily on their own.

Evidence that TAA and NAFTA-TAA training programs are useful is weak, at best (see Decker and Corson 1995; U.S. General Accounting Office 2000). Because workers typically enter training before getting a new job, there is a weak link between training and the skill needs of potential employers. This raises the possibility that workers may train for jobs that do not exist. This is not to say that training has no value to anyone. Classroom training can be of real value to some dislocated workers, but the share who benefit is quite small. Most workers acquire far more skill-enhancing knowledge on the job than in the classroom (see Jacobson 1998).

To move forward again, proactively, on the path of increasing economic integration, we must address the employment and earnings concerns of workers, along with strengthening the current set of programs. Jacobson (1998) articulated a set of clear primary policy goals, among them reducing the time it takes displaced workers to find new permanent jobs and offsetting the large and permanent earnings reductions associated with the loss of firm- or industry-specific human capital. The first of these goals can be met by the existing social safety net of TAA and NAFTA-TAA by providing job search assistance, assessing training needs and compatibilities, and providing training funds through grants and/or loans. Allowing part-time employment along with training participation would improve the support.

The second of Jacobson's goals, reducing long-term earnings losses, is more difficult and will require new programs. Time-limited earnings (or wage) insurance has been proposed by a number of authors, including Jacobson (1998), Burtless et al. (1998), and Kletzer and Litan (2001). Briefly, wage insurance is a program of financial assistance, upon re-employment, for workers who lose jobs, for any reason, through no fault of their own. The goal of a wage insurance program is to get workers back to work, while minimizing longer term earnings losses. A key aspect of the program, and difference between it and other adjustment assistance programs, is the employment incentive created by making benefits conditional on re-employment.[9]

Kletzer and Litan (2001) proposed a program that would be open to all workers who could provide documentation that they were "displaced" according to criteria similar to the operational definition of displacement used by the Bureau of Labor Statistics in its DWSs. This definition includes plant closing or relocation, elimination of position or shift, and insufficient work. Eligibility can be made contingent on a minimum period of service on the old job, perhaps two years. Workers re-employed in a new job that pays less than the old job (where both old and new job earnings can be documented through employer quarterly earnings reports that are filed with the states) would have a substantial portion of their lost earnings replaced, for up to two years following the date of initial job loss. For example, a displaced worker who once earned $40,000 per year, re-employed in a new job paying $30,000 per year would receive $5,000 per year, for a period from the time of re-employment to two years after initial job loss. Annual payments could be capped, perhaps at $10,000.

Kletzer and Litan provided cost estimates, based on DWS data, for a number of program scenarios. One of those scenarios, with a replacement rate of 50 percent of the earnings loss, a $10,000 annual payment cap, and eligibility limited to workers whose previous and new jobs were full time, would have cost about $3 billion in 1997, when the unemployment rate averaged 4.9 percent (the June 2001 unemployment rate was 4.5 percent).[10] These projected costs are a tiny fraction of the $500 billion in estimated benefits for the United States from freer trade.[11]

Wage insurance addresses some of the criticisms leveled at TAA and NAFTA-TAA. First, the structure of the program, with benefits available only upon re-employment, presents an incentive for workers to find new jobs. Second, workers' job search efforts may be broader, as entry-level jobs become more attractive to workers when the earnings gap is reduced. Third and relatedly, the program effectively subsidizes retraining on the job, where it is likely to be far more useful than in a training program where re-employment prospects are uncertain. Fourth, the program directly addresses the critical problem of earnings losses upon re-employment.

Free trade, open markets, and economic integration can facilitate economic growth. The benefits of free trade are considerable and widespread. But open engagement with the world does not help everyone. This study provides confirmation of the concentrated costs of free trade. Manufacturing industries offer striking differences in their sensitivities of employment change and job loss to changes in trade flows. Rising imports are associated with job loss. That the numbers may be small, or that the association is limited to a particular set of industries does not diminish the extent of the human costs. Proponents of expanded open trade and investment face an obligation to address the concerns of workers, companies, and communities who can be hurt by free trade.

Notes

1. NAFTA, starting with its negotiations in the early 1990s and continuing through its current outcomes, has been a prime source for the heated jobs debate. For an early view, see Hufbauer and Schott (1993). For a recent contribution, see Economic Policy Institute (2001).
2. Hufbauer and Goodrich (2001) estimated the consumer costs per job saved in the steel industry to be $360,000 annually and the estimated annual compensation per worker as $72,000.
3. However, it is possible that more active involvement in foreign markets comes with some risk. Regaining foreign markets may be more difficult than regaining domestic markets. I leave this question for future research.

4. See Kletzer (2001).
5. For more on the costs of job displacement, see Jacobson, LaLonde, and Sullivan (1993), and Kletzer (1998a).
6. See U.S. General Accounting Office (2000). This report is the source for the information that follows on workers certified.
7. The number includes workers certified under both programs.
8. See Kletzer (2001).
9. In the research literature, other proponents of wage insurance include Burtless et al. (1998) and Jacobson (1998).
10. Some of the cost of a wage insurance programs could be offset if it were incorporated into the TAA and NAFTA-TAA programs. One possibility would be to offer wage insurance to workers if they became re-employed within 26 weeks, the period before the extended income support from Trade Readjustment Allowances. Once receiving wage insurance, re-employed workers would be ineligible for income support and training allowances.
11. This estimated increase in U.S. economic welfare assumes global free trade, with all post-Uruguay Round trade barriers completely removed. See Brown, Deardorff, and Stern (2002).

Appendix A

MEASURES OF TRADE VOLUMES AND IMPORT PRICES

Data on U.S. import and exports, by four-digit SIC category, are available as part of the NBER Trade Database for the period 1958–1994. The import and export data file also reports the 1958–1994 value of domestic shipments from the NBER Productivity Database.[1]

The SIC-based industry trade data must be aggregated up to three-digit 1990 CIC codes in order to combine the trade information with CPS-based information on employment and job displacement.

Import price indices data are available for many four-digit SIC manufacturing industries starting in 1982–1983, with the SIC-based series currently ending with 1992. For a smaller set of industries, the price series provides reasonable information from 1980 forward. For industries where the three- or four-digit SIC import price information was missing, two-digit SIC price information was used to fill in the time-series gaps. The price measure is a fixed weight Laspeyres index with a 1985 base period.[2] Industry-specific Producer Price Indices, available from the Bureau of Labor Statistics, are used to obtain relative import prices.

MEASURING INDUSTRY EMPLOYMENT AND JOB LOSS USING THE CPS

Industry employment

Employment levels by industry were constructed from the March Annual Demographic File supplements to the CPS for the period of 1975–1996. These supplements contain information on labor market status and activities for the preceding calendar year (thus, the 1975–1996 files contain information for the period 1974–1995).[3] A number of important data construction issues arose in constructing the employment series. In the analysis sample, all industries are defined using

1990 CIC codes; concordances were employed to bring together the 1960, 1970, 1980, and 1990 three-digit CIC codes used in the various March supplements.

Job loss

The DWSs provide information on displacement. Available surveys, administered biennially as supplements to the CPS, cover displacements occurring over the period of 1979–1995. In each survey, adults (aged 20 years and older) were asked in the regular monthly CPS if they had lost a job in the preceding five-year period due to "a plant closing, an employer going out of business, a layoff from which he/she was not recalled, or other similar reasons." If the answer was yes, a series of questions followed concerning the old job and period of joblessness.

A common understanding of job displacement is that it occurs without personal prejudice; terminations are related to the operating decisions of the employer and are independent of individual job performance. In the DWSs, this definition can be implemented by drawing the sample of displaced workers from individuals who respond that their job loss was due to the reasons noted above. Other causes of job loss, such as quits or firings are not considered displacements.[4] This operational definition is not without ambiguity: the displacements are "job" displacements, in the sense that an individual displaced from a job and rehired into a different job with the same employer is considered displaced.

Some of the distinctions may be too narrow or arbitrary. The distinction between quits and displacements is muddied by the ability of employers to reduce employment by reducing or failing to raise wages. Wage changes may induce some workers to quit (and not be in the sample) while others opt to stay with the firm (and they get displaced and enter the sample).[5] This distinction means that the displaced worker sample will underestimate the amount of job change "caused" by trade. In addition, if the workers who stay on with the firm until displacement are those who face the worst labor market outcomes of all those at risk of displacement, then the displaced sample will be potentially nonrandom and it will overstate the costs of job loss. Without data on quits, these issues cannot be addressed.

The sample here is limited to workers (aged 20 to 64) displaced from manufacturing industries. Because the information is retrospectively gathered, it has potential recall error. Problems of recall are compounded by the overlapping coverage of years of displacement by surveys, with some years covered in two or three surveys.[6] This recall bias is thought to be significant. As Topel (1990) and Farber (1993) show, it is likely that the surveys seriously underestimate job loss that occurred long before the survey date due to inaccuracies in recall as well as question design.[7] This makes it desirable to have non-overlapping recall periods (that is, each year of displacement drawn from only one survey) that are relatively short. The sample was restricted to displacements occurring in the two-year period prior to each survey in order to incorporate these characteristics. A larger and more extended sample was drawn from the 1984 survey to extend the time-series coverage back to 1979.

Industry displacement rates were calculated by dividing the number of workers displaced from a three-digit CIC industry in a year by the number of workers employed in that industry in that year.

Appendix Notes

1. The 1958–1994 file combines data from the earlier NBER Trade and Immigration data file (described in Abowd 1991) with the NBER Trade Database (see Feenstra 1996).
2. These indices are described in more detail in U.S. Bureau of Labor Statistics (1992). They are based on a survey of actual transactions prices, and to the degree possible, they reflect c.i.f. (cost, insurance, freight) prices. When aggregation was needed, the SIC indices were weighted by their relative shares in total imports using the NBER Trade Database.
3. The employment counts were derived from the sample of individuals employed in private sector wage and salary jobs at the survey date, using information on industry in the previous calendar year and the CPS supplemental weights.
4. Individuals may also respond that their job loss was due to the end of a seasonal job or the failure of a self-employed business. These individuals are not considered displaced.
5. Jacobson, LaLonde, and Sullivan (1993) showed that wages fall for displaced workers before they are displaced.
6. The 1984 DWS covered the period 1979–1983; the 1986 survey, 1981–1985; the 1988 survey, 1983–1987; the 1990 survey, 1985–1989; the 1992 survey, 1987–1991; the 1994 survey, 1991–1993; and the 1996 survey, 1993–1995.
7. If more than one job was lost, information is gathered only for the job held longest. See Topel (1990) and Farber (1993).

Appendix A

Table A1 Basic Trade, Output, and Employment Statistics, U.S. Manufacturing Industries, 1979–1985

Industry (three-digit CIC)	Employment 1979 (000s)	Change in employ. 1979–85	Mean displace rate 1979–85	Import share 1979	Change in imp. share 1979–85	Export intensity 1979	Change in exports 1979–85
Electrical machinery	1255.2	−0.030	0.040	0.107	0.071	0.145	0.026
Apparel	1094.0	−0.175	0.054	0.132	0.103	0.023	−0.621
Machinery, exc. electric	1017.0	−0.113	0.053	0.085	0.052	0.139	−0.212
Furniture & fixtures	955.7	−0.010	0.023	0.046	0.048	0.014	−0.003
Motor vehicles	990.4	−0.115	0.064	0.173	0.086	0.091	−0.017
Printing, publishing	790.6	0.186	0.038	0.013	0.002	0.019	−0.068
Aircraft & parts	592.5	0.039	0.021	0.045	0.034	0.241	0.140
Blast furnaces	570.5	−0.634	0.084	0.119	0.074	0.033	−1.067
Misc. fabricated metal	532.2	−0.137	0.041	0.040	0.019	0.046	−0.358
Fabricated structural metals	516.3	−0.166	0.065	0.007	0.009	0.040	−0.742
Sawmills, planing mills	470.3	−0.089	0.047	0.135	0.003	0.063	−0.542
Yarn, thread	449.7	−0.291	0.052	0.045	0.040	0.072	−0.814
Industrial & misc. chemicals	426.4	−0.073	0.036	0.071	0.040	0.150	−0.128
Newspaper	420.1	0.069	0.039	0.001	0.002	0.000	0.812
Metalworking machinery	395.0	−0.178	0.038	0.108	0.061	0.095	−0.412
Office & acct. machines	385.5	0.260	0.009	0.079	0.083	0.183	−0.100
Construction & material moving machines	382.8	−0.414	0.081	0.059	0.091	0.270	−0.478
Electronic computing eqp.	369.5	0.521	0.027	0.103	0.086	0.939	0.586
Meat products	358.0	0.010	0.043	0.048	−0.008	0.044	−0.235

Misc. plastics products	340.1	0.015	N/A	0.032	0.013	0.051	-0.004
Metal forgings	300.7	-0.199	0.026	0.021	0.016	0.268	0.053
Misc. manuf. industries	273.6	-0.145	0.056	0.186	0.110	0.121	-0.740
Canned fruits	250.0	-0.104	0.043	0.038	0.023	0.031	-0.280
Cement, concrete, gypsum	248.7	-0.083	0.044	0.021	0.006	0.004	-0.335
Pulp, paper	245.8	-0.057	0.021	0.155	0.004	0.089	-0.129
Iron & Steel foundries	240.7	-0.532	0.085	0.017	0.024	0.011	-0.720
Beverage	237.9	-0.106	0.014	0.071	0.002	0.013	-0.315
Bakery	236.8	-0.091	0.025	0.005	0.005	0.002	0.150
Knitting mills	230.5	-0.139	0.023	0.061	0.097	0.016	-0.465
Ship & boat building	226.4	-0.193	0.077	0.019	0.018	0.028	-0.300
Paperboard	214.0	-0.084	0.020	0.004	0.003	0.007	-0.032
Plastics, synthetics	212.2	-0.210	0.024	0.023	0.024	0.145	-0.252
Misc. food	209.4	-0.067	0.035	0.049	0.006	0.160	-0.560
Glass & glass products	198.5	-0.240	0.050	0.055	0.038	0.056	-0.333
Drugs	192.5	0.066	0.021	0.052	0.012	0.077	0.175
Misc. fab. textile	189.2	-0.033	0.040	0.040	0.043	0.072	-0.729
Cutlery, handtools	183.9	-0.259	0.035	0.073	0.044	0.065	-0.336
Farm machinery & eqp.	182.3	-0.626	0.101	0.125	0.019	0.108	-0.547
Dairy products	179.8	-0.102	0.052	0.015	0.001	0.007	0.534
Household appliances	176.8	-0.274	0.058	0.071	0.050	0.081	-0.506
Misc. paper	174.4	0.109	N/A	0.014	0.009	0.027	-0.131
Petroleum refining	165.2	-0.156	0.030	0.075	0.026	0.016	0.764
Misc. nonmetallic mineral	157.9	-0.498	N/A	0.046	0.039	0.057	-0.149
Footwear	148.9	-0.406	0.110	0.348	0.219	0.018	0.078
Other rubber products	146.3	-0.169	0.054	0.086	-0.012	0.052	-0.233

158 Appendix A

Table A1 (continued)

Industry (three-digit CIC)	Employment 1979 (000s)	Change in employ. 1979–85	Mean displace rate 1979–85	Import share 1979	Change in imp. share 1979–85	Export intensity 1979	Change in exports 1979–85
Engines & turbines	145.1	−0.323	0.043	0.083	0.113	0.197	−0.256
Grain mill	144.1	−0.143	0.039	0.005	0.003	0.111	−0.361
Misc. wood products	139.6	−0.117	0.041	0.066	0.014	0.033	−0.325
Soaps & cosmetics	139.5	0.056	0.043	0.009	0.011	0.028	−0.237
Photographic eqp.	134.2	−0.090	0.031	0.121	0.052	0.144	−0.350
Scientific & controlling instr.	128.5	0.515	N/A	0.074	0.042	0.220	0.116
Tires & inner tubes	127.1	−0.303	0.050	0.130	0.038	0.044	−0.272
Toys & sporting goods	121.1	−0.242	0.084	0.229	0.148	0.093	−0.476
Screw machine products	115.9	−0.187	0.027	0.089	0.018	0.030	−0.327
Radio, TV	114.7	−0.315	0.189	0.151	0.046	0.090	0.107
Sugar products	112.8	−0.135	0.046	0.139	−0.031	0.022	−0.158
Other primary metal	109.6	−0.204	0.085	0.189	0.022	0.242	−1.139
Guided missiles	101.5	0.557	0.049	0.009	0.018	0.063	−0.002
Logging	88.5	−0.047	0.069	0.010	−0.004	0.309	−0.652
Wood bldgs. & mobile homes	83.4	−0.147	0.124	0.047	0.000	0.010	−1.592
Railroad locos.	74.3	−0.815	0.105	0.053	0.063	0.048	−0.260
Paints, varnishes	68.6	−0.079	0.040	0.002	0.006	0.025	−0.123
Primary aluminum industries	68.4	−0.296	0.079	0.048	0.045	0.044	−0.298
Misc. textile	66.4	−0.237	0.025	0.119	0.014	0.092	−0.230
Ordnance	63.7	0.197	0.047	0.041	0.003	0.176	−0.260

Floor coverings	60.5	−0.106	0.060	0.047	0.022	0.035	−0.524
Tobacco	55.9	−0.079	N/A	0.007	−0.002	0.065	−0.066
Cycles & misc. transport	54.3	−0.065	0.085	0.291	−0.022	0.145	0.410
Structural clay products	52.1	−0.329	0.070	0.092	0.032	0.045	−0.537
Leather products	50.8	−0.444	0.101	0.269	0.195	0.040	−0.555
Pottery & related	49.2	−0.237	0.079	0.313	0.105	0.071	0.061
Optical & health supplies	45.1	−0.133	0.206	0.064	0.008	0.107	0.137
Misc. petroleum	32.6	−0.215	0.083	0.050	0.024	0.055	−0.183
Watches, clocks	27.7	−0.812	0.091	0.387	0.226	0.088	−0.841
Leather tanning & finish	19.9	−0.296	0.049	0.160	0.073	0.156	−0.192
Mean	254.2	−0.114	0.057	0.086	0.040	0.094	−0.253

NOTE: Changes are log–changes from 1979 to 1985. Domestic demand and exports are deflated by the industry's Producer Price Index. N/A = not available. Import share is calculated as imports divided by domestic supply. Displacement rate is calculated as the number of workers displaced from an industry divided by the number of workers employed in that industry. Export intensity is calculated as exports divided by shipments.

SOURCE: Data on imports, exports, and shipments are from the NBER Trade Database, 1958–1994. Employment data are from the Bureau of Labor Statistics.

Table A2 Basic Trade, Output, and Employment Statistics, U.S. Manufacturing Industries, 1985–1994

Industry (three-digit CIC)	Employment 1985 (000s)	Change in employ. 1985–94	Mean displace rate 1985–94	Import share 1985	Change in imp. share 1985–94	Export intensity 1985	Change in exports 1985–94
Electrical machinery	1218.2	−0.072	0.038	0.178	0.135	0.129	1.146
Furniture & fixtures	985.8	0.023	0.024	0.095	0.038	0.013	1.478
Printing, publishing	952.0	0.108	0.037	0.015	0.006	0.014	1.038
Apparel	918.2	−0.222	0.052	0.236	0.146	0.012	1.965
Machinery, exc. electric	907.9	−0.000	0.037	0.137	0.050	0.121	0.757
Motor vehicles	883.1	0.029	0.038	0.259	0.016	0.088	0.800
Electronic computing eqp	622.3	−0.285	0.060	0.189	0.298	0.319	0.595
Aircraft & parts	616.2	−0.247	0.033	0.079	0.097	0.263	0.550
Office & acct. machines	500.2	−0.345	0.005	0.162	0.289	0.123	0.249
Misc. fabricated metal	464.2	0.002	0.027	0.059	0.026	0.035	0.952
Newspaper	450.1	−0.004	0.013	0.003	−0.003	0.001	0.307
Fabricated structural metals	437.2	−0.067	0.052	0.016	0.000	0.021	0.712
Sawmills, planing mills	430.4	0.070	0.031	0.138	0.005	0.036	0.949
Industrial & misc. chemicals	396.5	−0.076	0.028	0.111	0.021	0.147	0.477
Meat products	361.7	0.221	0.024	0.039	−0.006	0.032	0.944
Misc. plastics products	345.3	0.346	N/A	0.045	0.031	0.038	1.039
Yarn, thread	336.2	−0.159	0.036	0.086	0.022	0.036	0.871
Metalworking machinery	330.7	−0.026	0.032	0.169	0.068	0.084	0.900
Blast furnaces	302.6	−0.235	0.044	0.193	−0.003	0.020	1.084

Construction & material moving machines	253.0	−0.179	0.044	0.150	0.087	0.264	0.287
Metal forgings	246.5	−0.043	0.027	0.037	0.005	0.408	−0.801
Misc. manuf. industries	236.7	0.145	0.048	0.296	0.080	0.064	0.773
Pulp, paper	232.2	−0.057	0.024	0.159	0.010	0.072	0.772
Cement, concrete, gypsum	228.9	−0.056	0.030	0.027	−0.014	0.003	0.732
Canned fruits	225.4	0.086	0.026	0.061	−0.007	0.023	1.022
Bakery	216.3	−0.020	0.030	0.010	0.004	0.002	1.911
Scientific & controlling instr.	215.0	−0.161	0.016	0.117	0.112	0.199	0.593
Beverage	213.9	−0.192	0.026	0.074	−0.006	0.009	1.369
Drugs	205.6	0.246	0.022	0.063	0.030	0.081	0.889
Knitting mills	200.5	−0.003	0.016	0.158	0.061	0.011	1.907
Paperboard	196.8	0.088	0.027	0.007	0.006	0.007	1.519
Misc. food	195.9	0.099	0.043	0.055	0.011	0.083	0.445
Misc. paper	194.4	0.223	N/A	0.024	0.001	0.021	1.125
Ship & boat building	186.6	−0.165	0.074	0.037	0.003	0.022	1.165
Misc. fab. textile	183.0	0.171	0.033	0.083	0.065	0.028	0.891
Guided missiles	177.2	−0.500	0.093	0.027	0.030	0.032	0.075
Plastics, synthetics	172.0	−0.063	0.028	0.048	0.056	0.116	0.859
Dairy products	162.3	−0.092	0.041	0.016	0.001	0.011	0.493
Glass & glass products	156.1	−0.026	0.047	0.093	0.036	0.045	0.994
Soaps & cosmetics	147.5	0.039	0.029	0.021	0.019	0.022	1.459
Cutlery, handtools	142.0	−0.101	0.025	0.117	0.059	0.054	1.048
Iron & Steel foundries	141.4	−0.122	0.025	0.040	0.006	0.009	0.990
Petroleum refining	141.4	−0.261	0.023	0.101	−0.016	0.042	0.053
Household appliances	134.4	−0.090	0.035	0.121	0.047	0.051	1.108
Grain mill	124.9	0.028	0.027	0.008	0.011	0.059	0.495

Table A2 (continued)

Industry (three-digit CIC)	Employment 1985 (000s)	Change in employ. 1985–94	Mean displace rate 1985–94	Import share 1985	Change in imp. share 1985–94	Export intensity 1985	Change in exports 1985–94
Misc. wood products	124.2	0.098	0.033	0.080	0.022	0.022	1.050
Other rubber products	123.6	-0.036	0.050	0.074	0.169	0.042	1.124
Photographic eqp.	122.7	-0.329	0.028	0.172	0.088	0.111	0.378
Engines & turbines	105.1	-0.156	0.036	0.196	-0.007	0.200	0.798
Footwear	99.2	-0.544	0.081	0.567	0.140	0.024	1.297
Sugar products	98.6	0.012	0.031	0.108	-0.031	0.019	1.531
Farm machinery & eqp.	97.5	0.064	0.042	0.144	0.014	0.119	0.705
Screw machine products	96.1	-0.004	0.031	0.106	0.049	0.023	1.457
Misc. nonmetallic mineral	95.9	0.052	0.052	0.085	0.027	0.060	0.616
Toys & sporting goods	95.1	0.194	0.058	0.377	0.130	0.065	1.495
Tires & inner tubes	93.9	-0.177	0.034	0.167	0.058	0.036	1.316
Other primary metal	89.4	-0.119	0.071	0.211	-0.020	0.085	1.092
Logging	84.4	-0.028	0.052	0.006	0.014	0.140	0.679
Radio, TV	83.7	-0.297	0.086	0.197	0.101	0.063	1.205
Ordnance	77.6	-0.370	0.069	0.043	0.109	0.104	0.385
Wood bldgs. & mobile homes	72.0	0.021	0.089	0.047	-0.013	0.003	1.699
Paints, varnishes	63.4	-0.101	0.047	0.008	0.008	0.021	1.179
Floor coverings	54.4	0.161	0.040	0.069	0.002	0.020	1.244
Misc. textile	52.4	0.006	0.050	0.133	0.000	0.079	1.017
Tobacco	51.7	0.001	N/A	0.005	0.002	0.064	1.306

Cycles & misc. transport	50.9	−0.006	0.094	0.268	−0.041	0.186	0.565
Primary aluminum industries	50.9	−0.110	0.061	0.093	0.064	0.043	0.962
Optical & health supplies	39.5	2.038	0.080	0.072	0.043	0.082	1.232
Pottery & related	38.8	0.043	0.074	0.418	0.027	0.094	0.693
Structural clay products	37.5	−0.128	0.080	0.124	0.055	0.032	0.204
Railroad locos.	32.9	0.062	0.111	0.115	0.026	0.145	0.271
Leather products	32.6	−0.336	0.176	0.464	0.196	0.034	1.328
Misc. petroleum	26.3	0.034	0.038	0.074	−0.002	0.046	−0.005
Leather tanning & finish	14.8	−0.188	0.094	0.233	0.045	0.143	0.752
Watches, clocks	12.3	−0.381	N/A	0.613	0.187	0.083	0.793
Mean	227.6	−0.012	0.046	0.126	0.045	−0.073	0.898

NOTE: Changes are log–changes from 1985 to 1994. Domestic demand and exports are deflated by the industry's Producer Price Index. N/A = not available. Import share is calculated as imports divided by domestic supply. Displacement rate is calculated as the number of workers displaced from an industry divided by the number of workers employed in that industry. Export intensity is calculated as exports divided by shipments.

SOURCE: Data on imports, exports, and shipments are from the NBER Trade Database, 1958–1994. Employment data are from the Bureau of Labor Statistics.

Table A3 Industry Import Shares (Imports/Imports + Domestic Supply), 1975, 1980, 1985, 1990, and 1994

Industry	Mean 1975–94	1994	Rank	1990	Rank	1985	Rank	1980	Rank	1975	Rank
Watches, clocks	0.405	0.800	1	0.571	2	0.613	1	0.436	1	0.265	2
Footwear, ex. rubber & plastic	0.377	0.707	2	0.641	1	0.567	2	0.313	4	0.252	3
Leather products, ex. footwear	0.320	0.660	3	0.505	3	0.464	3	0.283	5	0.165	6
Pottery & related products	0.316	0.445	7	0.421	5	0.418	4	0.329	2	0.247	4
Toys & sporting goods	0.265	0.507	4	0.472	4	0.377	5	0.236	7	0.134	9
Cycles & misc. transport. equip.	0.264	0.227	19	0.234	13	0.268	7	0.328	3	0.278	1
Misc. manuf. industries	0.209	0.376	9	0.336	7	0.296	6	0.190	9	0.121	12
Motor vehicles	0.191	0.275	13	0.291	11	0.259	8	0.220	8	0.161	7
Electronic computing equipment	0.188	0.487	5	0.377	6	0.189	15	0.101	25	0.110	14
Leather tanning & finishing	0.172	0.277	12	0.303	10	0.233	10	0.128	17	0.089	19
Apparel & accessories	0.167	0.382	8	0.328	9	0.236	9	0.135	13	0.086	20
Radio, TV, & communication	0.158	0.298	11	0.217	14	0.197	12	0.143	12	0.121	11
Office & accounting machines	0.157	0.451	6	0.335	8	0.162	20	0.074	32	0.075	22
Other primary metal industries	0.156	0.191	22	0.176	22	0.211	11	0.244	6	0.106	16
Pulp, paper & paperboard mills	0.153	0.168	29	0.175	23	0.159	21	0.153	11	0.145	8
Electrical machinery, equip.	0.133	0.313	10	0.264	12	0.178	16	0.120	20	0.074	24
Blast furnaces, steelworks	0.130	0.190	23	0.154	29	0.193	14	0.125	18	0.117	13
Photographic equipment	0.129	0.260	14	0.214	16	0.172	17	0.116	22	0.075	23
Misc. textile mill products	0.128	0.133	38	0.131	33	0.133	27	0.131	16	0.124	10

Imports, Exports, and Jobs 165

Sawmills, planing mills	0.121	0.144	36	0.111	37	0.138	25	0.116	21	0.098	18
Tires & inner tubes	0.120	0.225	20	0.209	17	0.167	19	0.135	14	0.074	25
Sugar & confectionary products	0.120	0.078	50	0.093	44	0.108	34	0.159	10	0.169	5
Farm machinery & equipment	0.118	0.158	31	0.164	25	0.144	24	0.123	19	0.109	15
Metalworking machinery	0.114	0.236	17	0.196	19	0.169	18	0.113	23	0.066	27
Engines & turbines	0.114	0.189	24	0.162	26	0.196	13	0.134	15	0.062	30
Knitting mills	0.101	0.219	21	0.189	20	0.158	22	0.069	36	0.053	36
Machinery, ex. electrical	0.100	0.187	25	0.172	24	0.137	26	0.091	27	0.063	28
Construction & material moving machines	0.098	0.237	16	0.201	18	0.150	23	0.061	40	0.054	34
Scientific & controlling instrmnts	0.098	0.228	18	0.188	21	0.117	31	0.080	30	0.059	31
Other rubber products	0.096	0.243	15	0.217	15	0.074	47	0.096	26	0.054	33
Structural clay products	0.095	0.179	26	0.157	27	0.124	28	0.103	24	0.040	44
Household appliances	0.092	0.168	30	0.150	30	0.121	29	0.072	33	0.062	29
Cutlery, handtools	0.091	0.176	27	0.157	28	0.117	30	0.082	28	0.053	37
Screw machine products	0.088	0.156	33	0.137	32	0.106	35	0.081	29	0.076	21
Petroleum refining	0.083	0.085	48	0.093	43	0.101	36	0.068	38	0.102	17
Industrial & misc. chemicals	0.081	0.132	40	0.110	39	0.111	33	0.076	31	0.056	32
Glass & glass products	0.071	0.129	41	0.105	41	0.093	38	0.057	41	0.040	43
Primary aluminum industries	0.070	0.157	32	0.100	42	0.093	39	0.041	53	0.039	45
Aircraft & parts	0.069	0.176	28	0.147	31	0.079	44	0.070	34	0.043	41
Beverage industries	0.065	0.068	54	0.070	51	0.074	46	0.069	35	0.054	35
Misc. nonmetallic mineral	0.064	0.112	43	0.112	36	0.085	41	0.050	43	0.042	42
Optical & health supplies	0.064	0.115	42	0.108	40	0.072	48	0.062	39	0.048	38
Railroad locomotives	0.064	0.141	37	0.127	34	0.115	32	0.048	46	0.014	59
Yarn, thread, & fabric mills	0.063	0.108	44	0.093	45	0.086	40	0.048	47	0.037	47
Misc. wood products	0.063	0.101	46	0.083	46	0.080	43	0.068	37	0.044	40

Table A3 (continued)

Industry	Mean 1975–94	1994	Rank	1990	Rank	1985	Rank	1980	Rank	1975	Rank
Furniture & fixtures	0.061	0.133	39	0.111	38	0.095	37	0.047	48	0.032	51
Misc. fabricated textile products	0.060	0.148	35	0.120	35	0.083	42	0.046	49	0.029	54
Misc. petroleum & coal products	0.059	0.072	52	0.074	49	0.074	45	0.050	44	0.068	26
Drugs	0.051	0.093	47	0.075	48	0.063	50	0.050	45	0.038	46
Ordnance	0.050	0.153	34	0.076	47	0.043	57	0.039	55	0.037	48
Floor coverings	0.047	0.070	53	0.061	54	0.069	49	0.054	42	0.030	52
Misc. fabricated metal products	0.044	0.085	49	0.070	52	0.059	52	0.039	54	0.035	49
Misc. food preparations	0.044	0.066	55	0.054	57	0.055	53	0.043	51	0.044	39
Wood bldgs. & mobile homes	0.043	0.035	62	0.053	58	0.047	55	0.041	52	0.030	53
Plastics, synthetics, & resins	0.040	0.104	45	0.072	50	0.048	54	0.023	59	0.021	57
Canned and preserved fruits	0.040	0.054	57	0.060	55	0.061	51	0.035	56	0.025	55
Meat products	0.039	0.034	63	0.039	60	0.039	59	0.043	50	0.033	50
Misc. plastics products	0.038	0.076	51	0.066	53	0.045	56	0.031	57	0.021	56
Metal forgings	0.028	0.042	59	0.055	56	0.037	60	0.028	58	0.019	58
Iron & steel foundries	0.025	0.046	58	0.045	59	0.040	58	0.020	60	0.014	61
Ship & boat building & repair	0.022	0.040	60	0.021	65	0.037	61	0.016	61	0.010	64
Guided missiles, space vehicles	0.020	0.057	56	0.031	61	0.027	62	0.014	63	0.011	63
Logging	0.015	0.020	66	0.023	64	0.006	73	0.008	70	0.014	60
Misc. paper & pulp products	0.014	0.025	64	0.018	67	0.024	64	0.014	65	0.007	67
Cement, concrete, gypsum	0.014	0.012	73	0.023	63	0.027	63	0.014	64	0.009	66

Dairy products	0.014	0.017	68	0.016	68	0.016	67	0.015	62	0.010	65
Soaps & cosmetics	0.013	0.039	61	0.026	62	0.021	65	0.009	69	0.005	70
Printing, publishing	0.013	0.021	65	0.018	66	0.015	68	0.013	66	0.012	62
Fabricated structural metal	0.009	0.016	69	0.015	69	0.016	66	0.009	68	0.007	69
Grain mill products	0.009	0.018	67	0.013	70	0.008	71	0.005	72	0.005	71
Tobacco manufactures	0.009	0.008	74	0.004	74	0.005	74	0.011	67	0.007	68
Bakery products	0.007	0.014	71	0.011	71	0.010	69	0.006	71	0.004	72
Paints, varnishes	0.005	0.016	70	0.010	72	0.008	70	0.003	74	0.001	75
Paperboard containers & boxes	0.005	0.013	72	0.009	73	0.007	72	0.004	73	0.002	73
Newspaper publishing & printing	0.002	0.000	75	0.002	75	0.003	75	0.002	75	0.002	74
Mean (column)	0.096	0.171		0.148		0.126		0.090		0.066
Std. deviation	0.086	0.164		0.136		0.122		0.088		0.063

SOURCE: Author's calculations from the NBER Trade Database.

168 Appendix A

Table A4 Changes in Import Prices, by Industry

	Import price change 1980–85	Import price change 1985–92	Import price change 1980–92	Mean import share 1975–94
Watches, clocks	−0.366	0.222	−0.143	0.405
Footwear, ex. rubber & plastic	−0.182	0.084	−0.097	0.377
Leather products, ex. footwear	−0.182	0.084	−0.097	0.320
Pottery & related products	−0.214	0.585	0.370	0.316
Toys & sporting goods	−0.209	0.225	0.016	0.265
Cycles & misc. transport. equip.	0.037	0.199	0.237	0.264
Misc. manuf. industries	−0.087	0.265	0.178	0.209
Motor vehicles	0.025	0.178	0.203	0.191
Electronic computing equipment	−0.276	−0.074	−0.350	0.188
Leather tanning & finishing	−0.134	−0.022	−0.156	0.172
Apparel & accessories	−0.059	0.079	0.020	0.167
Radio, TV, & communication	N/A	0.002	N/A	0.158
Office & accounting machines	−0.276	−0.074	−0.350	0.157
Other primary metal industries	−0.255	0.038	−0.218	0.156
Pulp, paper & paperboard mills	−0.105	−0.073	−0.178	0.153
Electrical machinery, equip.	N/A	0.002	N/A	0.133
Blast furnaces, steelworks	−0.208	0.146	−0.062	0.130
Photographic equipment	−0.274	0.119	−0.155	0.129
Misc. textile mill products	0.050	0.244	0.294	0.128
Sawmills, planning mills	−0.204	0.074	−0.129	0.121
Tires & inner tubes	−0.049	−0.001	−0.050	0.120
Sugar & confectionary products	−0.455	−0.198	−0.653	0.120
Farm machinery & equipment	−0.249	0.249	−0.000	0.118
Metalworking machinery	−0.250	0.318	0.068	0.114
Engines & turbines	−0.249	0.200	−0.050	0.114
Knitting mills	−0.013	0.306	0.292	0.101
Machinery, ex. electrical	−0.249	0.262	0.012	0.100
Construction & material moving machines	−0.241	0.369	0.128	0.098
Scientific & controlling instrmnts	−0.290	0.232	−0.057	0.098
Other rubber products	−0.209	0.149	−0.061	0.096
Structural clay products	−0.125	0.396	0.270	0.095

Table A4 (continued)

	Import price change 1980–85	Import price change 1985–92	Import price change 1980–92	Mean import share 1975–94
Household appliances	N/A	0.242	N/A	0.092
Cutlery, handtools	N/A	–0.109	N/A	0.091
Screw machine products	–0.288	0.130	–0.158	0.088
Industrial & misc. chemicals	–0.083	0.002	–0.081	0.081
Glass & glass products	–0.125	0.396	0.270	0.071
Primary aluminum industries	–0.255	0.038	–0.218	0.070
Aircraft & parts	0.037	0.199	0.237	0.069
Beverage industries	–0.031	0.247	0.216	0.065
Misc. nonmetallic mineral	–0.125	0.396	0.270	0.064
Optical & health supplies	–0.290	0.232	–0.057	0.064
Railroad locomotives	0.037	0.208	0.246	0.064
Yarn, thread, & fabric mills	–0.013	0.290	0.276	0.063
Furniture & fixtures	–0.233	0.140	–0.093	0.061
Misc. fabricated textile products	–0.059	0.079	0.020	0.060
Drugs	–0.083	–0.392	–0.475	0.051
Ordnance	N/A	0.255	N/A	0.050
Floor coverings	–0.013	0.290	0.276	0.047
Misc. fabricated metal products	N/A	0.255	N/A	0.044
Wood bldgs. & mobile homes	–0.204	0.143	–0.061	0.043
Plastics, synthetics, & resins	–0.083	–0.060	–0.143	0.040
Canned and preserved fruits	–0.080	–0.077	–0.157	0.040
Meat products	–0.347	0.033	–0.315	0.039
Misc. plastics products	N/A	0.300	N/A	0.038
Metal forgings	N/A	0.315	N/A	0.028
Iron & steel foundries	–0.255	0.026	–0.229	0.025
Ship & boat building & repair	0.037	0.199	0.237	0.022
Guided missiles, space vehicles	0.037		0.237	0.020
Logging	–0.204	–0.136	–0.340	0.015
Misc. paper & pulp products	–0.105	–0.073	–0.178	0.014
Cement, concrete, gypsum	–0.125	0.396	0.270	0.014
Dairy products	–0.212	0.339	0.127	0.014
Soaps & cosmetics	–0.083	0.062	–0.021	0.013
Fabricated structural metal	N/A	0.251	N/A	0.009

Table A4 (continued)

	Import price change			Mean import share
	1980–85	1985–92	1980–92	1975–94
Paints, varnishes	–0.083	–0.008	–0.090	0.005
Paperboard containers & boxes	–0.105	–0.054	–0.159	0.005
Mean (column)	–0.148	0.140	–0.013	
Std. deviation	0.118	0.173	0.223	

NOTE: Changes are log changes. Where 1980 import price is unavailable, 1981 import price was used as a substitute (making the change "1981–85"). N/A = not available.
SOURCE: Author's calculations from the Bureau of Labor Statistics International Price Index and the NBER Trade Database.

Table A5 Industry Shares of Shipments and Exports, 1980, 1987, and 1994

	Industry share (1980)				Industry share (1987)				Industry share (1994)			
	Shipments	Rank	Exports	Rank	Shipments	Rank	Exports	Rank	Shipments	Rank	Exports	Rank
Meat products	0.033	8	0.012	23	0.032	9	0.017	14	0.032	8	0.016	15
Dairy products	0.018	18	0.002	60	0.019	18	0.002	56	0.016	21	0.002	59
Canned and preserved fruits	0.017	20	0.006	37	0.016	23	0.005	32	0.016	20	0.006	35
Grain mill products	0.013	28	0.017	15	0.015	25	0.012	20	0.015	24	0.009	25
Bakery products	0.010	36	0.000	74	0.009	35	0.000	73	0.008	39	0.001	70
Sugar & confectionary products	0.008	42	0.004	46	0.008	43	0.003	52	0.007	41	0.004	43
Beverage industries	0.021	13	0.003	55	0.020	15	0.003	50	0.019	14	0.004	45
Misc. food preparations	0.020	15	0.030	9	0.019	17	0.022	12	0.017	17	0.016	16
Tobacco manufactures	0.010	35	0.007	34	0.008	42	0.012	21	0.006	46	0.013	20
Knitting mills	0.006	49	0.001	63	0.006	51	0.001	67	0.006	47	0.003	53
Floor coverings	0.003	63	0.002	58	0.004	60	0.001	63	0.004	60	0.002	62
Yarn, thread, & fabric mills	0.012	31	0.009	30	0.011	32	0.005	36	0.010	31	0.005	40
Misc. textile mill products	0.003	68	0.003	53	0.003	66	0.003	49	0.003	64	0.003	49
Apparel & accessories	0.022	12	0.006	36	0.020	14	0.005	37	0.017	19	0.011	23
Misc. fabricated textile products	0.005	53	0.003	51	0.007	46	0.003	54	0.007	43	0.003	52
Pulp, paper & paperboard mills	0.019	17	0.023	12	0.020	16	0.024	11	0.018	15	0.018	13
Misc. paper & pulp products	0.014	25	0.004	44	0.015	24	0.004	38	0.015	23	0.006	37
Paperboard containers & boxes	0.011	33	0.001	66	0.011	33	0.001	62	0.011	29	0.002	57
Newspaper publishing & printing	0.014	26	0.000	75	0.013	28	0.000	74	0.009	36	0.000	75
Printing, publishing	0.032	9	0.007	33	0.040	4	0.008	29	0.036	6	0.009	24
Plastics, synthetics & resins	0.015	21	0.028	10	0.017	20	0.028	9	0.017	18	0.026	9
Drugs	0.015	22	0.012	24	0.016	22	0.017	15	0.018	16	0.018	14
Soaps & cosmetics	0.014	24	0.004	43	0.014	27	0.004	42	0.014	26	0.008	29
Paints, varnishes	0.005	55	0.001	61	0.005	52	0.002	60	0.005	53	0.002	56

Imports, Exports, and Jobs   171

Table A5 (continued)

	Industry share (1980)				Industry share (1987)				Industry share (1994)			
	Shipments	Rank	Exports	Rank	Shipments	Rank	Exports	Rank	Shipments	Rank	Exports	Rank
Industrial & misc. chemicals	0.036	5	0.063	6	0.033	7	0.068	5	0.029	10	0.049	6
Petroleum refining	0.060	2	0.014	20	0.053	2	0.020	13	0.046	4	0.014	18
Misc. petroleum & coal products	0.005	58	0.004	50	0.005	53	0.003	53	0.005	54	0.001	65
Tires & inner tubes	0.004	59	0.003	52	0.004	58	0.003	51	0.004	58	0.004	48
Other rubber products	0.005	54	0.003	54	0.005	54	0.003	48	0.005	51	0.004	46
Misc. plastics products	0.017	19	0.010	27	0.026	10	0.013	18	0.032	7	0.015	17
Leather tanning & finishing	0.001	73	0.002	59	0.001	74	0.002	57	0.001	73	0.002	61
Footwear, ex. rubber & plastic	0.003	64	0.001	70	0.002	67	0.001	66	0.001	70	0.001	66
Leather products, ex. footwear	0.002	71	0.001	71	0.001	72	0.000	69	0.001	74	0.001	68
Logging	0.005	57	0.010	28	0.005	56	0.009	28	0.003	61	0.007	32
Sawmills, planning mills	0.015	23	0.011	25	0.017	19	0.010	23	0.014	25	0.009	26
Wood bldgs. & mobile homes	0.003	65	0.001	73	0.003	65	0.000	75	0.003	65	0.000	74
Misc. wood products	0.004	62	0.001	62	0.004	59	0.001	61	0.004	56	0.002	63
Furniture & fixtures	0.013	29	0.002	57	0.015	26	0.002	55	0.013	27	0.005	42
Glass & glass products	0.007	45	0.005	39	0.007	45	0.004	43	0.006	45	0.005	41
Cement, concrete, gypsum	0.011	32	0.001	72	0.012	29	0.000	72	0.010	33	0.000	72
Structural clay products	0.001	72	0.001	68	0.001	70	0.001	68	0.001	71	0.000	73
Pottery & related products	0.001	74	0.001	67	0.001	73	0.001	64	0.001	72	0.001	67
Misc. nonmetallic mineral	0.007	48	0.005	41	0.006	50	0.004	39	0.005	52	0.004	47
Blast furnaces, steelworks	0.035	6	0.017	16	0.022	12	0.005	33	0.022	12	0.008	30
Iron & steel foundries	0.007	44	0.001	65	0.004	57	0.000	71	0.004	57	0.001	69
Primary aluminum industries	0.011	34	0.010	26	0.008	40	0.005	34	0.007	42	0.006	38
Other primary metal industries	0.014	27	0.033	8	0.012	30	0.016	16	0.011	28	0.019	11

Imports, Exports, and Jobs 173

Cutlery, handtools	0.006	50	0.005	38	0.006	49	0.004	41	0.005	50	0.005	39
Fabricated structural metal	0.019	16	0.010	29	0.017	21	0.004	44	0.015	22	0.004	44
Screw machine products	0.004	61	0.001	64	0.003	62	0.001	65	0.003	63	0.002	58
Metal forgings	0.003	67	0.007	31	0.002	68	0.009	27	0.001	68	0.002	60
Ordnance	0.003	69	0.004	48	0.003	63	0.003	46	0.002	67	0.003	50
Misc. fabricated metal products	0.024	11	0.014	19	0.021	13	0.010	24	0.020	13	0.012	21
Engines & turbines	0.009	40	0.022	13	0.006	47	0.015	17	0.006	48	0.019	12
Farm machinery & equipment	0.010	37	0.013	22	0.005	55	0.007	30	0.006	49	0.008	28
Construction & material moving machines	0.020	14	0.069	4	0.010	34	0.030	8	0.010	32	0.027	8
Metalworking machinery	0.013	30	0.015	17	0.008	38	0.011	22	0.008	37	0.012	22
Office & accounting machines	0.002	70	0.004	47	0.001	69	0.003	47	0.001	69	0.002	55
Electronic computing equipment	0.005	52	0.048	7	0.025	11	0.091	3	0.053	3	0.070	4
Machinery, ex. electrical	0.040	4	0.065	5	0.035	5	0.056	6	0.037	5	0.058	5
Household appliances	0.008	43	0.007	32	0.007	44	0.005	31	0.007	40	0.007	33
Radio, TV, & communication	0.026	10	0.024	11	0.033	6	0.030	7	0.030	9	0.046	7
Electrical machinery, equip.	0.041	3	0.069	3	0.048	3	0.089	4	0.073	2	0.114	1
Motor vehicles	0.068	1	0.074	2	0.085	1	0.097	2	0.093	1	0.108	2
Aircraft & parts	0.033	7	0.089	1	0.032	8	0.106	1	0.023	11	0.083	3
Ship & boat building & repair	0.007	47	0.004	49	0.006	48	0.002	58	0.004	55	0.003	51
Railroad locomotives	0.005	56	0.003	56	0.001	71	0.002	59	0.002	66	0.001	64
Guided missiles, space vehicles	0.007	46	0.005	40	0.011	31	0.004	40	0.006	44	0.002	54
Cycles & misc. transport. equip.	0.003	66	0.004	42	0.003	64	0.005	35	0.003	62	0.007	34
Scientific & controlling instrmnts	0.009	39	0.021	14	0.009	37	0.025	10	0.009	34	0.021	10
Optical & health supplies	0.006	51	0.006	35	0.008	39	0.010	26	0.010	30	0.013	19
Photographic equipment	0.009	41	0.015	18	0.008	41	0.012	19	0.008	38	0.008	27
Watches, clocks	0.001	75	0.001	69	0.001	75	0.000	70	0.000	75	0.000	71
Toys & sporting goods	0.004	60	0.004	45	0.004	61	0.004	45	0.004	59	0.006	36
Misc. manuf industries	0.010	38	0.014	21	0.009	36	0.010	25	0.009	35	0.008	31

SOURCE: Author's calculations from the NBER Trade Database.

174   Appendix A

Table A6 Industry Export Intensity (Exports/Shipments), 1975, 1980, 1985, and 1994

	Mean 1975–94	1994	Rank	1990	Rank	1985	Rank	1980	Rank	1975	Rank
Electronic computing equipment	0.615	0.167	22	0.271	7	0.319	2	0.811	1	1.842	1
Metal forgings	0.345	0.173	21	0.352	2	0.408	1	0.251	3	0.279	4
Aircraft & parts	0.304	0.449	1	0.379	1	0.263	4	0.246	4	0.282	3
Construction & material moving machines	0.303	0.344	3	0.302	4	0.264	3	0.319	2	0.343	2
Engines & turbines	0.244	0.394	2	0.264	8	0.200	5	0.229	5	0.213	6
Scientific & controlling instrmnts	0.233	0.295	4	0.273	6	0.199	6	0.213	7	0.226	5
Logging	0.210	0.266	5	0.278	5	0.140	11	0.199	8	0.205	8
Office & accounting machines	0.192	0.249	8	0.232	10	0.123	13	0.190	9	0.207	7
Cycles & misc. transport. equip.	0.183	0.265	6	0.189	12	0.186	7	0.149	15	0.140	14
Leather tanning & finishing	0.176	0.246	9	0.343	3	0.143	10	0.126	19	0.085	27
Electrical machinery, equip.	0.163	0.197	15	0.215	11	0.129	12	0.154	12	0.141	12
Industrial & misc. chemicals	0.160	0.208	13	0.174	16	0.147	8	0.162	11	0.133	15
Machinery, exc. electrical	0.155	0.199	14	0.178	13	0.121	14	0.150	14	0.158	10
Other primary metal industries	0.146	0.215	12	0.178	14	0.085	21	0.226	6	0.076	31
Ordnance	0.146	0.227	11	0.153	18	0.104	18	0.142	16	0.191	9
Plastics, synthetics & resins	0.144	0.191	18	0.178	15	0.116	16	0.173	10	0.098	24
Farm machinery & equipment	0.143	0.175	20	0.167	17	0.119	15	0.125	20	0.140	13
Photographic equipment	0.136	0.133	29	0.146	19	0.111	17	0.153	13	0.147	11
Tobacco manufactures	0.118	0.252	7	0.238	9	0.064	31	0.061	41	0.037	51

Imports, Exports, and Jobs 175

Metalworking machinery	0.117	0.176	19	0.140	21	0.084	22	0.106	24	0.116	19
Optical & health supplies	0.117	0.162	23	0.145	20	0.082	25	0.106	25	0.117	18
Misc. food preparations	0.113	0.114	35	0.093	35	0.083	24	0.140	17	0.113	20
Watches, clocks	0.110	0.237	10	0.107	28	0.083	23	0.083	31	0.086	26
Railroad locomotives	0.108	0.096	41	0.098	34	0.145	9	0.054	45	0.108	22
Motor vehicles	0.106	0.146	27	0.123	25	0.088	20	0.100	26	0.119	17
Toys & sporting goods	0.106	0.195	16	0.139	22	0.065	29	0.095	27	0.075	32
Misc. textile mill products	0.104	0.151	25	0.137	23	0.079	27	0.114	23	0.080	29
Pulp, paper & paperboard mills	0.103	0.126	31	0.122	26	0.072	28	0.115	22	0.122	16
Radio, TV, & communication	0.102	0.193	17	0.120	27	0.063	32	0.083	30	0.104	23
Misc. manuf. industries	0.099	0.111	36	0.106	29	0.064	30	0.132	18	0.086	25
Pottery & related products	0.098	0.146	26	0.125	24	0.094	19	0.075	34	0.044	48
Drugs	0.091	0.126	32	0.105	32	0.081	26	0.076	33	0.082	28
Grain mill products	0.085	0.080	44	0.070	43	0.059	34	0.121	21	0.109	21
Household appliances	0.084	0.117	33	0.101	33	0.051	36	0.087	28	0.076	30
Cutlery, handtools	0.081	0.135	28	0.105	31	0.054	35	0.078	32	0.068	33
Misc. nonmetallic mineral	0.069	0.100	39	0.084	37	0.060	33	0.064	39	0.054	37
Primary aluminum industries	0.064	0.102	37	0.106	30	0.043	39	0.085	29	0.041	49
Tires & inner tubes	0.064	0.116	34	0.092	36	0.036	43	0.073	35	0.052	42
Glass & glass products	0.062	0.096	40	0.083	39	0.045	38	0.061	42	0.046	47
Other rubber products	0.062	0.101	38	0.084	38	0.042	41	0.060	43	0.048	46
Sawmills, planning mills	0.058	0.075	47	0.068	45	0.036	44	0.069	37	0.053	39
Leather products, ex. footwear	0.055	0.152	24	0.069	44	0.034	47	0.043	54	0.020	62
Yarn, thread, & fabric mills	0.053	0.067	50	0.061	47	0.036	45	0.068	38	0.063	34
Misc. fabricated metal products	0.051	0.076	46	0.057	49	0.035	46	0.054	47	0.049	44
Ship & boat building & repair	0.050	0.076	45	0.076	41	0.022	56	0.049	50	0.031	54

Table A6 (continued)

	Mean 1975–94	1994	Rank	1990	Rank	1985	Rank	1980	Rank	1975	Rank
Misc. plastics products	0.049	0.059	52	0.050	51	0.038	42	0.053	48	0.058	35
Misc. petroleum & coal products	0.048	0.038	65	0.040	59	0.046	37	0.072	36	0.053	38
Guided missiles, space vehicles	0.048	0.048	58	0.041	57	0.032	49	0.060	44	0.040	50
Footwear, ex. rubber & plastic	0.047	0.127	30	0.082	40	0.024	52	0.022	63	0.009	70
Misc. fabricated textile products	0.045	0.048	59	0.035	63	0.028	51	0.063	40	0.056	36
Screw machine products	0.044	0.087	42	0.072	42	0.023	53	0.030	58	0.051	43
Meat products	0.044	0.065	51	0.058	48	0.032	48	0.035	56	0.029	55
Structural clay products	0.042	0.039	64	0.040	58	0.032	50	0.053	49	0.049	45
Floor coverings	0.041	0.056	54	0.051	50	0.020	62	0.054	46	0.034	52
Blast furnaces, steelworks	0.037	0.045	61	0.048	53	0.020	61	0.045	53	0.052	40
Sugar & confectionary products	0.037	0.074	48	0.062	46	0.019	63	0.045	52	0.024	59
Fabricated structural metal	0.035	0.036	66	0.026	67	0.021	60	0.046	51	0.052	41
Soaps & cosmetics	0.034	0.072	49	0.044	54	0.022	55	0.029	59	0.022	61
Canned and preserved fruits	0.034	0.050	57	0.039	61	0.023	54	0.032	57	0.028	56
Petroleum refining	0.033	0.039	63	0.048	52	0.042	40	0.021	64	0.015	64
Misc. wood products	0.032	0.045	62	0.039	60	0.022	57	0.035	55	0.024	58
Paints, varnishes	0.032	0.057	53	0.041	56	0.021	59	0.027	61	0.024	60
Apparel & accessories	0.030	0.082	43	0.042	55	0.012	66	0.025	62	0.013	66
Misc. paper & pulp products	0.030	0.050	56	0.037	62	0.021	58	0.029	60	0.025	57

Furniture & fixtures	0.022	0.048	60	0.031	65	0.013	65	0.017	68	0.012	67
Knitting mills	0.022	0.052	55	0.032	64	0.011	67	0.020	65	0.014	65
Printing, publishing	0.022	0.033	67	0.028	66	0.014	64	0.019	66	0.020	63
Iron & steel foundries	0.019	0.022	70	0.023	68	0.009	69	0.014	69	0.032	53
Beverage industries	0.015	0.029	68	0.019	69	0.009	70	0.013	70	0.008	71
Wood bldgs. & mobile homes	0.012	0.012	73	0.015	71	0.003	73	0.017	67	0.010	68
Paperboard containers & boxes	0.011	0.025	69	0.017	70	0.007	71	0.008	72	0.007	72
Dairy products	0.011	0.017	71	0.009	72	0.011	68	0.008	71	0.010	69
Cement, concrete, gypsum	0.004	0.005	74	0.005	74	0.003	72	0.005	73	0.004	73
Bakery products	0.004	0.012	72	0.007	73	0.002	74	0.002	74	0.001	74
Newspaper publishing & printing	0.001	0.001	75	0.001	75	0.001	75	0.000	75	0.000	75
Mean (across industries)	0.096	0.125		0.112		0.074		0.093		0.084	
Std. deviation	0.095	0.090		0.090		0.071		0.090		0.100	

NOTE: Across-industry mean and standard deviation uses industry shares of total value of shipments as weights.
SOURCE: Author's calculations from the NBER Trade Database.

Table A7 Industry Import Share and Export Intensities, 1980, 1987, and 1994

Industry	Mean trade overlap 1980–94	1980 Import share	1980 Export intensity	1987 Import share	1987 Export intensity	1994 Import share	1994 Export intensity
Footwear, ex. rubber & plastic	0.082	0.313	0.022	0.642	0.046	0.707	0.127
Logging	0.086	0.008	0.199	0.007	0.153	0.020	0.266
Leather products, ex. footwear	0.140	0.283	0.043	0.506	0.040	0.660	0.152
Watches, clocks	0.156	0.436	0.083	0.593	0.070	0.800	0.237
Apparel & accessories	0.174	0.135	0.025	0.285	0.019	0.382	0.082
Tobacco manufactures	0.233	0.011	0.061	0.006	0.123	0.008	0.252
Grain mill products	0.233	0.005	0.121	0.009	0.065	0.018	0.080
Knitting mills	0.253	0.069	0.020	0.151	0.011	0.219	0.052
Pottery & related products	0.312	0.329	0.075	0.444	0.094	0.445	0.146
Blast furnaces, steelworks	0.321	0.125	0.045	0.166	0.020	0.190	0.045
Toys & sporting goods	0.339	0.236	0.095	0.434	0.085	0.507	0.195
Wood bldgs. & mobile homes	0.346	0.041	0.017	0.059	0.002	0.035	0.012
Beverage industries	0.364	0.069	0.013	0.073	0.012	0.068	0.029
Aircraft & parts	0.393	0.070	0.246	0.088	0.270	0.176	0.449
Paints, varnishes	0.400	0.003	0.027	0.016	0.024	0.016	0.057
Furniture & fixtures	0.412	0.047	0.017	0.108	0.013	0.133	0.048
Misc. manuf. industries	0.415	0.190	0.132	0.305	0.090	0.376	0.111
Petroleum refining	0.442	0.068	0.021	0.097	0.032	0.085	0.039
Structural clay products	0.461	0.103	0.053	0.147	0.039	0.179	0.039

Cement, concrete, gypsum	0.465	0.014	0.005	0.026	0.002	0.012	0.005
Plastics, synthetics & resins	0.466	0.023	0.173	0.048	0.135	0.104	0.191
Tires & inner tubes	0.494	0.135	0.073	0.195	0.053	0.225	0.116
Screw machine products	0.500	0.081	0.030	0.124	0.026	0.156	0.087
Motor vehicles	0.540	0.220	0.100	0.294	0.094	0.275	0.146
Misc. wood products	0.579	0.068	0.035	0.084	0.025	0.101	0.045
Construction & material moving machines	0.584	0.061	0.319	0.201	0.241	0.237	0.344
Bakery products	0.586	0.006	0.002	0.011	0.002	0.014	0.012
Misc. fabricated textile products	0.592	0.046	0.063	0.096	0.032	0.148	0.048
Newspaper publishing & printing	0.595	0.002	0.000	0.004	0.001	0.000	0.001
Sugar & confectionary products	0.595	0.159	0.045	0.080	0.028	0.078	0.074
Ship & boat building & repair	0.601	0.016	0.049	0.043	0.025	0.040	0.076
Radio, TV, & communication	0.607	0.143	0.083	0.207	0.074	0.298	0.193
Ordnance	0.610	0.039	0.142	0.052	0.085	0.153	0.227
Iron & steel foundries	0.611	0.020	0.014	0.044	0.008	0.046	0.022
Fabricated structural metal	0.631	0.009	0.046	0.013	0.019	0.016	0.036
Sawmills, planning mills	0.638	0.116	0.069	0.123	0.049	0.144	0.075
Misc. food preparations	0.644	0.043	0.140	0.054	0.094	0.066	0.114
Other rubber products	0.654	0.096	0.060	0.088	0.051	0.243	0.101
Scientific & controlling instruments	0.679	0.080	0.213	0.152	0.218	0.228	0.295
Misc. petroleum & coal products	0.711	0.050	0.072	0.076	0.042	0.072	0.038
Engines & turbines	0.711	0.134	0.229	0.241	0.205	0.189	0.394
Soaps & cosmetics	0.714	0.009	0.029	0.022	0.024	0.039	0.072
Printing, publishing	0.721	0.013	0.019	0.017	0.016	0.021	0.033
Yarn, thread & fabric mills	0.722	0.048	0.068	0.095	0.037	0.108	0.067
Paperboard containers & boxes	0.729	0.004	0.008	0.008	0.009	0.013	0.025

Table A7 (continued)

Industry	Mean trade overlap 1980–94	1980 Import share	1980 Export intensity	1987 Import share	1987 Export intensity	1994 Import share	1994 Export intensity
Household appliances	0.736	0.072	0.087	0.142	0.064	0.168	0.117
Industrial & misc. chemicals	0.743	0.076	0.162	0.116	0.168	0.132	0.208
Misc. paper & pulp products	0.748	0.014	0.029	0.031	0.024	0.025	0.050
Cutlery, handtools	0.749	0.082	0.078	0.147	0.063	0.176	0.135
Drugs	0.752	0.050	0.076	0.073	0.083	0.093	0.126
Guided missiles, space vehicles	0.761	0.014	0.060	0.015	0.032	0.057	0.048
Office & accounting machines	0.762	0.074	0.190	0.257	0.191	0.451	0.249
Other primary metal industries	0.782	0.244	0.226	0.177	0.108	0.191	0.215
Primary aluminum industries	0.783	0.041	0.085	0.111	0.053	0.157	0.102
Railroad locomotives	0.783	0.048	0.054	0.216	0.135	0.141	0.096
Pulp, paper, & paperboard mills	0.794	0.153	0.115	0.163	0.099	0.168	0.126
Floor coverings	0.795	0.054	0.054	0.070	0.022	0.070	0.056
Electronic computing equipment	0.803	0.101	0.811	0.284	0.297	0.487	0.167
Photographic equipment	0.804	0.116	0.153	0.203	0.123	0.260	0.133
Canned and preserved fruits	0.806	0.035	0.032	0.055	0.027	0.054	0.050
Optical & health supplies	0.807	0.062	0.106	0.087	0.097	0.115	0.162
Dairy products	0.815	0.015	0.008	0.016	0.009	0.017	0.017
Metalworking machinery	0.816	0.113	0.106	0.198	0.108	0.236	0.176
Glass & glass products	0.825	0.057	0.061	0.099	0.050	0.129	0.096

Cycles & misc. transport. equip.	0.832	0.328	0.149	0.241	0.141	0.227	0.265
Metal forgings	0.833	0.028	0.251	0.044	0.418	0.042	0.173
Meat products	0.857	0.043	0.035	0.042	0.043	0.034	0.065
Misc. fabricated metal products	0.863	0.039	0.054	0.066	0.041	0.085	0.076
Electrical machinery, equip.	0.863	0.120	0.154	0.206	0.153	0.313	0.197
Misc. nonmetallic mineral	0.869	0.050	0.064	0.108	0.064	0.112	0.100
Misc. plastics products	0.875	0.031	0.053	0.053	0.042	0.076	0.059
Farm machinery & equipment	0.881	0.123	0.125	0.170	0.118	0.158	0.175
Machinery, ex. electrical	0.885	0.091	0.150	0.169	0.132	0.187	0.199
Misc. textile mill products	0.887	0.131	0.114	0.122	0.088	0.133	0.151
Leather tanning & finishing	0.887	0.128	0.126	0.242	0.178	0.277	0.246
Mean (unweighted)	0.613	0.089	0.096	0.139	0.080	0.171	0.124
Std. deviation (unweighted)	0.222	0.088	0.108	0.132	0.077	0.164	0.093

NOTE: Import share is calculated as imports divided by domestic supply; export intensity is calculated as exports divided by shipments. Trade overlap is defined in the text.

SOURCE: Author's calculations from the NBER Trade Database.

Table A8 Long-Period Changes in Industry Employment, Import Share, Exports, and Domestic Demand, 1979–1985

Industry	1979 employment share	Employ. change	Rank	Share of total mfg. employment losses/gains	Import share change	Rank	Export change	Rank	Domestic demand change	Rank
Electrical machinery	0.062	−0.030	61	0.015	0.071	16	0.026	61	0.217	63
Apparel	0.054	−0.175	30	0.070	0.103	8	−0.621	11	0.060	50
Machinery, ex. electric	0.050	−0.113	43	0.043	0.052	19	−0.212	44	0.027	44
Furniture & fixtures	0.049	−0.010	62	0.004	0.048	22	−0.003	59	0.138	59
Motor vehicles	0.049	−0.115	42	0.043	0.086	12	−0.017	57	0.161	60
Printing, publishing	0.039	0.186	70	0.199	0.002	66	−0.068	54	0.288	67
Aircraft & parts	0.029	0.039	65	0.029	0.034	33	0.140	68	0.259	65
Blast furnaces	0.028	−0.634	3	0.107	0.074	14	−1.067	3	−0.553	3
Misc. fabricated metal	0.026	−0.137	38	0.027	0.019	42	−0.358	24	−0.071	26
Fabricated structural metals	0.026	−0.166	32	0.032	0.009	54	−0.742	6	−0.162	16
Sawmills, planing mills	0.023	−0.089	50	0.016	0.003	62	−0.542	15	−0.241	11
Yarn, thread	0.022	−0.291	16	0.045	0.040	28	−0.814	5	−0.139	19
Industrial & misc. chem.	0.021	−0.073	55	0.012	0.040	29	−0.128	51	−0.102	23
Newspaper	0.021	0.069	68	0.037	0.002	67	0.812	75	0.197	61
Metalworking machinery	0.020	−0.178	29	0.026	0.061	18	−0.412	22	−0.183	13
Office & acct machines	0.019	0.260	72	0.141	0.083	13	−0.100	53	0.293	68
Construction machines	0.019	−0.414	8	0.052	0.091	10	−0.478	19	−0.334	8
Electronic computing eqp.	0.018	0.521	74	0.311	0.086	11	0.586	73	0.676	74

Imports, Exports, and Jobs 183

Meat products	0.018	0.010	63	0.005	−0.008	72	−0.235	41	−0.239	12
Misc. plastics products	0.017	0.015	64	0.006	0.013	50	−0.004	58	0.243	64
Metal forgings	0.015	−0.199	26	0.022	0.016	47	0.053	62	−0.048	30
Misc. manuf industries	0.014	−0.145	35	0.015	0.110	6	−0.740	7	0.028	45
Canned fruits	0.012	−0.104	46	0.010	0.023	39	−0.280	34	0.067	52
Cement, concrete, gypsum	0.012	−0.083	52	0.008	0.006	58	−0.335	27	−0.155	18
Pulp, paper	0.012	−0.057	58	0.005	0.004	60	−0.129	50	0.047	47
Iron & steel foundries	0.012	−0.532	5	0.040	0.024	38	−0.720	9	−0.543	4
Beverage	0.012	−0.106	44	0.010	0.002	65	−0.315	31	0.079	54
Bakery	0.012	−0.091	48	0.008	0.005	59	0.150	69	0.055	48
Knitting mills	0.011	−0.139	37	0.012	0.097	9	−0.465	21	−0.057	29
Ship & boat building	0.011	−0.193	27	0.016	0.018	45	−0.300	32	−0.037	34
Paperboard	0.011	−0.084	51	0.007	0.003	61	−0.032	56	0.038	46
Plastics, synthetics	0.011	−0.210	24	0.016	0.024	37	−0.252	39	−0.026	36
Misc. food	0.010	−0.067	56	0.005	0.006	57	−0.560	12	−0.118	21
Glass & glass products	0.010	−0.240	20	0.017	0.038	31	−0.333	28	−0.026	35
Drugs	0.010	0.066	67	0.016	0.012	51	0.175	70	0.301	69
Misc. fab. textile	0.009	−0.033	60	0.002	0.043	26	−0.729	8	0.197	62
Cutlery, handtools	0.009	−0.259	18	0.017	0.044	25	−0.336	26	−0.066	27
Farm machinery & eqp.	0.009	−0.626	4	0.034	0.019	43	−0.547	14	−0.589	2
Dairy products	0.009	−0.102	47	0.007	0.001	68	0.534	72	−0.013	37
Household appliances	0.009	−0.274	17	0.017	0.050	21	−0.506	18	0.011	41
Misc. paper	0.009	0.109	69	0.025	0.009	53	−0.131	49	0.084	55
Petroleum refining	0.008	−0.156	33	0.009	0.026	35	0.764	74	−0.129	20
Misc. nonmetallic mineral	0.008	−0.498	6	0.025	0.039	30	−0.149	48	−0.102	22
Footwear	0.007	−0.406	9	0.020	0.219	2	0.078	64	0.058	49

Table A8 (continued)

Industry	1979 employment share	Employ. change	Rank	Share of total mfg. employment losses/gains	Import share change	Rank	Export change	Rank	Domestic demand change	Rank
Other rubber products	0.007	−0.169	31	0.009	−0.012	73	−0.233	42	−0.012	38
Engines & turbines	0.007	−0.323	11	0.016	0.113	5	−0.256	38	−0.042	32
Grain mill	0.007	−0.143	36	0.008	0.003	63	−0.361	23	−0.011	39
Misc. wood products	0.007	−0.117	41	0.006	0.014	49	−0.325	30	−0.041	33
Soaps & cosmetics	0.007	0.056	66	0.010	0.011	52	−0.237	40	0.125	58
Photographic eqp.	0.007	−0.090	49	0.005	0.052	20	−0.350	25	0.096	56
Scientific & controlling	0.006	0.515	73	0.107	0.042	27	0.116	66	0.283	66
Tires & inner tubes	0.006	−0.303	13	0.013	0.038	32	−0.272	35	−0.180	14
Toys & sporting goods	0.006	−0.242	19	0.010	0.148	4	−0.476	20	0.064	51
Screw machine products	0.006	−0.187	28	0.008	0.018	46	−0.327	29	−0.171	15
Radio, TV	0.006	−0.315	12	0.012	0.046	23	0.107	65	0.445	73
Sugar products	0.006	−0.135	39	0.006	−0.031	75	−0.158	47	−0.047	31
Other primary metal	0.005	−0.204	25	0.008	0.022	40	−1.139	2	−0.248	10
Guided missiles	0.005	0.557	75	0.093	0.018	44	−0.002	60	0.767	75
Logging	0.004	−0.047	59	0.002	−0.004	71	−0.652	10	−0.101	24
Wood bldgs. & mobile	0.004	−0.147	34	0.005	0.000	69	−1.592	1	−0.356	7
Railroad locos	0.004	−0.815	1	0.017	0.063	17	−0.260	37	−1.396	1
Paints, varnishes	0.003	−0.079	53	0.002	0.006	56	−0.123	52	0.074	53
Primary aluminum industries	0.003	−0.296	15	0.007	0.045	24	−0.298	33	−0.304	9

Misc. textile	0.003	−0.237	22	0.006	0.014	48	−0.230	43	−0.157	17
Ordnance	0.003	0.197	71	0.017	0.003	64	−0.260	36	0.364	71
Floor coverings	0.003	−0.106	45	0.002	0.022	41	−0.524	17	0.026	43
Tobacco	0.003	−0.079	54	0.002	−0.002	70	−0.066	55	0.364	70
Cycles & misc. transport	0.003	−0.065	57	0.001	−0.022	74	0.410	71	0.006	40
Structural clay products	0.003	−0.329	10	0.006	0.032	34	−0.537	16	−0.088	25
Leather products	0.003	−0.444	7	0.007	0.195	3	−0.555	13	−0.063	28
Pottery & related	0.002	−0.237	21	0.004	0.105	7	0.061	63	0.022	42
Optical & health supplies	0.002	−0.133	40	0.002	0.008	55	0.137	67	0.403	72
Misc. petroleum	0.002	−0.215	23	0.003	0.024	36	−0.183	46	0.097	57
Watches, clocks	0.001	−0.812	2	0.006	0.226	1	−0.841	4	−0.415	5
Leather tanning & finish	0.001	−0.296	14	0.002	0.073	15	−0.192	45	−0.359	6

NOTE: Changes are log changes. Share of total mfg. employment losses/gains: if industry i employment change is negative, measure equals industry i employment change/total mfg. employment losses; if if industry i employment change is positive, measure equals industry i employment change/total mfg. employment gains.

Appendix A

Table A9 Long-Period Changes in Industry Employment, Import Share, Exports, and Domestic Demand, 1985–1994

Industry	1985 employment share	Employ. change	Rank	Share of total mfg. employment losses/gains	Import share change	Rank	Export change	Rank	Domestic demand change	Rank
Electrical machinery	0.066	−0.072	31	0.054	0.135	8	1.146	55	0.456	66
Furniture & fixtures	0.053	0.023	52	0.028	0.038	30	1.478	68	0.254	47
Printing, publishing	0.051	0.108	66	0.132	0.006	52	1.038	46	0.304	54
Apparel	0.050	−0.222	13	0.118	0.146	6	1.965	75	0.223	41
Machinery, ex. electric	0.049	−0.000	46	0.000	0.050	25	0.757	27	0.302	53
Motor vehicles	0.048	0.029	54	0.032	0.016	43	0.800	32	0.323	58
Electronic computing eqp.	0.034	−0.285	9	0.099	0.298	1	0.595	19	0.475	67
Aircraft & parts	0.033	−0.247	11	0.087	0.097	13	0.550	16	−0.026	6
Radio, TV	0.031	−0.297	8	0.094	0.101	12	1.205	58	0.014	8
Office & acct. machines	0.027	−0.345	5	0.094	0.289	2	0.249	6	−0.331	2
Misc. fabricated metal	0.025	0.002	48	0.001	0.026	37	0.952	40	0.180	32
Newspaper	0.024	−0.004	44	0.001	−0.003	64	0.307	9	0.128	23
Fabricated structural metals	0.024	−0.067	32	0.018	0.000	62	0.712	24	0.172	28
Sawmills, planing mills	0.023	0.070	61	0.038	0.005	53	0.949	39	0.494	68
Industrial & misc. chem.	0.021	−0.076	30	0.019	0.021	41	0.477	13	0.126	22
Meat products	0.020	0.221	72	0.109	−0.006	66	0.944	38	0.184	33
Misc. plastics products	0.019	0.346	75	0.173	0.031	32	1.039	47	0.556	72
Yarn, thread	0.018	−0.159	20	0.032	0.022	39	0.871	34	0.164	26
Metalworking machinery	0.018	−0.026	40	0.005	0.068	17	0.900	37	0.226	42

Imports, Exports, and Jobs

Blast furnaces	0.016	−0.235	12	0.041	−0.003	65	1.084	50	0.187	34
Construction & material moving machines	0.014	−0.179	16	0.027	0.087	15	0.287	8	0.061	11
Metal forgings	0.013	−0.043	36	0.007	0.005	54	−0.801	1	0.161	25
Misc. manuf. industries	0.013	0.145	67	0.045	0.080	16	0.773	29	0.410	64
Pulp, paper	0.013	−0.057	34	0.008	0.010	48	0.772	28	0.207	38
Cement, concrete, gypsum	0.012	−0.056	35	0.008	−0.014	71	0.732	25	0.121	18
Canned fruits	0.012	0.086	62	0.024	−0.007	69	1.022	45	0.236	44
Bakery	0.012	−0.020	41	0.003	0.004	55	1.911	74	0.189	35
Scientific & controlling	0.012	−0.161	19	0.039	0.112	10	0.593	18	0.244	46
Beverage	0.012	−0.192	14	0.024	−0.006	67	1.369	65	0.171	27
Drugs	0.011	0.246	74	0.070	0.030	34	0.889	35	0.754	74
Knitting mills	0.011	−0.003	45	0.000	0.061	20	1.907	73	0.353	61
Paperboard	0.011	0.088	63	0.022	0.006	51	1.519	70	0.301	52
Misc. food	0.011	0.099	65	0.025	0.011	46	0.445	12	0.121	19
Misc. paper	0.011	0.223	73	0.059	0.001	60	1.125	54	0.262	48
Ship & boat building	0.010	−0.165	18	0.018	0.003	56	1.165	56	−0.026	5
Misc. fab. textile	0.010	0.171	69	0.041	0.065	18	0.891	36	0.383	62
Guided missiles	0.010	−0.500	2	0.045	0.030	33	0.075	4	−0.316	4
Plastics, synthetics	0.009	−0.063	33	0.007	0.056	23	0.859	33	0.317	56
Dairy products	0.009	−0.092	28	0.009	0.001	59	0.493	14	0.111	16
Glass & glass products	0.008	−0.026	39	0.003	0.036	31	0.994	43	0.199	36
Soaps & cosmetics	0.008	0.039	56	0.007	0.019	42	1.459	67	0.264	49
Cutlery, handtools	0.008	−0.101	27	0.009	0.059	21	1.048	48	0.199	37
Iron & steel foundries	0.008	−0.122	23	0.011	0.006	50	0.990	42	0.121	21
Petroleum refining	0.008	−0.261	10	0.021	−0.016	72	0.053	3	−0.361	1

Table A9 (continued)

Industry	1985 employment share	Employ. change	Rank	Share of total mfg. employment losses/gains	Import share change	Rank	Export change	Rank	Domestic demand change	Rank
Household appliances	0.007	−0.090	29	0.007	0.047	27	1.108	52	0.173	30
Grain mill	0.007	0.028	53	0.004	0.011	47	0.495	15	0.297	51
Misc. wood products	0.007	0.098	64	0.016	0.022	40	1.050	49	0.520	71
Other rubber products	0.007	−0.036	37	0.003	0.169	5	1.124	53	0.394	63
Photographic eqp	0.007	−0.329	7	0.022	0.088	14	0.378	10	0.174	31
Engines & turbines	0.006	−0.156	21	0.010	−0.007	68	0.798	31	−0.010	7
Footwear	0.005	−0.544	1	0.027	0.140	7	1.297	61	0.028	9
Sugar products	0.005	0.012	50	0.001	−0.031	74	1.531	71	0.081	12
Farm machinery & eqp.	0.005	0.064	60	0.008	0.014	45	0.705	23	0.353	60
Screw machine products	0.005	−0.004	43	0.000	0.049	26	1.457	66	0.139	24
Misc. nonmetallic mineral	0.005	0.052	58	0.013	0.027	36	0.616	20	0.121	20
Toys & sporting goods	0.005	0.194	71	0.025	0.130	9	1.495	69	0.512	69
Tires & inner tubes	0.005	−0.177	17	0.010	0.058	22	1.316	63	0.035	10
Other primary metal	0.005	−0.119	24	0.006	−0.020	73	1.092	51	0.172	29
Logging	0.005	−0.028	38	0.001	0.014	44	0.679	21	0.514	70
Ordnance	0.004	−0.370	4	0.015	0.109	11	0.385	11	−0.325	3
Wood bldgs. & mobile	0.004	0.021	51	0.002	−0.013	70	1.699	72	0.325	59
Paints, varnishes	0.003	−0.101	26	0.004	0.008	49	1.179	57	0.240	45
Floor coverings	0.003	0.161	68	0.012	0.002	58	1.244	60	0.115	17

Misc. textile	0.003	0.006	49	0.000	0.000	61	1.017	44	0.308	55
Tobacco	0.003	0.001	47	0.000	0.002	57	1.306	62	0.231	43
Cycles & misc. transport	0.003	−0.006	42	0.000	−0.041	75	0.565	17	0.275	50
Primary aluminum industries	0.003	−0.110	25	0.003	0.064	19	0.962	41	0.091	14
Optical & health supplies	0.002	0.189	70	0.065	0.043	29	1.232	59	0.610	73
Pottery & related	0.002	0.043	57	0.002	0.027	35	0.693	22	0.317	57
Structural clay products	0.002	−0.128	22	0.003	0.055	24	0.204	5	0.105	15
Railroad locos	0.002	0.062	59	0.003	0.026	38	0.271	7	0.813	75
Leather products	0.002	−0.336	6	0.006	0.196	3	1.328	64	0.208	39
Misc. petroleum	0.001	0.034	55	0.001	−0.002	63	−0.005	2	0.089	13
Leather tanning & finish	0.001	−0.188	15	0.002	0.045	28	0.752	26	0.450	65
Watches, clocks	0.001	−0.381	3	0.003	0.187	4	0.793	30	0.215	40

NOTE: Changes are log changes. Share of total mfg. employment losses/gains: if industry i employment change is negative, measure equals industry i employment change/total mfg. employment losses; if if industry i employment change is positive, measure equals industry i employment change/total mfg. employment gains.

Table A10 Industry Displacements, Changes in Employment, and Changes in Import Share and Exports, 1979–1994

	Share of 1979 employment	Employ. change 1979–94	Total displaced 1979–94	Share of total displaced	Mean displace rate	Mean import share	Import share change	Import price change	Exports change
Electrical machinery	0.062	−0.102	822901	0.070	0.042	0.155	0.206	N/A	1.172
Apparel	0.054	−0.397	748325	0.064	0.052	0.194	0.250	0.020	1.343
Machinery, exc. electrical	0.050	−0.114	633346	0.054	0.044	0.113	0.102	0.012	0.544
Furniture & fixtures	0.049	0.013	374982	0.032	0.024	0.070	0.087	−0.093	1.476
Motor vehicles	0.049	−0.085	675574	0.057	0.051	0.217	0.101	0.203	0.783
Printing, publishing	0.039	0.294	580815	0.049	0.038	0.014	0.008	N/A	0.969
Aircraft & parts	0.029	−0.207	282846	0.024	0.029	0.080	0.132	0.237	0.690
Blast furnaces	0.028	−0.869	333094	0.028	0.061	0.143	0.071	−0.062	0.017
Misc. fabricated metal	0.026	−0.135	234805	0.020	0.032	0.050	0.045	N/A	0.594
Fabricated structural metals	0.026	−0.233	386332	0.033	0.056	0.011	0.009	N/A	−0.029
Sawmills, planing mills	0.023	−0.019	261766	0.022	0.039	0.124	0.008	−0.129	0.407
Yarn, thread	0.022	−0.450	237402	0.020	0.042	0.068	0.062	0.276	0.057
Industrial & misc. chem.	0.021	−0.149	188667	0.016	0.031	0.089	0.062	−0.081	0.349
Newspaper	0.021	0.065	163512	0.014	0.025	0.002	−0.001	N/A	1.119
Metalworking machinery	0.020	−0.203	177442	0.015	0.036	0.130	0.129	0.068	0.488
Office & acct. machines	0.019	−0.085	31820	0.003	0.008	0.181	0.372	−0.350	0.149
Construction & material moving machines	0.019	−0.593	251471	0.021	0.057	0.113	0.177	0.128	−0.191
Electronic computing eqp.	0.018	0.236	394949	0.034	0.046	0.214	0.384	−0.350	1.180
Meat products	0.018	0.232	197206	0.017	0.032	0.039	−0.014	−0.315	0.710

Imports, Exports, and Jobs   191

Misc. plastics products	0.017	0.361	293087	0.025	0.047	0.043	0.044	N/A	1.035
Metal forgings	0.015	-0.241	82316	0.007	0.027	0.032	0.021	N/A	-0.748
Misc. manuf industries	0.014	0.129	219224	0.019	0.054	0.234	0.190	0.178	0.033
Canned fruits	0.012	-0.018	115909	0.010	0.033	0.043	0.016	-0.157	0.742
Cement, concrete, gypsum	0.012	-0.139	122308	0.010	0.035	0.015	-0.008	0.270	0.397
Pulp, paper	0.012	-0.114	73250	0.006	0.023	0.154	0.014	-0.178	0.644
Iron & steel foundries	0.012	-0.654	123928	0.011	0.051	0.028	0.030	-0.229	0.270
Beverage	0.012	-0.299	69384	0.006	0.022	0.066	-0.003	0.216	1.054
Bakery	0.012	-0.111	93518	0.008	0.027	0.008	0.009	N/A	2.060
Knitting mills	0.011	-0.142	63980	0.005	0.020	0.114	0.159	0.292	1.441
Ship & boat building	0.011	-0.358	227173	0.019	0.075	0.025	0.021	0.237	0.865
Paperboard	0.011	0.004	74640	0.006	0.024	0.006	0.009	-0.159	1.487
Plastics, synthetics	0.011	-0.273	69623	0.006	0.027	0.044	0.081	-0.143	0.608
Misc. food	0.010	0.032	131110	0.011	0.040	0.047	0.017	N/A	-0.115
Glass & glass products	0.010	-0.266	125742	0.011	0.048	0.075	0.074	0.270	0.661
Drugs	0.010	0.312	68042	0.006	0.022	0.057	0.041	-0.475	1.064
Misc. fab. textile	0.009	0.138	96492	0.008	0.037	0.068	0.109	0.020	0.162
Cutlery, handtools	0.009	-0.359	47530	0.004	0.029	0.103	0.103	N/A	0.712
Farm machinery & eqp.	0.009	-0.562	110815	0.009	0.066	0.127	0.033	-0.000	0.158
Dairy products	0.009	-0.194	115101	0.010	0.044	0.015	0.002	0.127	1.027
Household appliances	0.009	-0.364	93327	0.008	0.047	0.105	0.097	N/A	0.603
Misc. paper	0.009	0.331	82257	0.007	0.028	0.016	0.010	-0.178	0.994
Petroleum refining	0.008	-0.417	41568	0.004	0.026	0.089	0.010	N/A	0.817
Misc. nonmetallic mineral	0.008	-0.446	61299	0.005	0.049	0.071	0.066	0.270	0.467
Footwear	0.007	-0.950	144385	0.012	0.091	0.436	0.359	-0.097	1.375
Other rubber products	0.007	-0.205	81614	0.007	0.051	0.111	0.157	-0.061	0.892

Table A10 (continued)

	Share of 1979 employment	Employ. change 1979–94	Total displaced 1979–94	Share of total displaced	Mean displace rate	Mean import share	Import share change	Import price change	Exports change
Engines & turbines	0.007	−0.479	59276	0.005	0.039	0.130	0.106	−0.050	0.541
Grain mill	0.007	−0.115	60978	0.005	0.033	0.009	0.013	N/A	0.134
Misc. wood products	0.007	−0.019	63757	0.005	0.036	0.069	0.035	N/A	0.726
Soaps & cosmetics	0.007	0.094	72412	0.006	0.035	0.015	0.030	−0.021	1.223
Photographic eqp	0.007	−0.419	40442	0.003	0.030	0.147	0.140	−0.155	0.028
Scientific & controlling	0.006	0.354	111831	0.010	0.024	0.111	0.154	−0.057	0.709
Tires & inner tubes	0.006	−0.479	60039	0.005	0.044	0.140	0.096	−0.050	1.044
Toys & sporting goods	0.006	−0.047	115307	0.010	0.068	0.301	0.278	0.016	1.019
Screw machine products	0.006	−0.192	22430	0.002	0.029	0.100	0.067	−0.158	1.130
Radio, TV	0.006	−0.380	279570	0.024	0.126	0.179	0.147	N/A	1.312
Sugar products	0.006	−0.122	45218	0.004	0.039	0.118	−0.062	−0.653	1.373
Other primary metal	0.005	−0.322	95218	0.008	0.076	0.168	0.002	−0.218	−0.047
Guided missiles	0.005	0.057	177594	0.015	0.080	0.023	0.048	0.237	0.073
Logging	0.004	−0.075	74568	0.006	0.060	0.013	0.010	−0.340	0.027
Wood bldgs. & mobile	0.004	−0.126	90571	0.008	0.099	0.043	−0.012	−0.061	0.107
Railroad locos.	0.004	−0.753	41625	0.004	0.108	0.076	0.089	0.246	0.011
Paints, varnishes	0.003	−0.180	24381	0.002	0.044	0.006	0.014	−0.090	1.055
Primary aluminum industries	0.003	−0.405	62610	0.005	0.070	0.074	0.109	−0.218	0.664
Misc. textile	0.003	−0.231	22612	0.002	0.042	0.124	0.015	0.294	0.788
Ordnance	0.003	−0.173	48565	0.004	0.059	0.055	0.112	N/A	0.125

Floor coverings	0.003	0.055		0.003	0.049	0.051	0.024	0.276	0.720
Cycles & misc. transport	0.003	-0.071	33619	0.005	0.094	0.271	-0.063	0.237	0.975
Structural clay products	0.003	-0.457	60810	0.001	0.084	0.106	0.088	0.270	-0.333
Leather products	0.003	-0.779	14464	0.004	0.142	0.361	0.391	-0.097	0.773
Pottery & related	0.002	-0.195	49057	0.002	0.072	0.347	0.133	0.370	0.754
Optical & health supplies	0.002	0.425	23462	0.011	0.126	0.072	0.051	-0.057	1.368
Misc. petroleum	0.002	-0.181	130452	0.001	0.074	0.064	0.022	N/A	-0.188
Watches, clocks	0.001	-0.697	8048	0.001	0.091	0.458	0.413	-0.143	-0.048
Leather tanning & finish	0.001	-0.296	7025	0.000	0.074	0.190	0.117	-0.156	0.560
			3530						
Mean (weighted)		-0.153	309515	0.026	0.043	0.104	0.097	-0.0125*	0.716
Std. deviation (weighted)		0.272	255785	0.022	0.018	0.077	0.098	0.2226*	0.525

NOTE: * = unweighted mean and standard deviation; N/A denotes not available.
SOURCE: Author's calculations from the Displaced Worker Surveys, the NBER Trade Database, and the Bureau of Labor Statistics International Price Index.

Appendix B

CONSTRUCTION OF INSTRUMENTS

Industry exchange rate indices

Industry exchange rate indices are constructed as follows:

$$\text{RER}_{k,t} = \frac{\sum_{i=1}^{j} \text{ERI}_{i,t} \times \text{SHIMP}_{k,i}}{\text{PPI}_{\text{US},t}}$$

where $\text{RER}_{k,t}$ is the real exchange rate index for industry k in year t, $\text{ERI}_{i,t}$ is the nominal exchange rate index for country i in year t, j is the number of countries that account for at least 2 percent of imports for industry k, $\text{SHIMP}_{k,i}$ is country i's share of total imports into the United States for industry k in 1984, and $\text{PPI}_{\text{US},t}$ is the U.S. producer price index for year t.

Nominal exchange rate indices are constructed in the following manner:

$$\text{ERI}_{i,t} = \frac{\text{ER}_{i,t}\, \text{ER}_{i,1990}}{\text{ER}_{i,1990}} \times 100 + 100$$

where $\text{ER}_{i,t}$ is the U.S.-country i bilateral nominal exchange rate (measured in national currency units per US\$) and $\text{ERI}_{i,1990}$ is set = 100.

Industry foreign cost indices

Industry foreign cost indices are constructed as follows:

$$\text{RFC}_{k,t} = \frac{\sum_{i=1}^{j} \text{PPI}_{i,t} \times \text{SHIMP}_{k,i}}{\text{PPI}_{\text{US},t}}$$

where $\text{RFC}_{k,t}$ is the real foreign cost index for industry k for year t,

$PPI_{i,t}$ is the producer price index for country i for year t, and the other variables are defined as above.

Data definitions and sources

The bilateral nominal exchange rates (U.S.-country i) for all countries, except for Hong Kong, and Taiwan, were taken from the International Monetary Fund's International Financial Statistics and cover the period 1978–1994. The nominal exchange rate for each country in year t is measured as an average of the monthly exchange rates (line rf in *International Financial Statistics*). The bilateral nominal exchange rates for Hong Kong and Taiwan were taken from the Penn World Tables and cover the period 1978–1992 for Hong Kong and 1978–1990 for Taiwan.

The consumer price index was used whenever the producer price index was unavailable. For all countries except for Hong Kong, Taiwan, and China, the price indices were taken from the International Monetary Fund's International Financial Statistics and cover the period 1978–1994, with the exception of Costa Rica (1978–1993), Nicaragua (1978–1992), Uruguay (1978–1993) and Romania (1978–1990).

Countries omitted

Macao, the Soviet Union, and Yugoslavia were omitted from the calculations because data for these countries was unavailable. Macao accounted for 4 percent of imports in SIC 239 and 2 percent of imports in SIC 394; the Soviet Union accounted for 17 percent of imports of SIC 287; Yugoslavia accounted for 3 percent of imports in SIC 259 and 2 percent of imports in SIC 348.

Data limitations

Source weights for the industry exchange rates were calculated from information on industry imports by country of origin. To minimize the degree of industry aggregation required in the calculations, only the subset of three-digit CIC industries that correspond to a single three-digit SIC industry was used to calculate the instruments. Thus, the IV import price analysis must be limited to this subset of industries.

First-stage estimates

First-stage estimates of the relationship between industry real import price and the two instruments, a source-weighted exchange rate and a source-weighted index of foreign production costs, are reported in Table B1. The fit of the first-stage regression is reasonable (R^2 = 0.324), and the signs of the estimated coefficients are as predicted and statistically significant. As the industry exchange rate increases (more national currency units per U.S. dollar), the import price index increases and, as foreign production costs increase, so do import prices.

Table B1 First-Stage Import Price Regression

Model:	1
No. obs:	290
Trade-weighted exchange rate	−0.3586**
	(0.1273)
Relative foreign costs	0.0405
	(0.2484)
Index of ind. production	0.0037*
	(0.0014)
Change R&D intensity	0.0066
	(0.0077)
ln(capital-output ratio)	−0.0064
	(0.0186)
Change ln(alternative wage)	−0.0320
	(0.0597)
Constant	−0.0378
	(0.0194)
Year effects	Yes
R^2	0.477
Exchange rate = 0: Pr > F	0.015
Relative foreign costs = 0: Pr > F	0.986

NOTE: Specification includes one lag in trade-weighted exchange rate and relative foreign costs. * = significant at the 5% level. ** = significant at 1% level.

References

Abowd, John M. 1991. "The NBER Immigration, Trade, and Labor Markets Data Files." In *Immigration, Trade and the Labor Market*, J.M. Abowd and R.B. Freeman, eds. Chicago: University of Chicago Press, pp. 407–422.

Abraham, Katherine G., and James A. Medoff. 1984. "Length of Service and Layoffs in Union and Nonunion Work Groups." *Industrial and Labor Relations Review* 38(October): 87–97.

Addison, John, Douglas A. Fox, and Christopher J. Ruhm. 1995. "Trade and Displacement in Manufacturing." *Monthly Labor Review* 118(April): 58–67.

Aho, C. Michael, and James A. Orr. 1980. "Demographic and Occupational Characteristics of Workers in Trade-Sensitive Industries." Economic Discussion Paper 2, U.S. Department of Labor, Bureau of International Labor Affairs (April).

Autor, David H., Lawrence F. Katz, and Alan B. Krueger. 1997. "Computing Inequality: Have Computers Changed the Labor Market?" Working paper 5956, National Bureau of Economic Research, Cambridge, Massachusetts.

Bartel, A., and F. Lichtenberg. 1987. "The Comparative Advantage of Educated Workers in Implementing New Technology." *The Review of Economics and Statistics* 69(1): 1–11.

Bednarzik, Robert W. 1993. "Analysis of U.S. Industries Sensitive to International Trade." *Monthly Labor Review* 116(2): 15–31.

Belman, Dale, and Thea M. Lee. 1996. "International Trade and the Performance of U.S. Labor Markets." In *International Trade: Theory and Measuremen*, Robert Blecker, ed. New York: M.E. Sharpe, pp. 61–107.

Berman, Eli, John Bound, and Zvi Griliches. 1994. "Changes in the Demand for Skilled Labor within U.S. Manufacturing Industries: Evidence from the Annual Survey of Manufacturing." *Quarterly Journal of Economics* 109(2): 367–397.

Berman, Eli, John Bound, and Stephen Machin. 1998. "Implications of Skill-Biased Technological Change: International Evidence." *Quarterly Journal of Economics* 113(4): 1245–1279.

Bernard, Andrew B., and J. Bradford Jensen. 1995. "Exporters, Jobs and Wages in U.S. Manufacturing: 1976–1987." *Brookings Papers on Economic Activity: Microeconomics,* pp. 67–119.

_____. 1997. "Exporters, Skill-Upgrading, and the Wage Gap." *Journal of International Economics* 42(1–2): 3–31.

Blanchflower, David G. 2000. "Globalization and the Labor Market." Paper commissioned by the U.S. Trade Deficit Review Commission, September.

Blanchflower, David G., and Matthew J. Slaughter. 1999. "Causes and Consequences of Changing Earnings Inequality: W(h)ither the Debate?" In *Growing Apart: The Causes and Consequences of Global Wage Inequality*, Albert Fishlow and Karen Parker, eds. Washington, D.C.: Council on Foreign Relations, pp. 67–94.

Borjas, George J., Richard B. Freeman, and Lawrence F. Katz. 1992. "On the Labor Market Effects of Immigration and Trade." In *Immigration and the Work Force: Economic Consequences for the United States and Source Areas*, G.J. Borjas and R.B. Freeman, eds. Chicago: University of Chicago Press, pp. 213–244.

———. 1997. "How Much Do Immigration and Trade Affect Labor Market Outcomes?" *Brookings Papers on Economic Activity*, no. 1: 1–90.

Brechling, Frank. 1978. "A Time Series Analysis of Labor Turnover." In *The Impact of International Trade and Investment on Employment*, William G. Dewald, ed. Washington, D.C.: Bureau of International Labor Affairs, U.S. Department of Labor, pp. 67–86.

Brown, Drusilla K., Alan V. Deardorff, and Robert M. Stern. 2002. "CGE Modeling and Analysis of Multilateral and Regional Negotiating Options." In *Issues and Options for U.S.-Japan Trade Policies*, R.M. Stern, ed. Ann Arbor: University of Michigan Press.

Burtless, Gary. 1995. "International Trade and the Rise in Earnings Inequality." *Journal of Economic Literature* 33(2): 800–816.

Burtless, Gary, Robert Z. Lawrence, Robert E. Litan, and Robert J. Shapiro. 1998. *Globaphobia: Confronting Fears about Open Trade*. Washington, D.C.: Brookings Institution.

Cline, William R. 1997. *Trade, Jobs and Income Distribution*. Washington, D.C.: Institute for International Economics.

Collins, Susan M., ed. 1998. *Imports, Exports and the American Worker*. Washington, D.C.: Brookings Institution Press.

Comanor, William S., and Thomas A. Wilson. 1974. *Advertising and Market Power*. Cambridge: Harvard University Press, pp. 88–92.

Council of Economic Advisers. 1999. *Economic Report of the President: transmitted to the Congress*. Washington, D.C.: Government Printing Office, February.

———. 2001. *Economic Report of the President: transmitted to the Congress*. Washington, D.C.: Government Printing Office, January.

Current Population Surveys. March 1962–1997. [machine-readable data files]/conducted by the Bureau of the Census for the Bureau of Labor Statistics. Washington, D.C.: Bureau of the Census [producer and distributor], 1962–1997. Santa Monica, California: Unicon Research Corporation [producer and distributor of CPS Utilities], 1998.

Davis, Steven J., John C. Haltiwanger, and Scott Schuh. 1996. *Job Creation and Destruction.* Cambridge: MIT Press.

Deardorff, Alan V. 1993. "Overview of the Stolper-Samuelson Theorem." In *The Stolper-Samuelson Theorem: A Golden Jubilee,* Alan V. Deardorff and Robert M. Stern, eds. Ann Arbor, Michigan: University of Michigan Press, pp. 3–6.

Decker, Paul, and Walter Corson. 1995. "International Trade and Worker Displacement: Evaluation of the Trade Adjustment Assistance Program." *Industrial and Labor Relations Review* 48(4): 758–774.

Dickens, William T. 1988. "The Effects of Trade on Employment: Techniques and Evidence." In *The Dynamics of Trade and Employment,* Laura D'Andrea Tyson, William T. Dickens, and John Zysman, eds. Cambridge, Massachusetts: Ballinger Publishing Company, pp. 41–85.

Economic Policy Institute. 2001. *NAFTA At Seven: Its Impact on Workers in All Three Nations.* Washington, D.C.: Economic Policy Institute.

Farber, Henry S. 1993. "The Incidence and Costs of Job Loss: 1982–91." *Brookings Papers on Economic Activity: Microeconomics* 1993: 73–119.

———. 1997. "The Changing Face of Job Loss in the United States, 1981–1995." *Brookings Papers on Economic Activity: Microeconomics* 1997: 55–142.

Feenstra, Robert C. 1996. "U.S. Imports, 1972–1994: Data and Concordances." Working Paper 5515, National Bureau of Economic Research, Cambridge, Massachusetts.

———. 1998. "Integration of Trade and Disintegration of Production in the Global Economy." *Journal of Economic Perspectives,* 12(4): 31–50.

———. 2000. *The Impact of International Trade on Wages.* Chicago: University of Chicago Press.

Feenstra, Robert C., and Gordon H. Hanson. 1997. "Productivity Measurement and the Impact of Trade and Technology on Wages: Estimates for the U.S., 1972–1990." Working Paper 6052, National Bureau of Economic Research, Cambridge, Massachusetts.

———. 1999. "The Impact of Outsourcing and High-Technology Capital on Wages: Estimates for the United States." *Quarterly Journal of Economics* 114(3): 907–940.

Feenstra, Robert C., Gordon H. Hanson, and Deborah L. Swenson. 2000. "Offshore Assembly from the United States: Production Characteristics of the 9802 Program." In *The Impact of International Trade on Wages,* R.C. Feenstra, ed. Chicago: University of Chicago Press, pp. 85–125.

Field, Martha K., and Emilio Pagoulatos. 1997. "The Cyclical Behavior of Price Elasticity of Demand." *Southern Economic Journal* 64(1): 118–129.

Freeman, Richard B. 1995. "Are Your Wages Set in Beijing?" *Journal of Economic Perspectives* 9(3): 15–32.

Freeman, Richard B., and Lawrence F. Katz. 1991. "Industrial Wage and Employment Determination in an Open Economy." In *Immigration, Trade, and the Labor Market*, J.M. Abowd and R.B. Freeman, eds. Chicago: University of Chicago Press, pp. 235–260.

Grossman, Gene. 1986. "Imports as a Cause of Injury: The Case of the U.S. Steel Industry." *Journal of International Economics* 20(3/4): 201–23.

———. 1987. "The Employment and Wage Effects of Import Competition." *Journal of International Economic Integration* 2(1): 1–23.

Grubel, H.G., and P.J. Lloyd. 1975. *Intra-Industry Trade: The Theory and Measurement of International Trade in Differentiated Products*. London: Macmillan.

Haveman, Jon D. 1998. "The Influence of Changing Trade Patterns on Displacements of Labor." *International Trade Journal* 12(2): 259–292.

Helpman, Elhanan. 1999. "The Structure of Foreign Trade." *Journal of Economic Perspectives* 13(2): 121–144.

Helpman, Elhanan, and Paul R. Krugman. 1985. *Market Structure and Foreign Trade: Increasing Returns, Imperfect Competition, and the International Economy*. Cambridge: The MIT Press.

Hufbauer, Gary C., and Ben Goodrich. 2001. "Steel: Big Problems, Better Solutions." *International Economics Policy Briefs*, PB01-9, July, Washington D.C.: Institute for International Economics.

Hufbauer, Gary C., and Jeffrey J. Schott. 1993. *NAFTA: An Assessment*. Washington, D.C.: Institute for International Economics, revised edition.

Jacobson, Louis. 1998. "Compensation Programs." In *Imports, Exports, and the American Worker*, Susan M. Collins, ed. Washington, D.C.: The Brookings Institution, pp. 473–537.

Jacobson, Louis, Robert LaLonde, and Daniel Sullivan. 1993. *The Costs of Worker Dislocation*. Kalamazoo, Michigan: W.E. Upjohn Institute for Employment Research.

Kletzer, Lori G. 1998a. "Job Displacement." *Journal of Economic Perspectives* 12(1): 115–136.

———. 1998b. "International Trade and Job Loss in U.S. Manufacturing, 1979–91." In *Imports, Exports, and the American Worker*, Susan M. Collins, ed. Washington, D.C.: The Brookings Institution, pp. 423–472.

———. 2000. "Trade and Job Loss in U.S. Manufacturing, 1979–94." In *The Impact of International Trade on Wages*, Robert C. Feenstra, ed. Chicago: University of Chicago Press, pp. 349–396.

———. 2001. *Job Loss from Imports: Measuring the Costs.* Washington, D.C.: Institute for International Economics.

Kletzer, Lori G., and Robert E. Litan. 2001. "A Prescription to Relieve Worker Anxiety." *International Economics Policy Briefs*, PB01-2, March, Washington, D.C.: Institute for International Economics.

Koutsoyiannis, A. 1984. "Goals of Oligopolistic Firms: An Empirical Test of Competing Hypotheses." *Southern Economic Journal* 51(2): 540–567.

Krueger, Alan B. 1997. "Labor Market Shifts and the Price Puzzle Revisited." Working Paper 5924, National Bureau of Economic Research, Cambridge, Massachusetts.

Krugman, Paul. 1995. "Increasing Returns, Imperfect Competition and the Positive Theory of International Trade." In *Handbook of International Economics*, Volume III, Gene M. Grossman and Kenneth Rogoff, eds. Amsterdam: Elsevier, pp. 1243–1277.

Krugman, Paul, and Robert Lawrence. 1993. "Trade, Jobs, and Wages." Working Paper 4478, National Bureau of Economic Research, Cambridge, Massachusetts.

Lawrence, Robert Z. 2000. "Does a Kick in the Pants Get You Going or Does It Just Hurt?: The Impact of International Competition on Technological Change in U.S. Manufacturing." In *The Impact of International Trade on Wages*, Robert C. Feenstra, ed. Chicago: University of Chicago Press, pp. 197–224.

Lawrence, Robert Z., and Matthew J. Slaughter. 1993. "International Trade and American Wages in the 1980s: Giant Sucking Sound or Small Hiccup?" *Brookings Papers on Economic Activity: Microeconomics* 1993: 161–210.

Leamer, Edward E. 1993. "Wage Effects of a U.S.-Mexican Free Trade Agreement." In *The Mexico-U.S. Free Trade Agreement*, P.M. Garber, ed. Cambridge, Massachusetts: MIT Press, pp. 57–125.

———. 1994. "Trade, Wages and Revolving Door Ideas." Working Paper 4716, National Bureau of Economic Research, Cambridge, Massachusetts.

———. 1998. "In Search of Stolper-Samuelson Linkages between International Trade and Lower Wages." In *Imports, Exports, and the American Worker*, Susan M. Collins, ed. Washington, D.C.: The Brookings Institution, pp. 141–214.

Leamer, Edward E., and James Levinsohn. 1995. "International Trade Theory: The Evidence." In *Handbook of International Economics*, Volume III, Gene M. Grossman and Kenneth Rogoff, eds. Amsterdam: Elsevier, pp. 1339–1394.

Lewis, Howard, III, and J. David Richardson. 2001. *Why Global Commitment Really Matters!* Washington, D.C.: Institute for International Economics.

Lovely, Mary E., and J. David Richardson. 2000. "Trade Flows and Wage Premiums: Does Who or What Matter?" In *The Impact of International Trade on Wages*, Robert C. Feenstra, ed. Chicago: University of Chicago Press, pp. 309–348.

MacPherson, David A., and James B. Stewart. 1990 "The Effect of International Competition on Union and Nonunion Wages." *Industrial and Labor Relations Review* 43(4): 434–446.

Mann, Catherine L. 1988. "The Effect of Foreign Competition in Prices and Quantities on the Employment in Import-Sensitive U.S. Industries." *The International Trade Journal* II (Summer): 409–444.

———. 1999. *Is the U.S. Trade Deficit Sustainable?* Washington, D.C.: Institute for International Economics.

Mincer, Jacob. 1991. "Human Capital, Technology and the Wage Structure: What do Time Series Show?" Working paper no. 3581, National Bureau of Economic Research, Cambridge, Massachusetts.

Murphy, Kevin M., and Finis Welch. 1991. "The Role of International Trade in Wage Differentials." In *Workers and Their Wages: Changing Patterns in the United States*, Marvin H. Kosters, ed. Washington, D.C.: The AEI Press, pp. 39–69.

National Science Foundation. 1981. *Research and Development in Industry, 1979*. NSF 81-324, Washington, D.C.: U.S. Government Printing Office.

———. 1989. *Research and Development in Industry, 1987*. NSF 89-323, Washington, D.C.: U.S. Government Printing Office.

———. 1999. *Research and Development in Industry, 1997*. NSF 99-358, Washington, D.C.: U.S. Government Printing Office.

Program on International Policy Attitudes. 2000. *Americans on Globalization: A Study of U.S. Public Attitudes*. College Park, MD: Program on International Policy Attitudes.

Revenga, Ana L. 1992. "Exporting Jobs? The Impact of Import Competition on Employment and Wages in U.S. Manufacturing." *Quarterly Journal of Economics* 107(1): 255–284.

Richardson, J. David. 1993. *Sizing Up U.S. Export Disincentives*. Washington, D.C.: Institute for International Economics.

———. 1995. "Income Inequality and Trade: How to Think, What to Conclude." *Journal of Economic Perspectives* 9(3): 33–56.

Richardson, J. David, and Karin Rindal. 1995. *Why Exports Really Matter!* Washington, D.C.: The Institute for International Economics and The Manufacturing Institute.

———. 1996. *Why Exports Matter: More!* Washington, D.C.: The Institute for International Economics and The Manufacturing Institute.

Sachs, Jeffrey D., and Howard J. Shatz. 1994. "Trade and Jobs in U.S. Manufacturing." *Brookings Papers on Economic Activity* 1994: 1–69.

———. 1998. "International Trade and Wage Inequality in the United States: Some New Results." In *Imports, Exports, and the American Worker*, Susan M. Collins, ed. Washington, D.C.: The Brookings Institution, pp. 215–254.

Salvatore, Dominick. 1998. *International Economics,* sixth edition. Upper Saddle River, New Jersey: Prentice-Hall.

Schoepfle, Gregory K. 1982. "Imports and Domestic Employment: Identifying Affected Industries." *Monthly Labor Review* 105(8): 13–26.

Slaughter, Matthew J. 2000. "What Are the Results of Product-Price Studies?" In *The Impact of International Trade on Wages*, R.C. Feenstra, ed. Chicago: University of Chicago Press, pp. 129–169.

Spence, Michael. 1976. "Product Selection, Fixed Costs, and Monopolistic Competition." *Review of Economic Studies* 43(2): 217–235.

Stolper, Wolfgang, and Paul A. Samuelson. 1941. "Protection and Real Wages." *Review of Economic Studies* 9(November): 58–73.

Topel, Robert. 1990. "Specific Capital and Unemployment: Measuring the Costs and Consequences of Job Loss." *Carnegie-Rochester Conference Series on Public Policy* 33(Autumn): 181–214.

United States Bureau of Labor Statistics. 1992. *BLS Handbook of Methods.* Bulletin 2414. Washington, D.C.: Government Printing Office.

United States General Accounting Office. 2000. *Trade Adjustment Assistance: Trends, Outcomes, and Management Issues in Dislocated Worker Programs.* GAO-01-59, October.

United States International Trade Commission. 1986. *U.S. Trade-Related Employment: 1978–84.* Washington, D.C.: Government Printing Office.

Wood, Adrian. 1994. *North-South Trade, Employment and Inequality.* Oxford: Clarendon Press.

———. 1995. "How Trade Hurt Unskilled Workers." *Journal of Economic Perspectives* 9(3): 57–80.

The Author

Lori G. Kletzer is Professor of Economics at the University of California, Santa Cruz. She received her Ph.D. in economics from the University of California, Berkeley, and she has held teaching and research appointments at Williams College, the University of Washington, the Brookings Institution, and the Institute for International Economics. In addition to the domestic labor market effects of globalization, her research has focused on the causes and consequences of job displacement, racial differences in the incidence of job loss, and the microeconomics of college choice, careers, and wages. She is also the author of a recent book that examines the costs to workers of trade-related job loss titled *Job Loss from Imports: Measuring the Costs,* published by the Institute for International Economics.

Subject Index

The italic letters f, n, and t following a page number indicate that the subject information is within a figure, note, or table, respectively, on that page.

Apparel industry, import and export shares and, 5, 6
Autarky, employment and wages in, 34

Barriers to trade. *See* Trade barriers
Benefits
　Lewis and Richardson on globalization and, 41
　under NAFTA-TAA and TAA, 148
Benefits of trade, wages, employment, and, 11–24
Bilateral trade agreements, 145–146

Capital
　as input, 13
　trade liberalization and, 15
Capital intensive industry, employment growth of, 109
Census of Population Industry Classification (CIC), 53, 54
Closed economy, 88
Cobb-Douglas production function, three-factor, 23
Comparative advantage, 12–14
　intra-industry trade and, 20
Competition, 5
　domestic employment and job loss link with, 11–24
　employment changes, job loss, and, 85
　import, 33, 144
　import by industry, 56–60
　import price changes as measure of, 60
　import share as measure of, 58
　monopolistic, 23
　See also Foreign competition

Competitiveness of domestic firms, industry import shares and, 22
Computer industry
　exports by, 61
　Sachs and Shatz on, 31
Conventional trade theory, vs. new trade theory, 18–20
Costs of trade
　for American employment, 123–125
　of free trade, 2
CPS. *See* Current Population Survey (CPS)
Cross-industry job loss, 136–137, 141–142
Cross-section estimates, of industry displacement rates, changes in sales, domestic demand, exports, and import share (1979–1994), 138–139t
Current Population Survey (CPS), 34, 76
　Annual Demographic File supplements to, 53–54
　measuring industry employment and job loss using, 153–193

Data
　definitions and sources, 196
　limitations of, 196
DC. *See* Developed country
Demand, 108
　employment-stimulating effect of rise in domestic, 89–90
　job loss and changes in, 132–141
　job loss rates and, 141
　shifts in, 88
　and supply of labor, 29–30

209

210 Index

Demand (continued)
  See also Domestic demand; Foreign demand
Developed country (DC)
  import share of, 108–109, 112–113
  U.S. trade with, 36–37
Developing country (LDC), import share of, 108–109, 112–113
Differentiated products, vs. conventional trade theory, 18–20
Disaggregated industry trade sensitivity, 38
Displaced Worker Surveys (DWSs), 53, 76
  displacement information in, 154
Displacement. *See* Job displacement; Job loss
Distribution
  affect of trade on level of, 28
  of employment change, 17
Distribution of income, trade liberalization and, 15
Dollar (U.S.)
  exchange value of, 49–52
  export intensity and, 64
  industry import shares and, 58–59
Domestic adjustment assistance policy, 147–150
Domestic demand
  changes in sales from, 105
  export sales and, 116
  import share, employment change, and, 112
  industry employment change and, 108
  job loss rates and, 141
  long-period changes in (1979–1985), 182–185*t*
  long-period changes in (1985–1994), 186–189*t*
  shift in, 89
Domestic labor, measuring industry trade sensitivity and, 21–23
Domestic price, industry relative, 119

Domestic supply, imports as share of, 56–58
DWSs. *See* Displaced Worker Surveys

Earnings
  recovering, 147
  workers' concerns over, 148–149
Earnings inequality, Wood on, 36
Economic integration, 1
Economies of scale. *See* Scale economies
Education, demand for, 35
Efficiency, of production, 13
Elasticity
  of domestic supply, 22
  of industry employment, 119
Eligibility, for displacement assistance, 149–150
Employment
  costs of trade for American employment, 123–125
  declining, 46, 70, 71–74
  and declining exports, 5
  effect of trade on level of, 28
  export declines and, 46
  exports, job loss, and, 40–41
  in factor-content approach, 33–34
  flexible wages and, 16
  import price changes and, 75–76
  import price competition and, 23
  import prices and, 90–91
  industry net change in, 6
  industry relative domestic price increases and, 119
  job displacement risk and, 7
  job loss and employment declines in, 6–7
  levels by industry, 53–54
  manufacturing and, 5, 45–82, 47*t*
  manufacturing sector employment and manufacturing employment as share of total employment (1975–1995), 47*f*
  outcomes of increases in foreign

competition on domestic
employment, 124–125
Sachs and Shatz on trade reduction
of, 35
services growth in, 53
trade flow changes and, 8
trends in, 12
in U.S. manufacturing industries
(1979–1985), 156–159*t*
in U.S. manufacturing industries
(1985–1994), 160–163*t*
workers' concerns over, 148–149
See also Full employment; Industry employment
Employment changes
and exogenous shifts in demand/supply, 87
imports, exports, and, 126–127*t*
in industry, 54–55
industry fixed effects and, 103–113
models of, 95
Murphy and Welch study of, 34–35
in 1979–1994, 190–193*t*
trade and, 85
variables affecting, 95
Employment decline, import share and, 105–108
Employment determination, industry model of, 86–95
Employment gain, industries with, 74
Employment growth
export growth and, 89–90
import share and, 109–112
Europe, factor-content studies and, 38
European Union, trade within, 66
Exchange value, of dollar, 49–52
Export(s)
changes in 1979–1994, 190–193*t*
changes in sales from, 105
changing percentage of, 1
concentration of, 61
declining, 5, 46
effects of changes on employment changes, 126–127*t*

employment, job loss, and, 40–41
employment enhanced by, 144
employment expansion and, 131
employment growth and, 75
as "engine of growth," 41
exchange value of dollar and, 52
in import-competing industries, 69–70
import competition changes and, 89
industry export activity and, 61–65
industry shares of (1980, 1987, 1994), 171–173*t*
job loss, import share, and, 80*t*
job loss from changes in, 8
job loss rates and, 134–135, 141
long-period changes in (1979–1985), 182–185*t*
long-period changes in (1985–1994), 186–189*t*
1975–1995, 49*f*
as percentage of GDP in manufacturing sector (1975–1995), 52*f*
promotion of, 145–146
rising, and employment decline, 71
trend toward growth in, 146
U.S. policy impeding, 146
Export decline, employment decline and, 71–74
Export demand, shift in, 89
Export growth, employment growth and, 89–90
Export intensity, 61–65
as composition measure, 65
cross-time correlation of industry quartile rankings by, 64*t*
in 1975, 1980, 1985, and 1994, 174–177*t*
in 1980, 1987, and 1994, 178–181*t*
of top exporting industries (1975–1994), 63*t*
Export penetration ratio, 21
Export sector, capital, labor, and, 13–14
Export shares, Freeman and Katz on, 38

Factor content of trade approach, 29–30
Factor-content studies, 27–28, 33–38
　criticisms of, 37–38
　European, 38
　trade flows and, 38–39
Factor endowments, 20
　differences in, 18
　Heckscher-Ohlin model and, 17–18
Factor price equalization (FPE), 15–17
Factors of production
　comparative advantage and, 12–14
　prices of, 13–14
　skill and unskilled labor as, 15
　two-factor model of, 12–14
　See also Inputs
Feasible generalized least squares (FGLS), as estimation technique, 92–93
Financial assistance, wage insurance as, 149–150
First-stage estimates, 197
Fixed effects model, 92
Foreign competition
　domestic employment outcomes of increases in, 124–125
　in industry employment, 70–75
　job displacement and, 131–150
　job loss and, 132–141
　See also Competition
Foreign demand, 104–105
　export sales and, 116
Foreign outsourcing, 32
Foreign-produced goods, as share of domestic supply, 59
FPE. *See* Factor price equalization
Free trade, 1–2
　costs of, 2
　in Heckscher-Ohlin-Samuelson model, 15–16
　opinions on, 143
　perfectly free trade, 15–16
Freeman, Richard B., 95, 96, 98
Full employment
　comparative advantage and, 13
　trade models and, 16–17
　See also Employment

Globalization
　ambivalence toward, 143
　immigration and, 36
　protests against, 2
Goods
　decrease in relative price and real wage of unskilled labor, 30
　exports and imports of (1975–1995), 49f
　production costs and, 12–13
　Stolper-Samuelson theorem and, 14–15
　U.S. international trade in (1975–1995), 50–51t
Government, domestic adjustment assistance policy, 147–150
Gross domestic product (GDP), manufacturing's share of, 48–59
Grossman, Gene, 33
Growth engine, exports as, 41
Grubel-Lloyd measure of trade, 66–69, 67–69t

Heckscher, Eli, 12
Heckscher-Ohlin-Samuelson model, 12, 15
　distributional impact of free trade in, 15–16
Heckscher-Ohlin theory, 12
　and country differences in factor endowments, 31
　new trade theory and, 17–18
　price measure and, 22–23
　product-price studies and, 30
　trade measurement and, 29
High-import industries, 56–58, 62
　import shares of (1975–1994), 57t
　long-period changes in employment, import share, exports, and domestic demand for, 72–73t
High skill labor, trade flows and, 35

Index 213

Immigration, globalization and, 36
Import(s)
  barriers to, 145
  Borjas, Freeman, and Katz on, 36
  changing percentage of, 1
  effects of changes on employment changes, 126–127t
  employment reductions and, 46, 131, 144
  exchange value of dollar and, 52
  immigration and, 36
  in 1975–1995, 49f
  price competition and industry employment link, 23
  prices in Heckscher-Ohlin-Samuelson model, 16
  rise in, 88–89, 141
Import-competing industries, 69–70
  employment decline, import share gain, export loss, and weak domestic demand in, 71
  by industry, 56–60
Import competition, 33
  changes in, 100–101
  increases measured as import price changes, 117–123
  long-period change in, 113
  modeling labor market responses to changes in, 85–130
  models of, 95
  protection from, 146
Import data, sources of, 108–109
Import-intensive industries, 33–34
Import penetration ratios, 21
  Freeman and Katz on, 38
Import prices, 75–76
  changes in, by industry, 168–170t
  elasticity for changes in total industry employment, 118
  and employment changes, 90–91
  import competition increases measured as changes in, 117–123
  measures of trade volumes and, 153–193
  setting of, 90–91
  trends in, 60–61
Import sector, capital, labor, and, 13–14
Import share, 21, 128–129
  displacement rates and, 8–9, 132, 135
  domestic demand, employment change, and, 112
  employment decline and, 71–74, 105–108
  employment growth and, 109–112
  foreign-produced goods and, 59
  increases in, 5–6, 75
  industrial relationships to, 7–8
  intensities in 1980, 1987, and 1994, 178–181t
  job loss and, 79–81
  for LDCs and DCs, 108–109
  within-industry effect of, 9
Import share changes, 88–89
  by country of origin, 137
  and export intensities (1980, 1987, and 1994), 178–181t
  long-period (1979–1985), 182–185t
  in 1979–1994, 190–193t
Income. *See* Distribution; Wage(s)
Increasing returns to scale, 18, 20
Industrialized countries (North)
  and newly industrialized countries (South), 65–66
  See also Developed country
Industry
  cross-time correlation of industry quartile rankings, by import share, 58t
  defined, 53–54
  displacement, import share, and exports in, 80t
  employment changes in, 7–8
  export activity in, 61–65
  export intensities of top (1975–1994), 63t
  import competition by, 56–60
  as importer and exporter, 66

Industry (continued)
  measuring trade sensitivity of, 21–23
  top export, 61
  trade and job loss by, 78–81
  See also Manufacturing; specific industries and issues
Industry displacements, in 1979–1994, 190–193*t*
Industry employment
  measuring using CPS, 153–193
  trade and foreign competition in, 70–75
  trade flow changes and, 103–130
  trade flows and domestic demand changes, 117
Industry employment changes, 54–55, 88, 90
  econometric specifications, 91–92
  long-period (1979–1985), 182–185*t*
  long-period (1985–1994), 186–189*t*
  long-period and annual, 113–117, 114–115*t*
  trade volume, foreign competition, and, 45
  See also Employment
Industry exchange rate indices, construction of instruments for, 195
Industry fixed effects. *See* Within-industry estimates
Industry foreign cost indices, construction of instruments for, 195–196
Industry import data, sources of, 108–109
Industry import prices, instrumental variables estimation of, 91
Industry import shares, 21–22
  in high-import industries (1975–1994), 57*t*
  in 1975, 1980, 1985, 1990, and 1994, 164–167*t*
  and U.S. dollar, 58–59
Industry model, of employment determination, 86–95

Industry prices, 90–91
Industry risk of job loss, import share changes and, 132
Inputs, capital and labor as, 13
Instruments, construction of, 195–197
Inter-industry trade, with homogeneous products, 19
Interest rates, exchange value of dollar and, 49
International trade. *See* Trade
International trade models, and indicators of international linkages, 23–24
International trade theories, 27
  impact of trade on workers and, 11–24
Internationalization, declining manufacturing employment, wage inequality, and, 41–42
Intra-industry trade, 65–70
  defined, 18–19
  Grubel-Lloyd measure of, 66
  increased trade volumes and, 46
  Lovely and Richardson on, 65–66
  See also New trade theory
Involuntary job loss
  trade volume, foreign competition, and, 45–46
  See also Job loss
Iron industry, 5

Job(s)
  domestic, 4
  fluctuations in foreign and domestic demand and, 146
  trade link with, 45–82
  trade reallocating of, 53
  See also Domestic labor; Employment; Workers
Job displacement
  adjustments after, 146–147
  eligibility for assistance, 149–150
  foreign competition and, 131–150
  import share and, 135, 141
  job loss measured through, 135

Index 215

in 1979–1994, 190–193*t*
role of imports and, 144
through trade, 131–132
See also Job loss
Job loss, 6, 45
above-average rates of, 6
across industry, 136–137
changes in composition of demand and risk of, 132–141
data on, 4–5
export changes and, 8, 134–135
exports, employment, and, 40–41
from free trade, 143–144
high-rate industries, 7
import share and, 8–9, 79, 80*t*
within industry, 132–135
manufacturing and, 45–82, 77–78
manufacturing employment and, 145
measuring using CPS, 153–193
rising exports and, 131
top job loss manufacturing industries (1979–1994), 78*t*
and trade, by industry, 78–81
trade and, 12, 76–78, 85
trade volume, foreign competition, and, 45–46
See also Job displacement

Katz, Lawrence F., 95, 96, 98
Krueger, Alan B., 31

Labor
as input, 13
skill levels in U.S. vs. Mexico, 32
skilled and unskilled, 15, 20
trade liberalization and, 15
See also Outsourcing
Labor demand
factors in, 39–40
and supply, 29–30
wage changes and, 35
See also Factor-content studies
Labor input coefficients, 38
Labor market
basic empirical model for product demand, import price competition, employment change, and job displacement changes, 95–101
international trade and domestic, 4
modeling responses to changes in trade and import competition, 85–130
product demand, import price competition, employment change, job displacement, and, 86–87
responses to changes in trade and import competition, 85–130
Labor supply
and demand, 29–30
high school and college graduates and, 35
Labor unions. *See* Unions
LDC. *See* Developing country
Less-developed country. *See* Developing country
Lovely, Mary E., 65–66
Low-skill labor
Sachs and Shatz on decline in manufacturing employment, 37
technological change and, 42
trade and, 34, 35

Mann, Catherine L., 23, 33, 95
Manufacturing
decline in employment in, 129
economic integration and, 1
employment, trade changes, and, 45–46
employment changes and, 54–55, 124, 145
employment in, 5
export intensity in, 61–62
importance of trade within, 52
job loss in, 77–78
sector employment and employment as share of total employment (1975–1995), 47*f*
as share of GDP (1975–1995), 48*f*
top loss industries (1979–1994), 78*t*

Manufacturing (continued)
  and total displacement rates, by year (1979–1994), 77f
  trends in international trade, employment, job loss, and, 45–82
  in U.S. (1975–1995), 47–53
  See also Industry
Market(s), opening to U.S. trade, 145–146
Market-clearing, vs. wages, 17
Market intervention, exchange value of dollar and, 49
Market share, quota restraints and, 23
Measures
  of industry employment and job loss using CPS, 153–193
  of trade volumes and import prices, 153–193
Mexico, skilled-unskilled wage gap in, 32
Monopolistic competition, quantity and, 23
Monopolistically competitive dominant/fringe model, 23
Multilateral trade agreements, NAFTA as, 145

NAFTA. See North American Free Trade Agreement
NAFTA-TAA. See North American Free Trade Agreement Transitional Adjustment Assistance
National Bureau of Economic Research (NBER), Trade Database of, 54, 108
Natural resources, 12
New trade theory, 17–20
Newly industrialized countries (South) intra-industry trade and, 65–66
  See also Developing country
North (industrialized countries), intra-industry trade and, 65–66
North American Free Trade Agreement (NAFTA), 3

North American Free Trade Agreement Implementation Act (1993), 147
North American Free Trade Agreement Transitional Adjustment Assistance (NAFTA-TAA), 147–148, 149

Offshore Assembly Program (OAP), 32
Ohlin, Bertil, 12
OLS estimates, 91, 92–93
Open economy, 88
Open trade, 2
Opportunity cost, of production, 13
Organization for Economic Cooperation and Development, technological change and, 39–40
Output
  in U.S. manufacturing industries (1979–1985), 156–159t
  in U.S. manufacturing industries (1985–1994), 160–163t
Outsourcing, 1
  foreign, 32
  job loss and, 137
  Northern, 66
Overhead costs, 18

Partial equilibrium modeling, of labor market responses to changes in trade and import competition, 85–130
Perfect competition, 21–22
Perfectly free trade, 15–16
Perot, Ross, 2, 3
Plaza Accord (1985), 49
Policy implications, 9, 143–150
  of labor market changes associated with increased trade, 45
  of opening markets to U.S. trade, 145–146
Price(s)
  declines for goods, 30
  as determinant of foreign and domestic supply, 23
  differences across countries, 12

employment, job loss, and, 85
global goods prices and domestic factor prices, 13–14
import, 60–61, 75–76
joint determination of, 85–86
as measure of effect of trade policy or foreign supply changes, 23
Price measure, Heckscher-Ohlin model and, 22–23
Price shocks, domestic displacement, import prices, and, 141
Principles of Political Economy (Ricardo), 12
Product demand
  Murphy and Welch on, 34–35
  trade-related components of, 87–88
Product differentiation, in new trade theory, 18
Product price studies
  Feenstra, Hanson, and Swenson on, 31–32
Product-price studies, 27, 29, 30–33
  Stolper-Samuelson on, 32
Product prices, trade, technological advance, and, 32
Production, comparative advantage and, 12–14
Production location, trade, technological advance, and, 32
Productivity, 12
Productivity growth, 5
  exports and, 41
Protection
  from import competition, 146
  trade barriers as, 147

Quantity, monopolistic competition and, 23
Quantity flows, trade measured as, 22
Quota protection, for industries, 23

Re-employment, 146–147
Readjustment allowances, 148
Real wages, declining, 28
Recall problems, 155

Relative prices
  of imports, changes within industry, 137–141
  Krueger on, 31
  Lawrence and Slaughter on, 31
Relative wages
  declining, 28
  trade, technological advance, and, 32
Research and development (R&D)
  job loss rates and, 135
  technological change and, 108
Resource(s), shifting, 2
Resource allocation, between industries and sectors, 29
Returns to scale. *See* Increasing returns to scale
Revenga, Ana L., 33, 95
Ricardo, David, 12
  country differences in technology and, 31
Richardson, J. David, 30, 65–66, 146

Sales
  employment responsiveness to changes in, 113
  and job loss, 134, 141
Scale economies
  increasing returns, benefits to trade, and, 20
  and trade in goods produced with identical proportions, 18–19
Scarcity of factors, in Heckscher-Ohlin-Samuelson model, 15
Services
  employment growth in, 53
  growth of services-producing industry, 48
  U.S. international trade in (1975–1995), 50–51*t*
Shipments
  import share, employment, and, 89–90
  industry shares of (1980, 1987, 1994), 171–173*t*

SIC. *See* Standard Industrial
  Classification categories
Skill-biased technological change, wage
  inequality and, 31
Skilled labor, 15
  declining wages of lesser skilled
    workers, 28
Solow, Robert, 95
South (newly industrialized countries),
  intra-industry trade and, 65–66
Standard Industrial Classification (SIC)
  categories, 54
Steel industry, 5
Stolper-Samuelson theorem, 14–15
  impact of trade on factor returns and,
    20
  product-price studies and, 30, 32
  trade liberalization and, 29
  wages and, 28
Supply
  and demand for labor, 29–30
  price as determinant of foreign and
    domestic, 23

TAA. *See* Trade Adjustment
  Assistance
Technological change, 39–40
  economic decline of lower skilled
    workers and, 42
  and industry employment changes,
    94–95
  R&D changes and, 108
  wage inequality and, 31
Technology
  capital, labor, and, 13
  Ricardo and, 12
  skill-biased change and, 146
TFP. *See* Total factor productivity
Three-factor Cobb-Douglas production
  function, price and, 23
Time-limited earnings (wage) insurance.
  See Wage insurance
Total factor productivity, 95
  job loss rates and, 135

Trade
  balanced advocacy of, 1–2
  benefits of, 11
  comparative advantage and, 13–14
  costs of, for American employment,
    123–125
  with developing countries, 36–37
  displacement through, 131–132
  employment change, job loss, and,
    85
  Grubel-Lloyd measure of, 66–69,
    67–69t
  increasing volumes of, 70
  in industry employment, 70–75
  intra-industry, 18–19
  job loss and (1979–1994), 76–78
  job loss by industry and, 78–81
  jobs link with, 45–82
  and low skill U.S. labor, 34
  manufacturing and, 45–82
  measurement of, 29
  measures of volumes and import
    prices, 153–193
  modeling labor market responses to
    changes in, 85–130
  perfectly free trade, 15–16
  as quantity flows, 22
  research on, 4
  Stolper-Samuelson theorem and,
    14–15
  technology and, 12, 32
  trends in, 11–12
  two-factor model of, 12–14
  U.S. international trade in goods and
    services (1975–1995), 50–51t
  in U.S. manufacturing industries
    (1979–1985), 156–159t
  in U.S. manufacturing industries
    (1985–1994), 160–163t
  Wood on earnings inequality and, 36
  See also Intra-industry trade
Trade Adjustment Assistance (TAA),
  147, 148, 149
Trade and wages literature, 27–42

Trade barriers, 145, 147
  free trade and, 16
  lack of, 14
Trade Expansion Act (1962), 147
Trade flows, 30
  changes in, 98–100
  domestic demand and, 89
  employment and, 8
  employment of high and low skill labor and, 35
  factor-content studies and, 38–39
  industry employment changes and, 103–130
  industry fixed effects and, 103–113
  intra-industry, 65–70
  joint determination of, 85–86
Trade liberalization, wage rate and, 14–15
Trade overlap, import share, export intensity, and, 67–69t
Trade sensitivity, by industry, 21–23
Trade sensitivity measures, 21–23, 38–39
  Davis, Haltiwanger, and Schuh on, 39
Trade shock, 29
Trade theory, intra-industry trade, new trade theory, and, 17–20
Training programs, TAA and NAFTA-TAA, 148
Two-factor model, of Heckscher-Ohlin, 12–14
Two-way trade, as intra-industry trade, 18

Unbalanced trade, trade flows and, 69
Unemployment. *See* Job loss; Job displacement
Unemployment compensation (UC), 146
Unions, 17
United States
  manufacturing in (1975–1995), 47–53

  See also Dollar (U.S.); specific issues
Unskilled labor, 15
  decrease in relative price of good and, 30
  impact of trade on, 20

Wage(s)
  comparative advantage and, 14
  exports, productivity, and, 41
  in factor-content approach, 33–34
  Heckscher-Ohlin-Samuelson model and, 16
  Heckscher-Ohlin theorem and, 14–15
  vs. market-clearing, 17
  Stolper-Samuelson theorem and, 28
  trends in, 12
  See also Trade and wages literature
Wage gap, in Mexico, 32
Wage inequality
  change estimate, 34
  international trade impact on, 31
  skill-biased technological change and, 31
  trade explanation of, 31
Wage insurance, 149–150
Within-industry estimates
  changes in employment
    domestic prices, import prices, 120–121t
    trade flows, 103–113
  changes in industry employment, sales, domestic demand, exports, and imports, 106–107t, 110–111t, 133t
  changes in industry employment and relative import prices, 122t
  changes in industry employment and relative import prices (1983–1992), 140t
  for relative import price changes, 137–141

Women, demand for education and, 35
Wood, Adrian, 36
Workers
  employment and earnings concerns of, 148–149
  employment of high and low skill, 35
  See also Employment; High skill labor; Low skill labor
World Trade Organization, protests against, 2

About the Institute

The W.E. Upjohn Institute for Employment Research is a nonprofit research organization devoted to finding and promoting solutions to employment-related problems at the national, state, and local levels. It is an activity of the W.E. Upjohn Unemployment Trustee Corporation, which was established in 1932 to administer a fund set aside by the late Dr. W.E. Upjohn, founder of The Upjohn Company, to seek ways to counteract the loss of employment income during economic downturns.

The Institute is funded largely by income from the W.E. Upjohn Unemployment Trust, supplemented by outside grants, contracts, and sales of publications. Activities of the Institute comprise the following elements: 1) a research program conducted by a resident staff of professional social scientists; 2) a competitive grant program, which expands and complements the internal research program by providing financial support to researchers outside the Institute; 3) a publications program, which provides the major vehicle for disseminating the research of staff and grantees, as well as other selected works in the field; and 4) an Employment Management Services division, which manages most of the publicly funded employment and training programs in the local area.

The broad objectives of the Institute's research, grant, and publication programs are to 1) promote scholarship and experimentation on issues of public and private employment and unemployment policy, and 2) make knowledge and scholarship relevant and useful to policymakers in their pursuit of solutions to employment and unemployment problems.

Current areas of concentration for these programs include causes, consequences, and measures to alleviate unemployment; social insurance and income maintenance programs; compensation; workforce quality; work arrangements; family labor issues; labor-management relations; and regional economic development and local labor markets.

612 624 0209